Film Noir, American Workers, and Postwar Hollywood

WORKING IN THE AMERICAS

UNIVERSITY PRESS OF FLORIDA

Florida A&M University, Tallahassee
Florida Atlantic University, Boca Raton
Florida Gulf Coast University, Ft. Myers
Florida International University, Miami
Florida State University, Tallahassee
New College of Florida, Sarasota
University of Central Florida, Orlando
University of Florida, Gainesville
University of North Florida, Jacksonville
University of South Florida, Tampa
University of West Florida, Pensacola

WORKING IN THE AMERICAS
Edited by Richard Greenwald, Drew University,
and Timothy Minchin, LaTrobe University

Working in the Americas is devoted to publishing important works in labor history and working-class studies in the Americas. This series seeks work that uses both traditional as well as innovative, interdisciplinary, or transnational approaches.
Its focus is the Americas and the lives of its workers.

Florida's Working-Class Past: Current Perspectives on Labor, Race, and Gender from Spanish Florida to the New Immigration, edited by Robert Cassanello and Melanie Shell-Weiss (2009)
The New Economy and the Modern South, by Michael Dennis (2009)
Film Noir, American Workers, and Postwar Hollywood, by Dennis Broe (2009)

Film Noir, American Workers, and Postwar Hollywood

Dennis Broe

Foreword by Richard Greenwald and Timothy Minchin

University Press of Florida
Gainesville · Tallahassee · Tampa · Boca Raton
Pensacola · Orlando · Miami · Jacksonville · Ft. Myers · Sarasota

Copyright 2009 by Dennis Broe
Printed in the United States of America.
All rights reserved
Frontispiece: Sam Masterson (Van Heflin), the resistant fugitive, in *The Strange Love of Martha Ivers*.

First cloth printing, 2009
First paperback printing, 2010

Library of Congress Cataloging-in-Publication Data
Broe, Dennis.
Film noir, American workers, and postwar Hollywood / Dennis Broe;
foreword by Richard Greenwald and Timothy Minchin.
p. cm. — (Working in the Americas)
Includes bibliographical references and index.
ISBN 978-0-8130-3322-8 (alk. paper); ISBN 978-0-8130-3549-9 (pbk.)
1. Film noir—United States—History and criticism. 2. Crime films—United States—History and criticism. 3. Working class in motion pictures. I. Title.
PN1995.9.F54B76 2008
791.43'6556—dc22   2008035071

The University Press of Florida is the scholarly publishing agency for the State University System of Florida, comprising Florida A&M University, Florida Atlantic University, Florida Gulf Coast University, Florida International University, Florida State University, New College of Florida, University of Central Florida, University of Florida, University of North Florida, University of South Florida, and University of West Florida.

University Press of Florida
15 Northwest 15th Street
Gainesville, FL 32611-2079
www.upf.com

To my two dads, mentors really: Jerry, my spiritual mentor, who believed that a book was possible long before I did; and Bill, my intellectual mentor, who also taught me How to Stop Worrying and (If Not) Love (at Least Not Detest) the New York Yankees.

Contents

Foreword ix

Preface xi

Acknowledgments xiii

Introduction: Let a Thousand Fetish Objects Bloom xv

1. The Home-front Detective as Dissident Lawman (and -woman): Hammett, Chandler, Woolrich, and 1940s Hollywood 1

2. Noir Part 1: Socialism in One Genre: Wildcat Strikers, Fugitive Outsiders, and a Savage Lament 30

3. Noir Part 2: Fugitive Kinds 54

4. The McCarthyite Crime Film: The Time of the (Quasi-Scientific) Toad (Criminal/Informer/Vigilante Cops versus Psychotic Fugitives) 80

5. The Neo-noirers: Fugitives, Surrealists, and the Return of the Degenerate Detective 105

Appendix: Crime Films of Each Film Noir Period 129

Notes 139

Bibliography 157

Index 171

Foreword

Working in the Americas is a series dedicated to presenting work in labor and working-class studies in the Americas. It publishes both traditional as well as interdisciplinary works that focus on the lives of workers and the transformation of work in the Americas.

Dennis Broe's *Film Noir, American Workers, and Postwar Hollywood* presents a new interpretation of film noir that is both a meditation on the relationship of class and culture and a sophisticated political analysis of Hollywood films in the 1940s. By combining a richly detailed discussion of the noir films to social and political history, we gain deeper insight into the culture of the mid- to late-1940s and see the period as a moment of hope for new democratic possibilities that are quickly closed off. For Broe, "the form itself becomes a lament for a broken promise of a hoped-for social change after the war that was never realized." Broe places the noir films of the 1945–1950 period into the social reality of the time through a careful discussion of the larger political changes that faced American workers. The postwar strike wave, Taft-Hartley, and the purge of the CIOs left-leaning unions form the backdrop needed to understand noir classics. The success of film noir is more than mere stylistic or cinematic. The noir hero, the anti-authoritarian, fugitive outsider is an American icon that was forged in the immediate postwar years as an expression of the new conformity, bureaucracy, and structured economic life.

More than a film history, Broe's cultural analysis moves the reader from gripping discussions of films and the structures of culture to the realm of social theory. And, he demonstrates that noir represents a promise, yet unfulfilled, that still has potency in post–9/11 America. It is for these reasons that *Film Noir, American Workers, and Postwar Hollywood* will change the way we view representations of class in film as well as the culture of the 1940s.

Richard A. Greenwald
Drew University

Timothy Minchin
LaTrobe University

Preface

To Foucault or Not To Foucault: The Micropolitics of Fear

This study began in the Clinton-era 1990s, when the cold war seemed a part of a distant past and the period of its onset could be viewed in a new light, shorn of previous prejudices. The ending of a period of war that had persisted through my entire life ideally made it possible to see how, in the Hollywood of the 1940s and in the country as a whole, the phrase *Communist menace* had often concealed labor's concerted attempt to assert itself and the repression that followed. This struggle was waged on the picket line, in the corporate boardroom, in Congress, and, more obliquely but importantly, on the movie screen.

Post–9/11 we are again in an undeclared war, the war on terror, where in an even more concerted way than in the previous cold war, we are constantly reminded that this unseen, unknowable menace can strike at any moment. While a certain strand of resistance, labeled biopolitics, fueled by the writings of Michel Foucault, explains that power is diffuse and thus can and must be contested on the micro level, the level of the everyday, a reactionary governmental and business cabal has answered this call with their own biopolitics of fear. Whereas in the cold war your neighbor might be a Communist plotting the takeover of the government, though more likely he or she was a labor organizer "plotting" how to be paid more fairly, today your neighbor might be a terrorist, who, in a more all-consuming new cold war, simply plots annihilation, though again, more likely he or she is simply an immigrant following the flow of wealth from the South to the North, hoping for a slightly better life for his or, more often, her family.

The post–World War II period, both in the working- and middle-class struggle against corporatism and in the slightly more oblique representation of that struggle on the screen, in what has subsequently been labeled "film noir," points to a moment of intense class division where a battle was waged and, for a period, won. Exposing the constructed nature of "the cold war" and its use in rolling back the progressive values and politics of the immediate postwar period in a perilous moment for capitalism (with domestic and international working classes actively contesting the goals of the system) points to the fact that in the same way just beyond the war on terrorism lie the contradictions of an equally perilous moment for global capital. (As I write, two entire continents, Europe and South America, are threatening to bolt from the system of American-led neo-liberalism in light of the no vote on the European Constitution, a vote expressly against global capital, and the left-led bloc in Latin America—Brazil, Argentina, Bolivia, Ecuador, Venezuela—attempting to form a united trade zone, to say nothing of the looming and far more devastating threat of a China that has chosen to follow its own path to capitalization.)

In this era, as Karl Marx wrote in the middle of a European industrialization that left the mass of humanity destitute, our duty is everywhere to engage in "ruthless criticism of the existing order" (*Early Writings* 207), not merely for the purpose of critique but to make "the world aware of its own consciousness, to show the world why it is struggling" (209). Ultimately, I hope, this study of a time of more open rebellion will contribute in some small way to this purpose. "Our task," the young Marx wrote, "is not to draw a sharp mental line between past and future but to complete the thought of the past" (209).

Acknowledgments

Many people are responsible for this book, that is, for the process that brought me to and sustained me in writing it. However, the errors, lapses of judgment, and vague formulations are, of course, all mine.

For giving me firsthand experience with unions and with the collectively radicalizing experience of a strike I would like to thank the rank and file and my fellow executive officers of the Long Island University Faculty Federation, especially Becky, Ed, Rhianon, Joe, and Melissa. A special thanks to Michael Pelias and Ralph Engleman, who did double duty as intellectual guardians and friends along this journey.

Thanks to the stalwarts of the New York University Department of Cinema Studies: Bob Sklar, whose words were more than encouraging; Bob Stam, whose conversation was always stimulating; and in absentia to William Everson, whose classes and screening nights in his apartment introduced me to many of the great films noir. Special thanks to Richard Allen, whose intellectual acumen is admirable; Marilyn Young, a remarkable historian and a wonderful compatriot; Michael Denning for his encouragement and participation; Bob Spiegelman for always being there; and finally Bill Simon, not only a wonderful and patient reader but a model teacher whose pedagogical rigor I strive to emulate.

Others who have aided my intellectual progress and been good friends in the process include Armond White, Michael Bentley, Annette Rubinstein, Terri Ginsberg, Pat Keaton, Paul Grant, and Antonino D'Ambrosio.

Writing a book is a journey that prompts emotional and spiritual changes, and those helpful in this area include, foremost, Jerry Mundis, without whose constant knowledge of the writing process this book would have been inconceivable; Bill, for his encouragement in Paris; and all those at the Cathedral in Paris and the Center in New York, two places where I found solitude. Thanks also to my parents for always helping out financially when I needed it in graduate school.

Finally, to my friends who asked little and gave a lot: Ed, Josh, Linda, Liz, Colleen, and Rich. And to my students and colleagues at Long Island University who helped me in ways too numerous and profound to define: Claire Goodman, Larry Banks, Stuart Fischelson, Kevin Lauth, Marjan Moghaddam, Maureen Nappi, Richard Hagen, Lydia, Christian, Rochelle, Rick, and many others.

Introduction

Let a Thousand Fetish Objects Bloom

He sits quietly at the bar nursing a drink and a grudge. Something has gone wrong, something is bothering him, something that the tall frame and those hands, callous, bulbous from the hard work they know will always be their lot, cannot conceal. Those hands slowly wrap themselves around the drink and clasp it as if for dear life. Perhaps he has just been fired, perhaps he just didn't get hired, perhaps he just found out the job he was counting on for the next six months is ending tomorrow. Who knows. What is apparent is that the breaks haven't gone his way for a long time. The equally anonymous someone behind the bar, for reasons known only in bars, starts suddenly to taunt him, to tease him for his crude manner, crude even in a bar. That's it. He can stand it no more. The tall hunk of a man suddenly rises off the bar stool and simply gives his anger free rein. He belts his tormentor, and that blow stands for all those who have tormented him in a life that though not long has been filled with struggle. The other man falls, quickly, dropping to the floor unconscious. No one is more surprised than the tall *fellow when a seedy bar rat emerges from the shadows and pronounces the bartender dead. Just another bad break, the striker thinks as he not quickly, as if he was guilty, but slowly, as if he knows that this break might bring him to the end of the line, sidles out of the bar and into the night. The night, the night, always the night, engulfing him and bringing its own dark solace where once there was promise.*

Bill Saunders, the "he" in the above description, played by Burt Lancaster in one of his first films, is brimming with working-class energy and remorse. The film, from 1948, is the aptly titled *Kiss the Blood Off My Hands*, and the film style described here is part of the amorphous entity that is film noir, one of Hollywood's most popular and enduring forms. Ever since French critics began using the term in the mid-1940s, what film noir is and how to define it has remained elusive.[1] Since there are so many definitions of the stylistics and thematics of these low-budget, dark, seedy, postwar crime films, many of which take place at night, most people perhaps just throw up their hands and, like Justice Stewart's definition of pornography, "know it when they see it."

But though the form is sometimes primarily defined visually, there is more to film noir than meets the eye. This study will argue for the central importance of class in the creation of film noir and will show that the form itself was developed and came to fruition during one of the most active periods of working-class agitation and middle-class antagonism in American history. In the period immediately following World War II, when the hopes and dreams of American working men and women seemed about to be realized, they were dashed. At the same time, the process of integrating formerly independent workers into a corporate structure was also raising anxiety in a burgeoning middle class. Film noir, in this reading, is a cultural formation that initially expressed working-class hope and middle-class agitation directly, then more fitfully as that hope was dashed by the forces of reaction, and finally functioned as a lament for a desired change that was not to be.

Film noir developed at what was becoming one of the centers of American capital, the Hollywood entertainment complex. Its particular expression was conditioned, as Freud, that grand old theorist of film noir, suggests, by its definition as a compromise formation.[2] The impulse for change after World War II, expressed as a series of strikes in every major industry, burst forward in the country as a whole and, perhaps most pointedly, in Hollywood, where an industry that had long been characterized by employee co-optation was directly challenged by its own workers, in both the craft unions and the creative guilds. But though the postwar strikes were a common experience shared in Hollywood—particularly the experience in the two years of almost continuous strikes between the spring of 1945 and the spring of 1947, a period concurrent with the development of film noir—the studio heads were adamant that no trace of working-class activism would be allowed to reach the screen. The resulting formation between the impulse for change and its repression on the screen conveyed the "structure of feeling" of this moment not directly in content about the strikes but in its style and also, and more pointedly, in the thematics of a consistent movement of the protagonist outside the law, a movement that became the predominant motif of the Hollywood crime film in the 1945–50 period. This permutation of the crime film is commonly called film noir.

The outside-the-law fugitive protagonist of the period, either male or female, is congruent with the figure of the outside-the-law unionist of the postwar period. The latter figure at first faced down the formidable opponents of business and the leaders of his or her own union in waging a series of strikes. They then had to contend with the government as well as their actions in fostering the strikes that were declared illegal in the Taft-Hartley Act. Finally, they were driven out of the many industries they had helped to organize in the "Communist" purges that followed the onset of the House Un-American Activities Committee (HUAC) and served largely as a cover for an attack on militant labor. As the labor figure moved further outside the law, so too did the film noir protagonist, who begins by ultimately proving his or her innocence and affixing blame where it belongs to an upper-class figure (*Somewhere in the Night*, 1947), then becomes more ambiguous and unable to so easily reconcile him- or herself with the society (the aforementioned *Kiss the Blood Off My Hands*, 1948), finally concluding the period in some cases not only dead in the end but doomed from his or her first moment on-screen (*Night and the City*, 1950), as the form itself becomes a lament for a broken promise.

The film noir period is preceded during the war (1941–45) by a (first) period that sets the stage for the outside-the-law protagonist. The lead figure of the crime film in this period is the hard-boiled detective, who, faithfully adapted from 1930s detective fiction, is new to Hollywood. This figure, standing between cop and criminal, though he is nominally a pseudo-representative of the law, is a transition figure between the 1930s lawman (in a series initiated in 1935 by *G-Men*) and the fugitive outsider. In contrast, what followed the film noir in the crime film in the (third) 1950–55 period was a backlash, a cultural counterrevolution in which the lead character, though still often working class, became a law enforcement official, either locally as a cop or nationally as a representative of a government organization, thus positively representing the direct hounding of Hollywood workers by federal agencies. The cop was also often an informer, and the narrative pattern involved validating infiltration and aligning the audience with the turncoat. But as we will see, the fugitive tradition persisted, despite this backlash, and continues to this day.

Class: The Return of the Structuring Absence

If we say that film noir is primarily an expression of class, and particularly of postwar American class tensions and class struggle, then it is necessary to define what we mean by class. Class, in the immediate postwar as represented in this study, reaches its optimal moment, as defined by Marx in *The German Ideology*, as class for-itself, that is, as class directly aware of its own interests and conscious of its struggle. The period of the birth of film noir is the greatest strike period in American history. From September 1945 until April 1946 nearly every major industry in the country was hit with a strike. In several mid-level cities the industry strike passed over into a general strike in which for at least a moment workers controlled the city (Lipsitz, *Rainbow*, 135). Thus, class expression in this instance, which parallels the genesis of the film noir protagonist, is extremely direct, that is, has passed over into class consciousness.

The postwar class struggle was often waged against the government, especially in its representation as the law. During the war, for the first time the government froze prices and wages and instituted a union no-strike clause, which was by the end of the war honored more in the breach than in the observance. After the war the government frequently attempted to contain the strikes, but then, after 1947, it enforced sections of the Taft-Hartley Act to break the organization of the strikes; subsequently, through HUAC and other governmental agencies, it sought to rid the unions of their militant members. Thus the film noir hero's struggle with the law recapitulates the labor rank and file member's battle for his or her own legitimacy in this era.

Not all the struggles of the period were so direct. The middle-class struggle at midcentury was bound up in a resistance to an ever increasing corporatization. The reality of working independently was fast fading as more and more workers were being compelled to enter the nine-to-five regimen. Once inside the corporation, workers found themselves trading their control over the conditions of their labor for money and a life that was more regulated and defined for them. The "structure of feeling" of this struggle is expressed in middle-class noirs such as *Double Indemnity* (1944), where insurance salesman Walter Neff looks regretfully over the stifling sameness of the corporate insurance office, and *The Big Clock* (1948), where editor George Stroud has a job that pays well but does not allow him even to take time off for his honeymoon.

Class is also a manner or mode of consciousness, class in-itself, which often, as Marx notes, preexists the actual coming to consciousness, class for-itself. The mode of consciousness, because of censorship—and especially so in the compromise formation of the Hollywood cinema, where direct expression of class consciousness is struck from the screen—exists in more oblique modes of representation alongside a more direct expression. Here, ways of being such as language (including working-class expressions), methods of comprehending the world, dress, mannerisms, and habits (in *Raw Deal*, 1948, a long discussion over getting or not getting a pack of cigarettes conveys one character's agony at losing another) converge to define working-class consciousness. These modes are intricately bound up with a discourse on "the common man" (and woman), a popular or "cultural front" discourse that stressed the "everyday" quality of the majority of Americans, which can be read as working class, or as an amalgam of a working- and middle-class consciousness in which to be ordinary or everyday is to throw oneself into the common lot of having to deal with the vicissitudes of life under corporate capitalism, including having to make a living in a wage scheme that was said to be a fair engagement of worker and owner but where in reality the cards were always stacked against the wage earner who did not own the means that ensured his or her livelihood. This sense of unfairness that is felt but not given voice in society is at least in part responsible for the cynical expressions of the tough guy and girl, language used as a way of warding off the harshness of a world controlled from above.

In terms of the Marxian categories, film noir is perhaps one of the few moments in American film when class in-itself becomes class for-itself, as film noir fugitive outsiders must actualize the modes of working-class consciousness in their suddenly being hunted by the law and in eventually proving either to society or just to themselves that they are innocent and the representatives of the class of order are guilty. The particular quality of this expression is the result of the compromise formation. The studio heads, whose unions and guilds were continually demanding more rights in this period, were adamantly against portraying any direct expression of this activity. Working within these limitations, writers, actors, and directors were nevertheless able to forge a genuine working-class representation.

This was part, as Michael Denning in *The Cultural Front* contends, of a general process he calls "the laboring of American culture," a legacy of the 1930s and a result in film noir of primarily four factors. First, many of these cultural workers were the sons and daughters of working-class immigrants who carried the values of their upbringing into the cultural industry. Second, many of them began their apprenticeship in the 1930s in the more class-conscious caldrons of the New York stage (with the working-class Yiddish theater and working-class-inflected Group Theater) or were immigrants who had watched a fascist crushing of the working class that made them aware of the importance of preserving these values. Third, in Hollywood itself many of these workers came to a specific class consciousness in this period, led by the militant crafts unions, whose Confederation of Studio Unions refused to be part of a sweetheart union and whose struggle both aided and strengthened the struggle of the writers, actors, and directors to forge their own guilds in the 1930s, a struggle that found them constantly being assaulted by the studios for having the audacity to even begin to organize outside the paternal structure of the entertainment corporation. Fourth, the legacy of 1930s culture promoted at least an adherence to the principle of the common man, a vague gesture which nevertheless meant that the studios themselves, in order to guarantee audience support, had to at least weakly echo that cry, and thus, until the coming of HUAC to Hollywood, were not able to entirely wrest artistic control from the crafts and creative workers.

Thus the crime film as a whole in the 1941–55 era and the film noir in particular cannot but bear the mark, or at least the repressed trace, of a time when heightened class conflict was in the forefront of American consciousness.

Crime and the Crime Film: Working- and Middle-Class Tough Guys and Girls

Hollywood has long linked crime and the working class, with working-class milieus being a favored setting for crime films from the first gangster film, D. W. Griffith's *The Musketeers of Pig Alley* (1912). Working-class milieus such as the seaside flophouses and warehouses of *Docks of New York* (1927), actual sites of working-class organization, have been legitimized as areas of scenic possibility by being presented as sites of crime. It was then ingenious on the part of the noir directors to, for a while, reverse this polarity while remaining within the ordinary iconography of the crime film. The fugitive outsider, middle or working class, hides out in these outré locales, the inner-city boardinghouses, bars, and backstreets, and often is aided, or at least not turned over, by the people who inhabit them, as the farm couple hides the escaped con in *Raw Deal*. In the 1950–55 period, conversely, these locales become not just sites of crime, of menace, but areas to be put under surveillance, either by the undercover cop or by the police dragnet, as in the manhunt for the killer on New York's Lower East Side in a film which formulates the police procedural, *The Naked City* (1948). In the light of the beginning of the purge of union activists, a location like the Lower East Side—a union stronghold and marker of demonstrations during the Depression, one of the places where the drive for union membership began—becomes, during the attack on labor that characterized the cold war, a hostile territory to be patrolled.

This counteracting of the characterization of the working class as criminal and the alternative of embracing the rebellious potential of the working class and its settings, which the noir directors in the 1940s accomplished visually and intuitively, was expressed theoretically in the 1950s and 1960s in the work of the British labor theorists who instituted cultural studies.

The most stirring chapter in E. P. Thompson's foundational cultural studies text, *The Making of the English Working Class* (1963), titled "Satan's Strongholds," details the ways working-class gatherings in the eighteenth century were criminalized and then points out how those gatherings could be seen instead as sites of class resistance. Protests against food shortages were termed "riots" and their participants "mobs" instead of being identified, as Thompson suggests, as protests by "revolutionary crowds" (62). Prostitutes, whose activity was labeled illegal, were often among the most class-conscious resisters of authority, while riots to protest the raising of prices at a plebeian theater indicated the strong sympathy for the French Revolution which the theater promoted.

Even more relevant to the film noir protagonist is Eric Hobsbawm's *Bandits* (1969). Hobsbawm characterizes bandits as pre-industrial peasant outlaws whom the lord and the state regarded as criminal but who remained within peasant society and were considered by their people as heroes. They were "champions, avengers, fighters for justice, perhaps even leaders of liberation, and in any case men [and women] to be admired, helped and supported" (13). The relation between the ordinary peasantry and the rebel is, for Hobsbawm, what makes social banditry interesting. He contends that modernization eliminates the conditions under which social banditry flourishes, but by his description of the social bandit one could make an excellent case that the film noir hero is the urban recollection of that older formation: the modern social bandit.

The bandit's career, like that of the sympathetic fugitive, "almost always begins with some incident which is not in itself grave, but drives him to outlawry; a police charge for some offence brought against the man rather than for the crime; false testimony; judicial error or intrigue; an unjust sentence to forced residence or one felt to be unjust" (Hobsbawm, *Rebels*, 16). This incident then leads the bandit, who is usually young, single, and without a family, to go on the run. He is felt to be honorable or a noncriminal by the population, and "once on the run he is protected by the peasants where 'our' [peasant] law stands against 'theirs' and 'our' justice against that of the rich" (*Rebels*, 16). Ultimately, when the error of the law is discovered, the "ex-bandit is easily integrated into society since only the state and the gentry considered his activities criminal" (*Rebels*, 18). This description might well be a synopsis of the plot of *Blue Dahlia* (1946), *Desperate* (1947), or *The Big Clock*, among others. The point here in Hobsbawm's terms is that "bandits share the values of the peasant world and are usually empathetic to its revolutionary surges" (Bandits, 85), the surges in the case of the immediate postwar being the working class striking for its share of wartime corporate profits and for the equality the war had promised, and a middle class striving for more control of its workplace conditions.

This view of crime as rebellion has been attacked (see, e.g., Platt's "Street Crime: A View from the Left") as a romanticization of an older mode of resistance that has been superseded by methods of industrial working-class organization. That critique sees what is sometimes called rebellion as instead a validation in the present of forms of disintegration (e.g., black-on-black street crime) that represent an extreme case of capitalist exploitation, as a part of "the universal market" that "destroys the material foundations of cooperative social relations" and "permeates even the private domain of personal life, setting husband against wife, neighbor against neighbor" (31).

This study, however, illustrates how the noir directors paralleled their outside-the-law hero not with the street criminal but with the working-class figure as a whole in the postwar era, thus reviving a pre-industrial mode of resistance for its rebellious potential in an industrial era. Their revival of this earlier form might more accurately be seen as a reaching into the past to recapture the collective spirit of a populace that was in the process of being broken down, disintegrated in the way that this critique describes.[3]

Why were the noir directors attracted to the crime film, and why did they use it to describe class conflict in the 1941–55 era? The beginning of the answer to this question lies in the role of the crime film as a genre. If, as various structuralist critics have maintained, following Lévi-Strauss's anthropological grouping of myths of various peoples, one function of literary and film genres is to mediate different aspects of social experience, the crime film is the genre that is concerned with the relationship of the individual and the law.[4]

The law is enforced by agents of the state for the preservation of the state, and in the 1941–55 period the role of the state vis-à-vis the law was expanding. To challenge the law during World War II—that is, to challenge government decrees such as the no-strike pact—was often portrayed as not only undesirable but traitorous. In the immediate postwar, workers in every major industry felt themselves outside the law as they staged strikes and then found these feelings materialized as the Taft-Hartley Act outlawed their actions.[5] Finally, in the later 1940s and 1950s, the HUAC investigations criminalized a much wider range of activity as "Communist." The law, or what one legal theorist calls "the language of the state" (Swidorski 178), entered daily life much more prominently, with actions that had not previously been a concern of the law now ruled criminal. With its various groupings of protagonists inside and outside the law, the crime film genre was ideally suited during this period to represent the tensions engendered by this expansion of government power.

Cultural front directors were also drawn to the crime film, because it had a history of expressing social problems as far back as *Musketeers of Pig Alley* (slum conditions) and including Fritz Lang's *You Only Live Once* (unemployment) and *Fury* (mob violence) in the 1930s. Indeed, immediately after the war, in films such as *Crossfire* (1947), with its references to a native American fascism in the form of anti-Semitism, these directors began to revive this tradition. They then were forced to retreat into more traditional generic patterns when *Crossfire*, specifically, was cited by HUAC.

Film Noir: Socialism in One Genre

Film noir has been defined in a variety of ways, none of which have previously centered on class. This study defines film noir as a permutation of the crime film that became the crime film dominant between 1945 and 1950, where the mainline of the genre consisted of a figure forced, usually, though not necessarily, through no fault of his or her own, outside the law. The main action of the film consists of the protagonist's attempt to prove his or her (or his *and* her, since men and women were as frequently class allies as antagonists) innocence, almost always against a foe whose class position was that of someone in charge, in control. The argument is that for one period, 1945–50, in one genre, ideas of the left were hegemonic, that they formed the core of the genre. Thus, for example, when Paul Schrader, in one of the earliest American writings on noir, says that good directors often did their best work in noir (Otto Preminger) and that even mediocre directors often did exemplary work in noir (John Farrow), this study posits the reason for that exceptional work as being that they were attuned to the left paradigm, which enabled this change in the crime genre to consistently convey ideas unusual in Hollywood, ideas such as the following: that because of society's latent inequality, the bottom could fall out of anyone's life at any time (economic precariousness); that most members of that society were involved in a struggle to survive, despite ideological premises that stated this wasn't so; and that the reason for this precariousness and this inequality could be located not in the working or middle classes but in a class that parasitically feasted off their labor and often arranged events to make these classes appear to be guilty.

A corollary of this definition of film noir is that not only does the protagonist move outside the law but the film itself creates what Murray Smith calls a "structure of sympathy" for that character; that is, the audience is sympathetic to the protagonist's struggle (see final section of this introduction). This definition of film noir is borne out by a statistical survey of the crime film in the 1945–50 period. Out of 441 crime films in the period, the dominant formation, 200 films, consists of the fugitive outsider.[6] The majority of the remaining films of the period fall into either the residual categories of the previous period's conventional or harassed detective or the emergent category of the police procedural, including films where the outlaw is a criminal informer or where the fugitive is now seen as a psychotic menace, films such as *White Heat* (1949) that establish, in contrast to the film noirs, a structure of antipathy toward their protagonist. (For a complete list see the appendix.)

In the voluminous literature in the field, class, though most often elided or vaguely hinted at, is cited only sporadically as having at least a tangential relation to film noir.[7] Paul Arthur sees the films as petit bourgeois cautionary tales about the danger of that class slipping into the working class, the "disavowed class" ("Gun" 98). Sylvia Harvey calls attention to noir as a middle-class formation expressing anxieties about "this feeling of being lost in a world of corporate values that are not sensitive to the needs and desires of the individual" (27). George Lipsitz stresses the parallel between the postwar wildcat striker and the film noir protagonist:

> The wildcat strike and mass demonstration circumvent legitimate channels to assert, however temporarily, the right to freedoms considered illegitimate by conventional standards. Similarly, film noir heroes break the law and avoid authorities to advance their own needs. They expect and fear disapproval and they battle enormous guilt, but they ultimately choose to be true to themselves even at the risk of appearing "illegitimate" to others. In film noir, the wildcat strike's rebellion against legitimacy becomes generalized into a means of survival and a standard of behavior for all the society. (*Rainbow* 178)

The present study argues that what occurs in the genre is the formation, in Gramsci's terms, of a hegemonic block of working- and middle-class positions that together call into question the (usually hegemonic) assumptions of the postwar American corporate class. That class responded to the Hollywood filmmakers with the HUAC hearings. The on-screen representation of that moment of repression is the generic work in the crime film of turning the film noir fugitive outsider into the 1950s working- or middle-class cop or the psychotic fugitive. American critics often make no distinction between the two periods, but that is not true of the most prescient students of film noir, the French critics Raymond Borde and Étienne Chaumeton, whose *Panorama du Film Noir Americain* in 1955 clearly identified the difference between the film noir told from "the point of view of the criminals" ("Definition" 20) with the fugitive viewed as "inglorious victim" (22), while the police, if they are featured at all, "are rotten," "sometimes even murderers" (21), and the later period's "police documentary," where the "investigators are portrayed as bright men, brave and incorruptible" (21).

The Return to a Working-Class Cultural Studies

Just as this study returns to the work of the early, more class-conscious, cultural studies movement in Britain for a description of class as active historical entity, so too does it return to the work of early cultural studies theoreticians for its theoretical grounding, foremost among them being Raymond Williams. Williams's concept of "structure of feeling" is useful in linking the social formation of labor history and the aesthetic representation of the crime film.

Williams defines "structure of feeling" as the representation through a cultural form of patterns of thought and emotion, most often by a subaltern group, that are not overtly articulated in the society at large. These structures, expressed through art and literature, or culture generally, are often not given voice in the bourgeois world, being "a kind of feeling and thinking which is indeed social and material, but [which exists] . . . in an embryonic phase before it can become fully articulate and defined exchange" ("Structures" 131).[8]

Thus, in each of the three periods the form of the crime film expresses the structure of feeling of labor as a whole: in the first period (1941–45), labor is harassed by the law, as is the detective who straddles the law; in the second period (1945–50), labor is defiant and outside the law; and in the third period (1950–55), labor is back inside the law policing its own as the working-class cops patrol working-class neighborhoods.[9] The structure of feeling is then used to provide a social context that helps to explain both the textual creation of a "structure of sympathy" during the noir period, when the audience is positioned with the fugitive outsider, and a "structure of antipathy" for the later "psychotic fugitive," where the audience participates voyeuristically in the destruction of the character[10] (both terms are explained more fully in the next section).

The second cultural studies formulation that illuminates this period of the crime film is derived from Antonio Gramsci. From his jail cell in the 1930s in Mussolini's Italy, Gramsci, particularly in a notebook titled "On the Margins of History," described the process by which, in William's terms, an "emergent" structure of feeling might become dominant. Gramsci's description of the subaltern, the marginalized of all kinds who could not speak in mainstream culture, included the working class whose culture had been devalued and silenced by upper-class intellectuals. This history was "necessarily fragmentary and episodic," especially since this history was usually written by those with little inclination to see this class move out of the shadows (qtd. in

Green 11).¹¹ In much the same way, working-class values had since the early 1920s begun to disappear from the Hollywood screen, replaced by a more middle-class gaze.¹²

Gramsci believed, though, that subaltern groups, including the proletariat, could become the dominant group and that their values could become hegemonic if they succeeded in creating a system of class alliances through promoting values that would "mobilize the majority of the working population against capitalism and the bourgeois state" (qtd. in Green 18).¹³ Following Gramsci, this study argues that in one genre, the crime film, in one period, 1945–50, in that permutation of the crime film known as film noir, this emergent structure of feeling of the militant working class became the dominant mode of the crime film, and that it became so through a working- and middle-class alliance against the threat of U.S. corporatism, an alliance directly observable on-screen.

But how could this moment occur, and what can it mean, given that this cultural formation was part of an industry owned and governed by corporate interests? To begin to answer this question, we must view this phenomenon as part of a wider process, a process that Michael Denning terms the "laboring of American culture," in effect the "proletarianization" of American culture, which consisted of "the increased influence on and participation of working-class Americans in the world of culture and the arts" (xvii). This phenomenon, which Denning terms the "cultural front," took place from 1934 to 1948 and coincided with the rise of the Congress of Industrial Organizations, taking that mass unionization movement as its popular base. Denning details how the sons and daughters of working-class parents moved into what Theodor Adorno termed the "culture industry" and effected change across the cultural spectrum, including Hollywood, so that two processes were taking place concurrently. Adorno describes a process of cultural commodification and intensification of cultural control from above at the same time that Denning describes an equally intense process of working-class contestation of cultural forms from below, which is to say, à la Gramsci, that the culture industry in this period was a contentious "site of (class) struggle."

In addition, in Hollywood in the 1940s three main currents of creative artists from milieus that were already highly politicized entered the industry, all three drawn to the crime film. First, writers came either from the directly working-class proletarian fiction that dominated the 1930s (A. I. Bezzerides, W. R. Burnett, Albert Maltz, Daniel Mainwaring) or from its close cousin the hard-boiled detective novel (Dashiell Hammett, Raymond Chandler, James M. Cain, Cornell Woolrich). Second, veterans of the highly politicized New York stage of the 1930s brought their commitment to social themes with them to Hollywood and found the crime film a congenial place to express these themes. This group included directors Orson Welles, Jules Dassin, Nicholas Ray, Joseph Losey, and Anthony Mann and actors John Garfield and Joseph Cotton. The third group included émigré directors fleeing fascism, most with a highly developed sense of class from both a stronger European tradition of class consciousness and from a sense that fascism was strongly anti-labor and anti-union.[14] Many of these directors, including Fritz Lang, Otto Preminger, Jean Renoir, Curtis Burnhardt, Stuart Heisler, Robert Siodmak, William Dieterle, and Boris Ingster (Naremore, *More Than Night*, 124), had worked in the crime film in Europe and found it a natural vehicle for expressing class antagonism. To this influx must be added the radicalizing experience of the early to mid-1940s in general where many members of the writers, actors, and directors guilds supported the militant struggle of the craftsworkers in the industry and were involved in constant struggles in their own guilds.[15]

Against a current of criticism that sees little or no evidence of this struggle on the screen, there has been a developing counter-trend in critics of film noir who find the films indeed evidencing working-class concerns. Denning asserts that these cultural front artists were continually trying to make films of "social significance" and that the "*noir thrillers*" were perhaps "the most lasting emblems of the culture industry radicals . . . of the 1930s and 1940s" (86). Brian Neve, in *Film and Politics in America*, claims that these "modestly budgeted crime films of the era were able to tell some home truths, as well as allowing some filmmakers on the left . . . to attempt more pointed comments on what [Thom] Andersen calls the 'injuries of class'" (170).[16]

However, the argument that working-class ideas were hegemonic has never been fully articulated. In "From the Nightmare Factory: HUAC and the Politics of Noir," Philip Kemp implies that the structure of the genre had changed in the noir period and that this change conditioned the possible responses of the crime film directors. Kemp asks how admittedly conservative writers like Leo Rosten, a firm critic of the Communists in Hollywood, and directors like John Farrow, a Catholic so devout he was appointed Knight of the Holy Sepulchre (268), could have collaborated on *Where Danger Lives*, a noir from 1950 that he claims illustrates Marx and Engels's dictum from the *Communist Manifesto* that the bourgeoisie "has left remaining no other nexus between man and man than naked self-interest, than callous 'cash payment'" (266).

Paul Schrader also, in his 1973 seminal article on noir, in a far more disguised way, perhaps indicates that this more socially and class-tinged change in the genre had breathed new life into it when he asked what it was about film noir that enabled writers and directors to do their best work, so that good directors made great film noirs and even mediocre directors made good film noirs (62). Finally, in a recent major study of noir, *More Than Night*, James Naremore, in making the most direct case for noir being a more straightforward working-class formation, points to "several junctures at which classic film noir is nearly indistinguishable from Odets-style social realism and from the larger history of the proletarian or 'ghetto' novel" (103).

This study, then, will outline how these ideas, which come to the surface through the lens of the cultural studies theorists Williams, Gramsci, and Denning, first emerge in the war, develop into a moment of hegemony with the noir protagonist representing a bloc of working- and middle-class characters, and then are repressed in the cold war period.

Through a Glass Darkly: Sympathetic and Psychotic Fugitives

In their seminal study of film noir in 1955, Borde and Chaumeton call attention to how the narration, that is, the overall process of telling the story, treats the protagonist. They claim that the primary distinguishing mark of film noir is "sympathy aroused during the greater part of the narrative for unsympathetic characters," these unsympathetic characters usually being criminals ("Definition" 21).

In describing both the individual films and the movement of the crime film genre as a whole in the 1941–55 era, this study, taking its cue from the French critics, employs Murray Smith's concept of "structure of sympathy." According to Smith, the text, through its narration, often creates structures of both sympathy and antipathy for its characters and does this primarily in two ways: first, alignment, which is bound up with the formal concept of "narrative discourse,"[17] and second, allegiance, which is tied more integrally to the story itself.

Alignment describes how the audience is placed in proximity to the character in terms of physical presence contributing to knowing what that character thinks and feels, with the idea being that, most often, the more the audience is in the presence of the character and the more the audience knows about the character, the stronger the sympathy. Alignment may be both spatial and subjective. Spatial alignment has simply to do with presence on the screen or through which character the story is told or, in Gérard Genette's term, focalized (M. Smith, "Altered States" 41). The classic example of an intense spatial alignment is the detective film in which the detective is present in almost every scene, since it is through his or her eyes that the crime is detected and solved.

The second form of alignment is subjective access, where the narrative discourse gives the audience a greater or lesser degree of access not only to the physical presence of the character but to what he or she is thinking and feeling. It is no mistake that some of the most striking experiments in subjective access in the Hollywood film are the techniques associated with film noir, such as voice-over narration at the beginning and throughout the film. A more intensified form of subjective access Smith terms "perceptual alignment" places the audience in the position of the lead character through such devices as point-of-view shots and subjective camera ("Altered States" 41). Perhaps the two most glaring examples of this technique in American film history take place in the noir period in *Lady in the Lake* (1947) and *Dark Passage* (1947), the former linking the audience with the detective harassed by the law and the latter linking the audience with the escaped convict to intensify sympathy for his attempts to elude the law.[18]

The second element in Smith's schema, allegiance, often acts in conjunction with alignment to more intensely promote the structure of sympathy. Allegiance is the attempt by the film to create agreement with the character's ideological position. This level of sympathy is produced dynamically in the course of the film through a number of different devices that suggest the desirability of the character's actions, thoughts, and feelings (M. Smith, *Engaging Characters* 188).[19] The most important way the text promotes allegiance is by validating character action—especially in Hollywood, where "character is virtually synonymous with character action" (192). Character action is often validated through the protagonist's relations with other characters. This includes both actions that are generally regarded as sympathetic, such as the generous treatment of weaker characters by a more dominant protagonist, and less acceptable actions that are made understandable through the character's explanation of those actions.

For example, Joe, the escaped convict in *Raw Deal*, is persistently challenged by the middle-class figure of Ann, but he consistently defends himself by proclaiming the social reasons for his "tough" background (he grew up in an orphanage, etc.); at the same time, in his actions, including his loyalty to his working-class ally Pat, he shows much warmth, or working-class solidarity, for those around him. Thus his words and actions promote allegiance for a position, that of the escaped convict, that would not ordinarily elicit audience sympathy. In the 1960s return of the postwar fugitive protagonist in the television series *The Fugitive* (covered in detail in chapter 5), at the end of the pilot, the convicted murderer Richard Kimble, fleeing the police, stops to pick up and pet a stray kitten. The gesture, which also points to his future life on the series as being like that of the stray or alley cat, presents Kimble as naive, childlike, and in a pun on the show's overarching legal formulation, as *innocent*.

Besides character action, there are at least four other ways of engendering allegiance, both intra- and extradiegetic, that is, both part of the story on the screen and outside it. Intradiegetic allegiance may be produced through iconography and character names, and extradiegetic allegiance is often engendered through music and star persona.

The iconography of the crime film (including the character's physical attributes and dress, and props associated with them) is deployed in *Raw Deal* as Joe, the everyman fugitive, associated with prison, gas stations, and flophouses, dresses in slacks, open shirt, and light jacket, while Rick, the gangster-businessman, lounges in a gaudily decorated townhouse and wears a smoking jacket with white shirt and tie. Character names in film noir also cue audience reaction. Joe is one of the most common names of the 1940s (giving rise to the sobriquet "ordinary Joe"), as is Sam, the detective's name in *The Maltese Falcon* (1941). The latter's full name, Sam Spade, also indicates someone who speaks plainly ("calls a spade a spade").[20] In contrast, the name of Spade's opponent, Casper Gutman, functions both to characterize his upper-class ostentatiousness, including his superfluous language, and, literally in the last name, his enormous girth, a sign of the overindulgence of the rich.

The extradiegetic Hollywood symphonic score in the film noir is repeatedly used to produce allegiance for the criminal outsider. In one of the earliest noirs, *Double Indemnity* (1944), both the scene where the frustrated insurance agent, Walter Neff, and the rich man's wife, Phyllis Dietrich, murder the husband and a later scene where Phyllis is nearly caught by the insurance investigator, Keyes, visiting Neff's apartment, are heightened by the discordant music that attempts to produce in the audience an anxiety over whether the lawbreakers will succeed, an anxiety that places the audience squarely on the side of the lawbreakers. Another key extradiegetic category is the shifting connotation of the Hollywood actor, his or her star persona, developed by the studios to create various kinds of character sympathy or, for villains, antipathy.[21] Humphrey Bogart had consistently been a sneering, amoral gangster in the 1930s (a role that is ultimately reprised at the end of the decade in *Roaring Twenties*, 1940), but at the beginning of the next decade his persona began to change with both *High Sierra* (1941), in which the gangster dies saving a crippled girl, and *They Drive by Night* (1940), in which he plays a working-class truck driver. Thus, in *The Maltese Falcon*, Bogart's hard-bitten detective, who at first is a murder suspect himself, also has a softer, romantic edge, and the gritty remarks he trades with the upper-class-aligned villains recall the working-class persona under construction as he speaks plainly and counters their flowery obsequiousness.

The hard-boiled detective film, with its lead character who is both inside and outside the law, features a strong spatial alignment with the detective, who is in almost every scene of the film, plus a gradually developing allegiance as the audience, which at first may find characters like Sam Spade (who borders on the criminal) unsympathetic, comes to accept his judgments. The film noir, with its fugitive outsider, features a strong spatial and exceptionally strong subjective alignment and a gradually shifting allegiance such that the audience comes to understand, accept, and value the lead character's position outside the law. Finally, the cold war police procedural and psychotic fugitive films, in their rewriting of the film noir, produce a more complicated combination of allegiance and alignment and a shift from a structure of sympathy to a structure of antipathy for the fugitive. These films are often split between the police, with whom there is limited spatial and almost no subjective alignment but strong allegiance, simply because they represent the law, and the fugitive, with whom there is again a strong spatial and sometimes even subjective alignment, but because of the viciousness of his or her acts, which are clearly labeled "criminal," an allegiance that shifts from initially sympathetic to ultimately condemnatory. Films such as *Niagara* (1953), examined in depth in chapter 4, begin with the assumption from the film noir period that the outsider character, who narrates his feelings in voice-over, is sympathetic, then dynamically in the course of the film moves to generate antipathy for that character so that at the end the audience "sees" the need for his elimination, in this case in order that the corporate world function more smoothly without the militant labor figure.

Chapter 1 outlines the wartime labor struggles, when actively protesting conditions on the job might be labeled traitorous, and traces the emergent moment in the first-period crime film (1941–45) of the hard-boiled detective, him- or herself often outside the law.

Chapters 2 and 3 first describe the postwar period (1945–50) of strikes in the country as a whole and most pointedly in Hollywood, a period that is followed by the actions of the strikers being directly declared illegal in the Taft-Hartley Act, then traces the parallel rise to dominance of the film noir fugitive outsider. This figure is described in all his or her class positions as under-class, working class, and middle class through such instances as the criminal fugitive, the amnesiac war veteran, the Depression-era drifter, and the detective now a criminal him- or herself.

Chapter 4 deals with the immediate aftermath of the film noir period (1950–55), describing the rollback in the country as a whole and in Hollywood in particular of the militant labor position through the use of the Communist menace and the concomitant turn in the crime film to an embracing of all modes of law enforcement. The working-class cop of the police procedural at first rebels and becomes a fugitive him- or herself, but then transforms into an upstanding member of a society charged with subduing the threat of "psychotic" outsiders (the remade figure of the 1940s sympathetic fugitive), and finally moves outside the law him- or herself, but this time in order to more strongly defend it as a vigilante cop.

Chapter 5 describes the persistence of the sympathetic fugitive, often countering the persistently reoccurring counter-figure of the working-class cop from the police procedural. The fugitive reemerges first in a forty-year dispute on television between producer Roy Huggins's outsiders (*Maverick*, *The Fugitive*, *Rockford Files*) and Jack Webb's institutional stalwarts (*Dragnet*, *Adam-12*, *Dragnet* again); continues in the Reagan-Bush era in neo-noir proper, most prominently in David Lynch's critiques of a reactionary indolence in *Blue Velvet* and *Twin Peaks*; and persists on television in the 1990s until being silenced in the visual media in the post-9/11 new cold war in the wake of an overwhelming return to the police procedural as television series such as *24* were rewritten to transform the fugitive cop into a vigilante.

Yet still the anti-authoritarian fugitive outsider and the critique of the existing order persist in the detective fiction of the new millennium as a promise waiting to be kept in the visual media, just as 1930s detective fiction begat the noir cycle in 1940s Hollywood.

chapter 1

The Home-front Detective as Dissident Lawman (and -woman)

Hammett, Chandler, Woolrich, and 1940s Hollywood

The self-employed detective Sam Spade prowling the mean streets of San Francisco in search of a golden bird would not on the surface appear to have much in common with the man or woman on the assembly line working overtime to produce the weapons and devices needed to fight fascism, but this chapter will argue that in their inner life, in the crucial way they characterized authority, and in their modes of making sense of reality and dealing with pressures from above, there was a world of similarity between the wartime or home-front detective and his or her labor counterpart. This detective, like the worker on the assembly line who engaged in various job actions, at first straddled the law and later went outside it, ultimately reworking the law to fit his or her own morality and in the process paving the way for the fugitive outsider and the labor equivalent, the postwar militant striker.

Labor's Untold Story Told and Revised

Although on the Hollywood screen World War II was largely fought on the battlefield, in reality the war was largely fought in the factories by working men and women who produced the weapons and materials necessary for first the Russians and then the Allies together to fight and defeat the fascist powers. One of the earliest accounts of working people's side of the war, *Labor's Untold Story*, published by the left-led Electrical Workers Union, celebrates this anti-fascist effort, adding the astounding fact that there were more wartime casualties in American factories than on the battlefield (88,000 killed and 11,112,600 injured on the home front, eleven times as many as those in combat) (Boyer and Morais 334).

This was a period of great sacrifice, not only by the 3.25 million men and women in uniform but in the factories as well. *Labor's Untold Story* proudly relates how workers, convinced of the validity of the anti-fascist cause, maintained a no-strike pledge throughout the war, went on a forty-eight-hour workweek, and accomplished ever greater feats of production. The war was also a period of growing strength for organized labor, as union enrollment jumped from 8.9 million in 1940 to 14.7 million men and women in 1945.

But if labor was strong, business was stronger. Not only profits but also business power grew during the war as business and government interests overlapped ever more tightly. Corporate profits during the war were 250 percent higher than before the war, averaging $22 billion per year during the war, a figure which exceeded that of 1929, until then the most profitable year for American industry (Boyer and Morais 333). These gains were primarily the result of two factors: first, a 45 percent rise in prices and a corresponding freeze on wages during the war, such that wages rose only 15 percent over the 1941 level in the five years of the war; and second, direct government participation in this upward redistribution of wealth with the freeze on wages and the no-strike pledge both being Roosevelt initiatives. Millions in taxes were handed to business in the form of government war contracts and tax-free war plants, with the revenue appropriated from a 10 percent War Bond and a 5 percent Victory Tax coming out of workers' salaries (Boyer and Morais 319).

Thus, alongside the feelings of contributing to a collective struggle went the growing feeling that the sacrifices were all going one way: workers were sacrificing, and corporations were profiting. John Dos Passos describes this growing recognition after visiting a United Auto Workers gathering in 1943: "The gist of it was that the men couldn't get over the suspicion that the great automobile concerns were using the war emergency for their own purposes: When it was over they were the ones who would come out on top" (qtd. in Lichtenstein 119).

There was also a growing ambiguity in labor's relation to government, expressed, as the war progressed, as an ever-accelerating tendency of labor to go outside the law. Though Roosevelt's New Deal was often seen, especially in its recognition of the right to collective bargaining, as aiding the cause of labor, a revisionist wave of historians viewed New Deal attempts to resolve class conflicts and antagonisms through the trade union movement and the Democratic Party as concerned with creating "the structural forms which regulated future capital accumulation and class conflicts" (Levine 172).[1] In this sense, the structural role of the state in managing labor greatly accelerated during the war, when a large-scale movement of business directly into government resulted in the "transformation of government as a key instrument for asserting the hegemony of large corporations over American society" (Lipsitz, *Rainbow* 7).

Corporate executives presided over the War Board, which was responsible for all wartime industrial planning, and the result for labor was a combination of no-strike pledge, an agreement to settle for minimal wage increases, increased overtime at minimal increase of pay, and a drive for increased productivity. Business interests had long craved these changes; what was unique here was the government's direct collusion. Since all the changes were claimed as necessary for winning the war, opposition to any element of this package could be portrayed as not only unpatriotic but even treasonous. One war poster proclaimed that "the day after payday is no time to relax," suggesting that to relax when one's subsistence requirements are satisfied or when one has a certain level of material possessions contributes to the rising number of military casualties (Kessler-Harris 116).

"Patriotism" became a way of enforcing these decrees and the concept came to signify combined business and government pressure on workers. In this era, then, for the first time, corporate policy began to acquire the added legitimacy of the law because it had the backing of government. To oppose that policy meant in a dangerous sense during the war to be outside the law. As an example of this new collusion, during one strike against an airplane defense plant in California, federal troops were called in to end the job action. Once the strike was ended, the troops patrolled the plant floor for weeks afterward. The strike leaders were deposed by the army but continued to command fierce loyalty from the workers in the plant (Lichtenstein 62).

Thus, both sides hardened in the course of the war, as business sought increasingly larger gains and labor became increasingly discontent and rebellious. At the onset of the war, in 1941, defense planning was orchestrated through the Defense Mediation Board composed of business and labor representatives in what was viewed as a joint effort. Quickly this board gave way to the War Production Board with no labor representation,[2] headed first by the more consumer-oriented and liberal Sears Roebuck director Donald Nelson but later by the more hard-line General Electric chairman Charles Wilson, an architect of the cold war (Van Der Pijl 114).[3]

Correspondingly, during the first half of the war (1941–43) workers were more likely to toe the line and to create short slowdowns and work stoppages over issues other than wages, issues that were more likely to concern workers' relative freedom at the plant and the safety conditions of the plants. "Workers generally supported the no-strike pledge but as a practical matter they refused to allow it to interfere with their struggle against intolerable working conditions," writes Lipsitz (*Rainbow* 31). By 1943, though, workers became more militant and began a series of wildcat strikes. In response, Roosevelt issued a dramatic "hold-the-line" order to prevent the strikes from destroying the wage controls (Van Der Pijl 133). This resistance was no doubt fueled by the fact that though there was full employment during the war, wages were at their lowest point in twenty years (114).

These new strikes were mostly wildcat strikes waged against the confluence of forces that were thought to be impinging on the workers, an array that now included for the first time not only government and business but also union leaders,[4] who were increasingly operating as guarantors of union docility.[5] The strikes, which broadened in impact to contest wages as well as work conditions, increased enormously in number from 1943 to 1944; by the end of the war the number of strikes had exceeded even the high strike year of 1937 (Lichtenstein 119–21).

One of the most remarkable descriptions of how the war did not paper over the conditions or the resentment in the factories was provided by the African American author Chester Himes in *If He Hollers Let Him Go*. Written at the end of this period, the novel is based on Himes's experiences in the defense shipbuilding industry in Los Angeles, the city itself a booming combination of the two industries—defense and entertainment—that would fuel the American economy for the next fifty years and would often support each other. Himes's novel centers on the particular pain experienced by his African American lead character, but this initial description applies as well to all workers in the factory.

> The decks were low and with the tools and equipment of the workers, the thousand and one lines of the welders, the chippers, the blowers, the burners, the light lines, the wooden staging, combined with the equipment of the ship, the shapes and plates, the ventilation trunks and ducts, reducers, dividers, transformers, the machines, lathes, mills, and such, half yet to be installed, the place looked like a littered madhouse. I had to pick every step to find a foot-size clearance of deck space, and at the same time to keep looking up so I wouldn't tear off an ear or knock out an eye against some overhanging shape. Every two or three steps I'd bump into another worker. The only time anybody apologized was when they knocked you down. (16)

This contradiction of supporting the war effort while experiencing its ill effects affected the petite bourgeoisie and middle class as well. During the war, large corporations, through their position in government on the War Board, which allowed them to determine business policy, waged war against their smaller, independent rivals by awarding contracts to larger firms, thus wiping out more and more small businesses and increasing the concentration of corporate power. According to historian George Lipsitz, the war was the beginning of the closing down of the long-held American dream of independent employment (*Rainbow* 7).

Thus while the goal of defeating the fascist powers was the same for both business and labor, the rationale for fighting and engaging in the war was very different, and from the midpoint to the end of the war the antagonism of working- and middle-class employees toward those whom the war was benefiting became increasingly pronounced and more openly expressed.

Hollywood Labor's Untold Story

Consistently during the years from 1941 to 1955, a period when labor was at the forefront of American life, Hollywood labor relations were far more than just a microcosm of American labor relations. They were the epitome of labor relations, as virulent and vociferous both in their militancy and in the repression that militancy engendered as in any other sector of the economy.

It is important to understand two major factors about Hollywood labor in the 1940s. First, it was divided between the crafts and creative workers, and second, before the 1940s it had been mostly docile and plagued by either no unions or, worse still, corrupt or sweetheart workers organizations. The artificial distinction between "crafts" workers and "creative" workers—the names themselves implying which group was more highly valued—helped divide the Hollywood labor market. As Herb Sorrell, the leader of a group of rebellious locals who would eventually attempt to link all the workers, said, in pointing to this false dichotomy, what is a set decorator (a "crafts" worker) but "a man who studies periods of furniture, periods of architecture, knows what kinds of rugs (to place) into certain castles, what kinds of furnishings to (place) in certain kinds of homes. . . . He is in a way an artist" (qtd. in Horne 158).

The crafts unions at the onset of the war were represented by the International Association of Theatrical and Stage Employees (IATSE), a member of the American Federation of Labor. Not only was the IATSE a union strongly accommodating to management (historians Larry Ceplair and Steven Englund characterize it as consistently more sensitive to the needs of the studio executives than to those of its rank and file), but IATSE members also made themselves available to the studios as "scabs, strike-breakers, and thugs" both during and increasingly after the war (Ceplair and Englund 87). The height of this corruption was illustrated in a series of trials from 1940 to 1943 of the IATSE head George Browne and his mob compatriot Willy Bioff. During the trials there was testimony that the studios were paying the mob to infiltrate the union to halt strikes, and one witness estimated that the mob influence saved the studios $1.5 million in funds not lost to strikes or to increased wages (Friedrich 65, 80).[6]

As for the "creative" workers, the war years were a period of consolidation for the fledgling writers, actors, and directors guilds, all finally acknowledged as legitimate bargaining units but also constantly under studio attack. The Screen Writers Guild (SWG) was founded in 1933 but was not initially recognized by the studios, and it was nearly crushed when the studios instead backed their own counter-unit, the Screen Playwrights, in 1937. The government in the form of the National Labor Relations Board intervened in 1938, ruling that an election for a union should be held, and the SWG won the election. Still, it was not until 1940 that the studios agreed to a first union contract and not until 1941 that regular bargaining sessions began, with that session being marked by Jack Warner having to be escorted out of the room screaming "You goddamn Commie bastards . . . want to take my goddamned studio" (Friedrich 73–77). To give an idea of the resistance to the formation of independent creative unions, Fox's Darryl Zanuck, regarded as a liberal within the industry, at the time when the SWG was first asserting itself as a collective bargaining agent, remarked, "If those guys set up a picket line and try to shut down my studio, I'll mount a machine gun on the roof and mow them down" (Friedrich 74).

The Screen Actors Guild received its first contract in 1937, and by 1940 it included nearly 50 percent of all actors (May 128), though it was constantly fighting battles with the studios over contracts. The contract situation, described by anthropologist Hortense Powdermaker as "more like the medieval power relationships of lord and serf than of the employer and employee in the modern world" (Friedrich 194), was so exploitative that Olivia de Havilland won her freedom from a Warner Brothers contract because the courts ruled that the studio had violated a California law which stated that servitude for more than seven years constituted slavery (196). Elsewhere, the Screen Directors Guild was in existence longer but was a much less effective union body.

Both the crafts and creative workers (henceforth referred to as the unions and the guilds, respectively) strongly supported the war as an anti-fascist effort. The no-strike pledge held in the Hollywood unions until the last year of the war, when it broke down dramatically, and the guilds were leading contributors to the war efforts, led by the SWG, whose members created the Hollywood Writers Mobilization (HWM). The HWM provided propaganda assistance to the government, including scripts for war-bond drives, documentary scripts for the War Department, and speeches for government officials (Ceplair and Englund 186).[7]

As with industry as a whole, the film industry profited enormously from the war. Just as the new prestige of the heads of other industrial sectors was tied to their capacity to create the products of war, so too did increased prestige accrue to the studios because of their role in making fictional war films and documentaries and training films for the government. The studios welcomed this role as official and unofficial propaganda dispensers, a role that made criticism of what previously might have seemed a trivial "entertainment" industry unpatriotic.

Government also greatly supported the growth and the monopolization of the industry during the war, as it did with industry as a whole. Though the industry's monopolistic practices of blind and block booking of films in theaters was outlawed in 1938, the outlawing was not enforced, and by 1944 the theater owners were back in court finally forcing the government to act against the studios for violating the Sherman Antitrust Act. Even after this action, the ruling had not begun to be enforced until 1948 (Friedrich 197).

Government contracts for "voluntary" studio propaganda work helped keep productive capacity, despite the loss of key overseas markets in Europe, at near prewar levels. The government work, dispensed by Fox Studio head Darryl Zanuck, reinforced the monopoly system as well, since Zanuck handed out the majority of the work to his own studio and three other majors (RKO, Paramount, MGM) (Friedrich 78) and did it in such a way as to compensate for down time lost to decreased production. In addition, to compensate for workers lost to the armed forces, the studios increased the workweek from thirty-six to forty-eight hours, taking advantage of the climate for extra work created by the mandatory forty-eight-hour workweek that was declared for all defense industry workers in Los Angeles County, one of the centers of the defense industry (Friedrich 73). Finally, movies themselves became more popular than ever domestically. Theaters stayed open around the clock to accommodate the staggered shifts in the factories. Patriotism, then, for the studios, was synonymous with profit.

Like American labor as a whole, Hollywood labor grew more and more suspicious and antagonistic during the war as it watched the studios prosper while the workers, now working harder than ever, were told that agitating or striking for a share of these profits was greedy and traitorous (Buhle and Wagner 161). The guilds and independent owners also watched as the government-studio union, with mob collusion, increased the power and centralization of the five major studios.

As early as 1941, though, things began to change. A cartoonists strike at Disney resulted in the birth of a militant crafts movement as the local refused to comply with the IATSE guidelines.[8] Herb Sorrell, the strike's leader, saw the future as an organization of locals who would fight the IATSE leadership, and in 1943, when IATSE head Richard Walsh, a defender of the mob-tainted former IATSE head Browne, signed a contract giving the IATSE the right to bargain for all studio locals, three more locals joined Sorrell's fledgling organization (Horne 137). By March 1945, before the war had ended, the Confederation of Studio Unions (CSU) was ten thousand members strong, as opposed to sixteen thousand IATSE members. It was the CSU that began the American strike wave of that year even before the war had ended, a strike wave that was to encompass almost every American industry from September 1945 to April 1946.

Thus, in Hollywood as in the nation as a whole, the wartime antifascist consensus by the middle of the war and increasingly from then on collided with the sense that, under the guise of patriotism, the law was increasingly being used as a device to bludgeon working people into participating at no benefit to themselves in the increased prestige, profits, and power of American business.

The Hollywood Detective Film: From Over Easy to Hard-boiled

The crime film of the 1930s followed a pattern that is typical of Hollywood film history as a whole. The decade began with an opening, a daring moment, followed by a repression of that moment, and concluded with a tentative step toward a reopening.

From 1930 to 1932, with the onset of the Depression, the gangster film was the crime film dominant. Most pointedly in three canonical films (*Little Caesar*, 1930; *Public Enemy*, 1931; *Scarface*, 1932), the narration, though at first sympathetic and then antagonistic to the gangster, nevertheless was almost entirely focalized through the outside-the-law figure who never repents from beginning to end. Allegiance toward the gangster is promoted because of his position as underprivileged child of the streets, like Tom Powers (James Cagney) in *Public Enemy*. This allegiance is ultimately withdrawn, often because of the way the gangster in his rise to power betrays his origins in the streets, as Powers kills Putty Nose, whom he has known since they were kids, because Powers has been told that his boyhood companion "thinks you're soft." Thus allegiance here is both solicited and withdrawn because of the protagonist's degree of class alliance.

The official outcry over the popularity of these films resulted in their banishment from the screen a scant two years later with the enforcement of the Hollywood production code in 1934.[9] As a further reaction to this moment, in the latter half of the decade the Hollywood crime film was instead focalized through the lawman, with the films often deliberately rewriting the earlier sympathy for the gangster's working-class roots. Cagney, though keeping his street origins, in *G-Men* (1935) was transformed into an FBI agent, hunting down the type of character he formerly portrayed, then further repudiating his past when, as a gangster in *Angels with Dirty Faces* (1938), he replaced his once tragic death as farce with his breaking down before being executed as part of a pithy "crime doesn't pay" moral. This moment continues as Edward G. Robinson, the sociopathic "Ricco" (of "Is this the end of Ricco") in *Little Caesar*, appears as an informer cop in *Bullets and Ballots* (1936), and it reaches its apotheosis when gangster-on-the-lam Robinson enters a monastery and, miraculously, decides to stay in *Brother Orchid* (1941).[10]

This trend is countered only in two remarkable films by German émigré Fritz Lang, both of which question the ability to pursue the American dream and presage the noir period. In the first, *Fury* (1936), the Spencer Tracy everyman (or every American), whose commonness is stressed both by the casting of the down-to-earth Tracy and by his humble dreams of owning his own business and having a happy life with "his girl," is nearly lynched when he is mistaken for a fugitive and ends the film completely disillusioned with society for its inability to guarantee his (exceedingly humble) dream. *You Only Live Once* (1937) goes further in its siding with the everyman character; here a convict, prototypically played by the even more quintessential American Henry Fonda, fails in his quest to go straight after two previous convictions. This character's flirtation with the American dream of being married and owning a house is even shorter lived than Tracy's in *Fury*, and his fate is worse. His death at the hands of nebulous but menacing cops, whose uniforms resemble those of Nazi storm troopers, is depicted as a crucifixion. With the coming of the war, the gangster was banished from the screen in the U.S. propaganda effort to show crime as being stamped out along with poverty and struggles around work. "Movies," critic Carlos Clarens says, "supplied the public with the image of a seamless democratic society, free of dissent" (172).

However, help in returning the crime film to its more class-conscious roots in the early sound era arrived from an unexpected source. The detective subgenre was established in the post-production-code moment as consisting mainly of what William Everson termed "the dapper detective," a mainly upper-class character for whom crime was essentially a parlor game. Among the screen detectives of this cycle were the dashing Bulldog Drummond, played by Ronald Colman and Ralph Richardson, who reigned on the screen from 1934 to 1937; the "ineffably cultured" Philo Vance, played by William Powell, whose persona suggested fast-paced comedy; and the dilettante Nero Wolfe, "a self-proclaimed genius who detested work" (Rimoldi 172). The debonair sleuths seldom involved themselves personally in the case, which they solved primarily with their "exceptional powers of imagination and…deduction" (172). Ironically, the most famous of the classical debonair detectives was the Dashiell Hammett–adapted *Thin Man* series (1934–41 with two later entries in 1944 and 1947), with Dick Powell and Myrna Loy as a couple in the midst of the Depression flaunting a decadent upper-class lifestyle and detecting on the side, with the villains in the series often carrying undertones of those who threatened their wealth from below.

The production history of *The Maltese Falcon* is emblematic of the change in the detective film from the production-code-induced denial

Figure 1. Sam Spade under pressure from the law in *The Maltese Falcon*.

of the Depression of the mid-1930s to the turn to more contemporary, hard-edged themes at the onset of the war in the early 1940s. The first (1931) version of the film starred Ricardo Cortez, doing his best Rudolph Valentino as a suave, dapper adventurer who operated not out of a dingy office but out of a lavishly decorated bachelor apartment where he was clad not in rumpled trench coat but in silk dressing gown (Friedrich 79). This "Queer Eye for the Straight Detective" version was followed in 1936 by the Bette Davis vehicle *Satan Met a Lady*. The first version played Spade's stark and unromantic turning over of the damsel in distress, Brigid, to the police for murder at the end as the beginning of a soon-to-be-requited love affair, and the second reinterpreted the ending from the melodramatic point of view of the suffering murderess. Both distorted Hammett's novel, and neither was successful at the box office (Friedrich 79).

When John Huston chose *The Maltese Falcon* for his first directorial project, the producers, Hal Wallis and Henry Blanke, were surprised at his wanting to remake a two-time failure, but in Huston's view "*The Falcon* had never really been put on the screen" (Friedrich 80). The Hollywood legend is that Huston asked a secretary to draft a first version of the book, which she did by cutting out the dialogue and pasting it onto a story board (Luhr, *Falcon*). The result was one of the most faithful renderings of a book on the screen. In so doing, Huston highlighted Hammett's tough, working-class-aligned language and Spade's ambiguous position toward the law, including his run-ins with the police and the district attorney and the audience's suspicion that he is the murderer. Just as Hammett had changed the detective novel (as Raymond Chandler put it, "Hammett gave murder back to the kind of people that commit it for reasons, not just to provide a corpse; and with the means at hand, not with handwrought dueling pistols, curare, and tropical fish . . . put these people down on paper as they are and . . . [made] them talk and think in the language they customarily used for these purposes" [Cawelti 309]), so too Huston, with his direct adaptation of Hammett, changed the detective film.

What Huston accomplished, what Chandler's description points to, was to bring the class contradictions manifest in the detective film to the fore. Spade's attitude toward money (his constant demand to get paid), his direct language (as opposed to the ostentatious language of his upper-class opponents), and his antagonism to the law (to the point of being a suspect himself) add to the already established concentration of the detective on the process of work and invest this character with a working-class-inflected mode of relating to the world. In addition, not only would the Hollywood detective film move away from its upper-class, Sherlock Holmes–style 1930s leanings, but as the war continued, in tandem with the dissatisfaction of the workers toward the government's no-strike clause, the detective would become more antagonistic to the law as the main detective adaptee moved from Hammett to Chandler.

World War II's Mean Streets

The anticipation of U.S. engagement in World War II and that engagement itself prompted a change in the content of Hollywood films. Screenwriter Robert Rossen's opinion expressed in *New Masses* that "In many quarters there was an expectation that war would now allow the movies to deal more fully with the real issues that concerned ordinary Americans" (qtd. in Stead 141) became a limited reality. Films made immediately before and during the war tended far more than in the period of the mid- to late 1930s to deal with contemporary subjects, but they put a patriotic gloss on the treatment of those subjects.[11]

The Hollywood genre that exhibited this new realism most stridently was the war film. The war film, and particularly its most common variant, the platoon film, tended to concentrate on the individual unit of the platoon and the ethnic types who inhabited it. Platoon life, not only in its anti-fascist purpose but also in its organization and lived experience, validated American democracy, with the point of the film being the platoon's banding together to overcome the enemies of its own form of democracy.[12]

For the most part, home-front contemporary films tended to show patriotic citizens of the democracy banding together, though there were a few notable exceptions. The early noir films challenged this syrupy portrayal of the inner lives of Americans and instead pointed to the class contradictions that the war, far from alleviating, in some ways exacerbated.[13] The left-wing labor-aligned writers in Hollywood worked on both types of films, the combination of which often presented a kind of schizophrenic view of American society as illustrated in the work of two future Hollywood Ten members. Lester Cole's *Objective Burma* (1945) has a swashbuckling Errol Flynn leading his multiethnic troops in a charge in the Pacific theater, while the early noir *Among the Living* (1941) suggested in its critique of southern post-plantation life within a degenerate family that the residue of slavery was still very much alive. Albert Maltz's *Destination Tokyo* (1942), in which the democratic battlefield platoon is reconfigured on a submarine with captain Cary Grant, finds its negative expression in the same year in the doomed loneliness and alienation of Alan Ladd's hit man who in the end has more integrity than his fascist employer in *This Gun for Hire*.

The mainline of the crime film in the 1940–45 period saw the genre at first groping toward the hard-boiled detective who challenged the law. With *Maltese Falcon* and *Murder My Sweet* (1943) that movement was codified and then became a standard most strongly enforced by subsequent multiple adaptations of Raymond Chandler.

Both *Stranger on the Third Floor* (1940) and *Among the Living* featured protagonists who, though not detectives, were forced to make sense of crimes in which they were potentially involved. *Stranger*'s reporter, Mike Ward, attempts to move up the social ladder by testifying against a taxi driver in a murder case, then suffers from what might be a guilty hallucination and is himself accused of a second murder with the same MO. He is then saved by his fiancée-turned-detective, who discovers Peter Lorre's *M*-influenced killer, also presented sympathetically as more mentally disturbed than evil. In the end the reporter, his girlfriend, and the taxi driver celebrate their working- and middle-class connection rather than using each other for upward mobility.[14] *Among the Living* features both a protagonist, John, who is a double of his murderous brother Paul (whose acts, like those of the Peter Lorre figure in *Stranger*, are attributed to the degeneracy of Southern post-plantation society and not to him), and an angry southern lynch mob which functions as the embodiment of a law that the film sees as tainted by its past exploitation through slavery, a not-so-abstract cause of the degeneracy of the present.[15]

While the hard-boiled detective represented a toughening of the dapper detective, the impetus for the realization of this figure also came from a corresponding softening of the gangster. In *High Sierra*, which immediately preceded *Maltese Falcon*, Bogart's sometimes psychotic gangster of the 1930s, here named "Mad Dog" Earle, is transformed into a largely sympathetic figure whose death in a typical shootout with the police occurs not because of his isolation and increased greed but because he sticks around to donate his loot for an operation to benefit a crippled woman who is in love with him. The next year featured Alan Ladd as Raven, a highly romanticized and sympathetic contract killer who is introduced in the process of performing a killing in *This Gun for Hire*, a script adapted from the Graham Greene novel.[16] Raven's work, though not condoned, is explained in part by his brutal treatment as a youth. He is caught between the law, in the figure of a cop who arranges his death partly because Raven has stolen the cop's girlfriend (Veronica Lake), and his employer, a chemical magnate who wants to profit from the war by selling a formula to the Nazis. Raven turns detective to find the identity of the industrialist and then kills him just prior to being killed himself. This double bind—the worker for hire caught between the law (or government) and a war-profiteering corporatism—restructures the gangster film to accommodate the structure of feeling of the wartime proletariat. Ladd subsequently appeared in *The Glass Key* (1942), another Hammett adaptation, which this time crossed the gangster and detective film more directly with Ladd as smooth consigliore Ned Beaumont, a kinder, gentler Karl Rove–like adviser to his gangster turned political candidate boss who might have been framed for a murder or may be guilty.

Early 1940s detective series also reflected this change to the lawman now straddling the law. Whereas in the 1930s these series consisted of the rigorously law-abiding *Thin Man*, *Charlie Chan*, and *Mr. Moto*, wartime series included the transposition into the Mike Shayne series, in an entry titled *Time to Kill* (1942), of the plots of one of the most class conscious of Chandler's Philip Marlowes, *The High Window*, which details the generations of murder required to amass and retain a family fortune and the creation of the Boston Blackie character, a reformed safecracker who, for example, in *Chance of a Lifetime* (1943), takes the murder rap for an escaped con and then proves him innocent. This trend continues immediately after the war with the increased importation of Chandler's Marlowe, including 1946's *Big Sleep* and 1947's *Lady in the Lake* and *The High Window*, this time featuring Marlowe and renamed *The Brasher Doubloon*. (For a more thorough listing of outside-the-law detective films of the World War II period, see the appendix.)

Hammett and Chandler: Class as Crime

This section, by examining the two seminal crime films of the wartime period, *The Maltese Falcon* and *Murder My Sweet*, will focus on five ways that this more faithful adaptation of the hard-boiled detective to the Hollywood screen introduced elements of class antagonism into the products of an industry where elsewhere there was only class harmony, elements that, taken together, made for an alignment or congruence of the position of the detective straddling the law and organized labor itself in this period. The elements, all key to the hard-boiled detective narrative, were a focus on money and "getting paid"; a corresponding focus on the process of work; the detective's use of language as plain speaking where many around him use it for obfuscation; a resentment toward the rich and the upper-middle professional classes; and an increasingly antagonistic relationship to the law. These elements indicate not only a congruence in terms of class position but also a similarity in the ways each made sense of the world.

This increasingly class-conscious attitude was aided by the link in the 1930s and 1940s between the detective and proletarian novels, a form featuring worker protagonists that developed in the wake of the Depression.[17] Proletarian novelist Benjamin Appel, who himself wrote stories that included a gangster element, stressed this link: "Some of the best of the tough guy novels were also among the best of the proletarian novels" (qtd. in Denning 221). In addition, in the 1940s, as the crime story in both film and fiction became a site of more direct expression of outrage against the law, "a number of writers connected to the proletarian-literature movement . . . turned to detective and mystery fiction" (Denning 257). Hammett himself was not above political allegory in the detective novel, most strikingly in *Red Harvest* (1929), where the detective is called in to clean up a town of gangsters originally employed by the industrialist who owns the town to break a strike by the Wobblies (International Workers of the World). The thugs break the strike, but then, in a parallel Hammett draws with Mussolini in Italy, stay around to take over the government (see Marcus).

Getting Paid

The classical detective was most often independently wealthy or at least never deigned to introduce the vulgar subject of his own income into the investigation. In contrast, Spade and Marlowe are highly concerned (and Spade is at times obsessed) with how often and how much they will be paid for their work. Thus the detective's romantic quest for justice is here also seen as ordinary work, grounded in the capitalist relations of employer and employee.

Spade's relation with Brigid O'Shaughnessy and the other treasure hunters in *The Maltese Falcon* is permeated by his concern and *need* to be paid. When Brigid initially hires him, she puts a hundred-dollar bill on his desk. He stares at her with no comment, and under this scrutiny she adds a second hundred-dollar bill. "Will that be enough?" she asks. Bogart's Spade for the first time smiles slightly as he takes her money. She mouths the word "Thanks" and he replies, "Not at all."

Later, when Spade discovers she has been lying to him and that the work is more dangerous than he first assumed, he asks, "How much money have you got?" "Five hundred dollars," she replies. "Give it to me," he barks. Finally, when her money is all gone and the work is now even more dangerous, she asks, "What else is there I can buy you with?" He replies by kissing her. She can buy him with sex. They do later sleep together, and though it is presented in the middle-class terms of romantic love, a feature of the relationship is the impossibility of separating sex from the necessity of money, a much more working-class conception of the deed.

Spade continues to bargain for money with the other seekers of the Falcon, Gutman and Cairo, in the end taking a thousand dollars from Gutman for his time, but perhaps the ultimate expression of Spade's unwillingness to dissociate his need to be paid from the romantic quest of the detective occurs in the final moments of the film when he explains why he is turning Brigid over to the police for the murder of his partner in spite of the fact that he has feelings for her. She asks if he would have turned her loose if the Falcon had been real and he answers, not disingenuously, "A lot more money would have been one more item on your side of the scales."

Marlowe in *Murder My Sweet* is less concerned with getting paid, but he does describe the doggedness of his pursuit of the murderer of his client in economic terms: "I'm just a small businessman in a very messy business, but I'd like to follow through on the sale." In addition, money, or the lack of it, dictates when and how often he must work. In the opening of the film he is so broke he has to take a divorce job he doesn't like ("The only reason I took the case was that my bank account was trying to crawl under a duck"), and then, long after his workday is through, he has to cancel a date and instead go with Moose Malloy to a bar to look for a missing person because he is offered twenty dollars. The cop, Randall, notices this obsession and accuses him of being focused on money: "You're not a detective, you're a slot machine."

Detection as Work

The detective novel and subsequent film is one of the few, if not the only, American genre whose primary focus is on process, that is, on the actual performance of work. Much of the enjoyment of the genre is generated from the way the detective pursues his activity. This is especially true of the more democratic hard-boiled detective who discovers the truth as much through dogged pursuit and through his ability to psychologically grasp personality and his innate understanding of how power works in the world as through his absolute reason.

It is true that this detective is never figured directly as working class. He dresses in a suit, operates privately out of an office, is hired on a client-by-client basis, and is a solitary figure—all attributes of "a marginal professional" whose "salary and mode of life is that of lower middle class" (Cawelti 144). But in Hollywood the working class is seldom awarded a hero drawn from its own ranks, instead frequently being represented by a stand-in one class above, as so many of the postwar noir working-class figures are petit bourgeois.[18]

In contrast to the middle-class markings of the detective, Bogart in *The Maltese Falcon* exhibits a strong working-class bearing, seen in the slow but determined gait in his apartment to receive the Falcon—a kind of walk conditioned by those who must trudge through work and yet endure it—and, as is discussed below, in his plain speaking. The Bogart persona, though being made up mainly of amoral gangster villains (the epitome of this characterization is *Roaring Twenties*, 1939), also had within it a working-class component from both the previous year's *They Drive by Night*, which featured Bogart as a much more working-class-defined truck driver who fits in with the other drivers, as opposed to George Raft's hardened individual, and *Black Legion* (1937), where Bogart plays a factory worker tempted by a racist organization.[19]

Finally, in his conception of work, Spade, and less so Marlowe, evokes a vision of a collective. Spade begins his final speech to Brigid, in which he reveals his true motives for undertaking the case, in what is perhaps the most famous moment of the book and the film, by evoking this collective: "When a man's partner's killed, he's supposed to do something about it. It doesn't make any difference what you thought of him, he was your partner and you're supposed to do something about it." Christopher Mettress reads Spade as attempting to "overcome his own destructive embracing of self-interest . . . to seek a greater collective identity" (99), with Spade's end position relating him more to a group of workers and distancing him from the capitalist treasure hunters Gutman, Cairo, and Brigid, whose ethos is expressed explicitly in Gutman's exhortation to Spade, "I do like a man who tells you right out he's looking out for himself." In continuing his explanation of why he will turn Brigid in, Spade evokes more sharply the language of association, perhaps the closest Hollywood gets to the cooperation of a union: "it happens we're in the detective business. Well, when one of your organization gets killed, it's bad business to let the killer get away with it; bad all around; bad for every detective everywhere."

Language as Plain Speaking

The detective's use of language to tell the truth rather than to obfuscate is one of the primary ways he is aligned with the working class. In the case of Hammett's detective, this use is even alluded to in his name; calling a spade a spade is truth telling.

Spade's direct language is in stark contrast to the three treasure hunters' use of words. As one critic put it, Spade reduces "their flowery thoughts to bold statements" and punctures their words with "the flat rasping cynicism of the private eye who has seen it all before and knows it is phony" (Cawelti 165). One after another, Spade takes on Brigid's discourse of the romantic heroine, Cairo's delicate pleasantries, and Gutman's quasi-academic obfuscation. Their language as a whole is designed to disguise their baser needs and desires and the way they go about getting what they want. By exposing them, Spade levels them, stripping away degrees of (affected) upper-class pretentiousness.

The first time Spade and Gutman meet, in a low-angle shot that accents the latter's girth and pomposity, Gutman says, "I'll tell you right out, I'm a man who likes talking to a man who likes to talk." Spade punctures this pompousness with a simple "Will we talk about the black bird?" Gutman is then reduced to stammering in reply. In their next meeting Gutman recites the complex romanticized history of the Falcon in quasi-mystical terms; in a later scene, Spade counters by referring to the object as a "dingus," a term that was street slang for a gadget and removes the mystical quality from the bird. Gutman's rival and sometimes accomplice Joel Cairo expresses himself in euphemisms or his words simply trail off, delicately refusing to describe the unpleasant acts that the words conceal. Spade counters by filling in Cairo's lapses. When the question of a per diem comes up, with Spade pretending to go to work for him, Cairo says, "Shall we say . . . one hundred dollars?" and he squirms a little with nervousness at the supposed outlandish thought of anyone with his taste and refinement hiring someone to do his criminal bidding. Spade answers immediately, "No, we shall say two hundred," as he reaches over to grab another hundred.

Brigid's language is that of the damsel in distress. Spade, as the detective, is supposed to play the knight who comes to her rescue with the narrative built around his ultimate rejection of that role. His language deconstructs her romantic discourse. To her plea for aid ("Be generous, Mr. Spade. You're brave. You're strong. You can spare me some of that courage and strength, surely. Help me, Mr. Spade"), he replies, "You won't need much of anybody's help. You're good. It's chiefly your eyes I think and that throb you get in your voice when you say things like 'Be generous, Mr. Spade.'" The end point of the confrontation is the single interchange in which Brigid exhorts him to follow the dictates of the romantic tradition by letting her go, though she is guilty of murdering his partner. "You don't love me," she says when he refuses. "I won't play the sap for you," he replies with brutal honesty. His use of the word "sap" is deliberate working-class argot which suggests that for the non-privileged classes "love" is sometimes simply a device to compound their oppression.

Marlowe, on the other hand, while following in Spade's footsteps, also sometimes uses language in the opposite way; that is, he talks tough in order to conceal that underneath he is playing the knight in shining armor. It is in the next two categories that his congruence with the working class exceeds Spade's.

(Upper-) Class Antagonism

One of the most pronounced characteristics of the World War II and immediate postwar crime film was that "the criminal is frequently a person of considerable political and social influence" (Cawelti 148). These films even exceeded their origins in pulp detective fiction, which, Cawelti notes, exposed "the corrupt relationship between the pillars of the community and the criminal underground" (148), "the unholy alliance between business, politics and organized crime" (155). *Murder My Sweet* goes further than its pulp source. It eliminates the shadowy underworld gambling kingpin Laird Burnette and instead calls attention to the negligence of the police, the corruption of Marlowe's upper-class employer, and the fascist control exerted by the upper-middle-class professionals who take the place of the usual criminal

Figure 2. Spade applying some pressure of his own in *The Maltese Falcon*.

underground. This "depiction of evil in places higher than the underworld" (Clarens 195) focuses attention away from crime being an element of the criminal class and suggests that crime is instead "endemic to the social order" (Cawelti 151), or, one might say, integral to a social order whose very basis is the systemic crime of inequality.

In *The Maltese Falcon*, the three treasure hunters, though not wealthy themselves, exhibit the characteristics of a kind of foreign wealth that in the moment of 1941 might be read not only as upper class but as also pro-fascist. Gutman's strong affectation in language and appearance of a British gentleman, Brigid's evocation of the British romantic damsel in distress, and Cairo's German or at least Eastern European accent and mannerisms might be read as exemplary of a British upper class that had before the war strongly supported German fascism[20] and in Cairo's case as the trace of that fascism itself.[21]

Chandler presented the upper classes directly. In addition to *Farewell My Lovely*, two of his novels open with Marlowe's encounter with a wealthy client (Mrs. Murdock in *The High Window* and General Sternwood in *The Big Sleep*). In each case the evil either originates directly in a concealed crime of the rich (the covering up of Mrs. Murdock's original murder of her first husband by pushing him out a window causes the subsequent crimes in *The High Window*) or is seen as growing out of that decadent milieu (General Sternwood's daughter, the murderer, as Sternwood's dark side in *The Big Sleep*). At the end of *The High Window*, the animosity Marlowe feels toward the wealthy but morally bankrupt Murdock family far exceeds Spade's more limited snide attitude toward the bourgeois pretensions of his foes. Marlowe tells Mrs. Murdock's son: "I've been working for your mother and whatever right to my silence that gives her she can have. I don't like her. I don't like you, I don't like this house" (Chandler, *High Window* 196). Both novels later became films with the critique of the rich intact.

The film *Murder My Sweet* reproduces Marlowe's contempt for the rich, expressed in the book when, upon sighting the Grayle mansion, Marlowe says, "The house itself was not so much. It was smaller than Buckingham Palace, rather gray for California and probably had fewer windows than the Chrysler Building" (122). In the film, Marlowe's voice-over as his car careens up the long driveway blunts the book's more overt, because more specific, class criticism slightly but nevertheless expresses its essence: "It was a nice little front yard, cozy, only you'd need a compass to go to the mailbox." Once inside, Marlowe is shown in long shot dwarfed by a hall that he describes as "like waiting on a crypt in the mausoleum." He then meets the frail, aging owner of this unfathomable wealth, Mr. Grayle, and his young, vivacious wife, yet another accoutrement of the mansion. Indeed, Marlowe's description of the hall as a crypt will be apt, as much death and destruction will radiate out from the old man's necrophiliac acquisition of a much younger bride and Mrs. Grayle's subsequent attempt to hold onto this wealth. Marlowe shows his disdain for the entire milieu, which he correctly perceives as trapping its owners, when, upon leaving, he asks the butler, "How do you get out of this box?"

The class antagonism in *Murder My Sweet* also extends to upper-middle-class professionals (psychiatrists and doctors). Here, in the middle of the war, they are seen not only as a group that polices the lower and lower middle classes but also as bearing the traces of the corrupt gangsterism that characterized fascism's leaders on the Continent. The well-to-do psychiatrist Dr. Amthor, whom Marlowe correctly accuses of being a blackmailer, replies, in a thick German accent,

"Your thinking is untidy, like most so-called thinking today." After Marlowe has been pummeled into unconsciousness, Amthor, staring at his body, comments with the disdain of the fascist aesthete, calling him a "dirty, stupid little man in a dirty, stupid world." The language is similar to Gutman's in *The Maltese Falcon*, though far more pointedly Hitlerian. Later, Marlowe is drugged by another member of the gang, the doctor (with the Aryan-sounding name Sonderberg), whose words supposedly offering the solace of his profession, "You've been a sick man, sir, a very sick man," are in actuality designed to work in tandem with the drugs to *induce* Marlowe to faint. The professional classes here are simply the mental appendage of the criminal classes.[22]

The Lawman Harassed by the Law

The first four categories have stressed the detective's general congruence with working-class attitudes and ways of making sense of the world. The fifth, the lawman's increasingly antagonistic relationship with the law, concerns more acutely the contemporary parallel between the detective, often outside the law, and working-class unionism in the period of the war. At the onset of the war, as labor maintained Roosevelt's no-strike pact, thereby indicating its agreement with the war's initial anti-fascist goals but still feeling the pact as pressure and aware that business was profiting from the use of the law to regulate it, the detective, in the Hammett version, exists in a parallel world where in the end his morality coincides with the law, though he takes pains to indicate that his choice is for different reasons. Later in the war, as union resistance to the pact grew and as business profits guaranteed through government regulation of union resistance became more apparent, the detective, in Chandler's version, more openly defies the law and adopts his own morality.

French critic Nino Frank, observing this break in the detective film in 1946, wrote that the protagonist of both films has "nothing to do with the government and is in fact outside the law" (qtd. in Palmer, introduction 22). For a later observer, John Cawelti, the detective, far from being a representative of the law, takes on the characteristics of the criminals, including "a penchant for violence, alienation from society and rejection of conventional values coupled with an adherence to a personal code of ethics" (59).

Spade experiences the "thuggish" quality of the police firsthand in the form of Lieutenant Dundy, who pressures, interrogates, and finally punches him.[23] Likewise, the district attorney, who represents a higher rung on the law-and-order ladder, attempts to do verbally what Dundy has done physically to Spade, telling him, "I'm a sworn officer of the law twenty-four hours a day, and neither formality nor informality justifies you withholding evidence of crime from me," to which Spade responds by telling him to back off. Though Spade reacts with a great deal of calm throughout the film, in the last scene with Brigid he is at great pains to convey to her the pressure they are under as the law must be appeased: "Both of us, right now, are sitting under the gallows."

Marlowe, in the later film in the middle of the war, is under intense pressure from the start. The film begins with a more formal interrogation than that of Spade, which in the previous film is conducted by two officers in three shots, in Spade's bedroom with Huston's framing with Spade's back to the audience simulating a police station interrogation. In *Murder My Sweet*, the audience, in the first shot, is subjectively aligned with Marlowe, put in his place, made to sit in his seat under the interrogation lamp, hearing the cold, impersonal voice of the law telling him they are arraigning him for a killing and later commanding him to tell the entire story "From the beginning." The first-person narration, a convention of the detective novel, is new to the crime film and here is motivated by Marlowe telling his story under pressure, attempting to clear himself of two murders. In the course of the story, and similar to Spade, Marlowe is harassed by a hard-nosed cop named Randall who believes Marlowe is a part of a blackmailing operation. Later, Marlowe reveals to his client Helen Grayle that he had worked for the district attorney and was fired, not for corruption, but for "talking back." Both Spade and Marlowe are harassed by authority, and the films delight in describing their characters "talking back" to that authority.

There are three main ways in which the antagonism of and toward the law increases from one film to the next. The first has to do with alignment. Both films feature a protagonist who is in nearly every scene and through whose consciousness much of the information is filtered—that is, there is a strong spatial alignment. However, *Murder*

My Sweet also features Marlowe's voice-over narration throughout the film. This is not as strongly subjective as the later film noirs, because the voice-over is Marlowe's testimony in front of the police, but it is still an added layer of subjectivity intended to invest the audience with sympathy for the outside-the-law character.[24]

The second is the role of the police. In *The Maltese Falcon*, Spade is harassed by a hard-nosed but honest cop, Dundy. The Los Angeles police in *Murder My Sweet* fulfill this role, but in Bay City there is a corrupt cop, Randall, who also opposes Marlowe. Admittedly, this is a dim shadow of the rampant and systematic corruption depicted by Chandler in the book, corruption tied to and emanating from the wealthy. Upon leaving the Grayle mansion, Marlowe reflects: "I've got to watch my step. This Grayle packs a lot of dough in his pants. And law is where you buy it in this town. Look at the funny way the cops are acting [about a murder that involves the family]" (139).[25] Yet, there is still in the film's Bay City more than a hint through Randall, Amthor, and Sonderberg of a city corrupt at its core and not merely overly authoritarian.

The third, and most crucial, way the relation between the protagonist and the law changed had to do with the hard-boiled detective's acceptance of the parameters of the law. Unlike the classical detective, who always accepts the law as a given, the hard-boiled detective is "forced to define his own concept of morality and justice, frequently in conflict with the social authority of the police" (Cawelti 143). While Spade's actions place him outside the law for much of the film, in the end his morality coincides with that of the law; Marlowe's, on the other hand, does not.

In the film's last sequence, in a speech adapted word for word from the book, Spade explains to Brigid why he is going to turn her over to the police for the killing of his partner. This "betrayal" is the moment of his ultimate conformity. He solves the three murders, alerts the police to pick up Gutman, Wilmer, and Cairo, and watches as the elevator gates slam shut on Brigid, metaphorically figuring her imprisonment and sealing her under the sign of the law. As he says in the speech, on the one side is his moral obligation. On the other side is his desire ("maybe you love me and maybe I love you"), and at this point (we might say, at this point in the war effort), duty and obligation win out over desire for this working-class-aligned figure. In the end, Spade will not let Brigid go because "all of me wants to." In a sense the gates/cell slamming shut on Brigid confine Spade as well; he is a prisoner of the wartime consensus.

Marlowe, in contrast, does not trust in the police to administer justice. Instead, he brings all the parties together, not, as in the classical detective story, to reveal the killer, but to allow Moose Malloy, his original client, and his double or dark side, to meet Velma, Moose's long-lost love, who years before had assumed the identity of Mrs. Grayle. Moose has killed the phony psychiatrist Jules Amthor, but Marlowe understands that the killing was not intentional and so, instead of turning him in, takes him to meet Velma. At the meeting, Moose, Grayle, and Velma are killed, in a sense wiping away the evil web woven by the Grayle money.[26]

Thus, at the beginning of the war, the hard-boiled detective, as the lead figure in the crime genre, is a working-class-aligned figure who conforms, as does labor, to the dictates of the law, or government, which is now tied directly to business through the War Board. By the middle of the war, though, this figure is much more questioning of the ability of the law, or of a government so strongly tied to promoting profit, to administer justice.

Coda: Cornell Woolrich's Nightmare Detectives: Evil Isn't Always a Lady

Although both films point to the corrupting influence of upper-class wealth and the law that aids it, both also locate ultimate evil in the figure of the woman. Both Spade and Marlowe act in the role of the classical detective when in the end they unveil the true killer, revealing that the original murder of Spade's partner was by Brigid and that the murder of the amorous playboy Marriot, which begins a string of murders, was committed by Mrs. Grayle. What's more, the women are guilty not only of murder but of treachery; they do their killing, as Spade says, "up close," in a way that trades on feelings of intimacy that they evoke in the victim. Brigid has Spade's partner, Miles, follow her down an alley where she shoots him point-blank, and Velma/Helen Grayle clubs her sometimes lover Marriot to death in the back of his car.[27]

In addition, each woman's "crime" is the desire to be upwardly mobile. Brigid gives her name first as Wonderly, an Anglo-Saxon name implying old wealth that goes along with the English gothic damsel in distress. That name gives way, though, to O'Shaughnessy, an Irish name that, along with her behavior (e.g., scratching and then kicking Cairo), implies a much more working-class background underneath the veneer. But while Spade's working-class affectations are viewed with affection, Brigid's class survival skills, when exposed, contribute to her being labeled a criminal. In *Murder My Sweet* the locus of crime is the wealthy Mrs. Grayle and her attempts to conceal that she is Velma, a former saloon singer. The psychiatrist Amthor treats her for a "speech impediment," code for her attempt to erase her class origins; the impediment, which Amthor gives a psychological explanation, is an impediment not to communication but to her social advancement. Both films, then, criticize the woman who attempts class mobility. In relation to her, the detective functions as a full-fledged agent of the law, patrolling the boundaries of gender and mobility.[28]

Beginning during the war and dominating the postwar noir period in terms of adaptations was a series of novels by Cornell Woolrich that went some way toward righting the masculinist predisposition of the detective films. Woolrich more properly belongs in the next chapter, but I will consider him here because of the change his works occasion. Rather than bearing the strong image of the independent detective, Woolrich's male protagonists, never even quasi-representatives of the law, are instead pressed into detecting because they were accused of a crime, often being dazed victims who needed the help of others to clear themselves (*Street of Chance*, 1942; *Deadline at Dawn*, 1946; *Fall Guy*, 1947). In contrast, his female protagonists, in a parallel series of films (*Phantom Lady*, 1944; *Black Angel*, 1946; *I Wouldn't Be in Your Shoes*, 1948), were drawn into a treacherous male underworld to clear a wrongly accused lover or husband, proving themselves quite resourceful in making their way through it, their resourcefulness a testament to the newly acquired independence won by working women during the war.

In the novel *Black Angel* (1940), Woolrich details the journey of a wife racing to prove that her convicted husband did not kill his girlfriend by entering the lives of a series of men whom the victim knew to see which of them wanted her dead. The journey in the book involves the woman, Alberta, masquerading as a drug addict, a prostitute, and a con woman, positioning herself outside the law to right a social wrong. The film cleans up the implications of Woolrich's dark night of the soul somewhat while still concentrating on the resourcefulness of the young wife. In both *Phantom Lady* and *Black Angel*, the treacherous female villain is replaced by a treacherous male companion who had seemed to help the woman (a male artist in *Phantom Lady*, a jazz musician in *Black Angel*), but in the end only for the purpose of deceiving her. Ultimately, though, it is in a little-discussed Woolrich adaptation, *I Wouldn't Be in Your Shoes*, that gender equality in the detective film is most strongly asserted. Here, the female partner of a song-and-dance team makes the underground journey to clear her partner, accompanied by yet another devious male companion, only this time the trusted guide is a police detective who himself turns out to be the murderer. Not only is the woman in charge of the investigation, but she is also finally able to place blame on the male representative of the law as the source of wrongdoing.

Thus, in Woolrich, the outside-the-law detective figure culminates in a female representative of the wartime assembly line as the hardboiled detective who in class solidarity sets out to aid her wronged male counterpart and in the process discovers that true villainy resides with the law*man*. Here, in a refusal to displace the crimes of power onto the woman, the detective film sheds its archaic patriarchal past.

chapter 2

Noir Part 1

Socialism in One Genre: Wildcat Strikers, Fugitive Outsiders, and a Savage Lament

> Mitchell: What's happened? Has everybody suddenly gone crazy . . .
> Or is it just me?
> Keeley: No, it's not just you. The snakes are loose.
> *Crossfire*

As defined in this study, "film noir" denotes the moment in the history of the crime film where ideas of the left dominated and, for a brief moment, dictated the structure of the genre. This left hegemony, in one genre of the culture industry for one short period (1945–50), represented on the screen the coming together of a dominant bloc of working- and middle-class interests. It appeared at a moment when working-class consciousness was heightened by a series of strikes, both in the nation as a whole and in Hollywood in particular, and when middle-class anxiety over increasing corporatization was acute. The formation expressed itself on the screen as a multitude of sub-working-class, working-class, and middle-class male and female fugitives forced to flee the law, usually for a crime they felt at least in some way innocent of, ultimately exposing the real criminal as the upper- or business-class foe who torments them.

In addition, there is a sub-period grouping within this five-year span both in labor as a whole and in Hollywood labor and in its expression on screen in the crime film. The period immediately after the war begins with the hope of change in society, expressed in labor through a series of strikes and in the crime film through a turn to a more direct dealing with social problems. Labor is then frontally assaulted through the Taft-Hartley Act and through HUAC, with the effect of this assault on the crime film being the retreat of the crime film directors into a more covert expression in the form of the generic dominant of the outside-the-law fugitive. Finally, by the end of the period, labor has ousted its militant members, the Hollywood blacklist is fully in effect, and the crime film directors respond with films that function as a lament for a lost opportunity for radical change.

Postwar Labor: Revolt and Counter-revolt

For labor, the three sub-periods were the postwar strikes, which ignited mass strikes as well (1945–47); the reaction against these strikes, initially on the legislative front in the Taft-Hartley Act (1947–48); and then, more broadly, the wide-scale attack on labor under the all-purpose label of "Communism," which culminated in the CIO's expulsion of eleven of its most radical unions (1949–50).

Coming out of the war, labor was extremely organized and extremely disaffected. By the end of the war, 69 percent of workers in industrial production were unionized (Brecher 223) and many had gained experience in striking, with 1944 boasting the most strikes ever up to that point in U.S. history (225). During the war they watched business profits rise while wages remained stagnant, and after the war, expecting a pay increase, they saw instead, largely because of the cancellation of wartime overtime, their income decline from 15 percent (Lichtenstein 221) to 30 percent (Lipsitz, *Rainbow* 99). Worse yet, the end of the war occasioned the overnight cancellation of $24 billion in government contracts, leading to massive layoffs (2 million by 1 October 1945 and by winter one-quarter of the U.S. workforce [Lipsitz, *Rainbow* 99]) in a wartime economy that had seen full employment for the first time in U.S. history. Add to this workforce the 10 million returning servicemen and -women, and the specter of a new depression loomed large.

The presence of a disaffected but organized workforce resulted in the twelve-month period after V-J Day being the greatest strike period in U.S. history (Lipsitz, *Rainbow* 99). During that year, 4.6 million workers participated in strikes (Richter xii), and the strikes kept building momentum; the number of workers on strike doubled from August to September 1945, doubled again in October, and then became in the first six months of 1946 "the most concentrated period of labor management strife in the country's history" (Brecher 228). Most major sectors of U.S. industry went on strike, with a strike by railroad workers in May 1946 bringing trains to a halt and a strike by 750,000 steelworkers being the largest strike in U.S. history (Richter xii).

The strikers generally had the support of the country, with a *Fortune* poll revealing that public support for the strikes was greater at the end than at the beginning of the strike year (Lipsitz, *Rainbow* 116). This support also resulted in general strikes in a number of medium-size cities, including Rochester, Pittsburgh, Oakland, and Houston, with each case resulting in citywide shutdowns (149). In Oakland the entire downtown area was closed; no one without a union card was allowed in the area, and workers determined which stores remained open (149). In his book *Strike*, Jeremy Brecher characterizes this period as "the closest thing to a national general strike of industry in the twentieth century" and says that "the potential capacity of workers to paralyze . . . the entire country was demonstrated" (230).

Though the strikers may have had popular support, they did feel themselves, and were made to feel, outside the law. Arrayed against them were the forces of business, government, and for the most part their own union leaders. In the strikes, workers were demanding an average increase in wages of 30 percent. Management was often willing to concede, as in the case with the United Auto Workers (UAW), up to a 17 percent increase, but in exchange for increased control of the production line (Lipsitz, *Rainbow* 111). The UAW argued that, based on wartime profits, the auto industry could afford the wage increase with no new increase in prices. This they originally demanded because they foresaw that the wage increase would be passed onto the populace and the union would be blamed for it (113). The ruling elites characterized such demands as a challenge to their authority, with *Business Week* calling the demands and the strikes not "a series of isolated battles for isolated gains" but instead "part of a long-term, irrepressible struggle for power" (Brecher 240).

The federal government also opposed the strikes, initially calling on workers to maintain the wartime no-strike clause, which labor now opposed and officially rejected in October 1945 (Lichtenstein 222). President Truman, while threatening to back a bill that would draft workers who went on strike, also used the powers of the government to seize oil wells, packinghouses, and coal mines to end strikes, and he frequently threatened to call out the army against the strikers. Truman later characterized the strikes as treason: "We used the weapons we had at hand in order to fight a rebellion against the government" (Brecher 229).

For the most part, the strikes were also opposed by the strikers' union leadership, who recognized during the war that their power came from their ability to control their members. In the UAW strike, union head Walter Reuther was ordered to remove his demand for no price increase by the head of the CIO, Philip Murray, who had signed a pact of labor peace with the U.S. Chamber of Commerce in March 1945, declaring that "only chaos and destruction of our industrial life will result if . . . labor unions have to resort to widespread strikes to defend their existence and the living standards of their members" (Lichtenstein 217). In the UAW strike, Reuther and the union leadership not only complied with Murray's order, "transforming the strike from a socially responsible assault on corporate power to a justified, but limited, exercise in self-interest" (Lipsitz, *Rainbow* 113), but also then pledged as part of the settlement to fine future wildcat strikers (227).

Though the strike period resulted in millions of workers having "a shared experience of defying the law and striking against the government" (Lipsitz, *Rainbow* 116), of being outside the law, the wage increases won by the workers were passed onto the populace (prices rose 16 percent after the strikes, while wages rose on average 7 percent [Lichtenstein 230]), and the increased prices created the climate for the election in the fall of 1946 of a Republican Congress charged with taking away workers' ability to strike.

This they quickly attempted, passing, in February 1947, the Taft-

Hartley Act, designed to curb organized labor by criminalizing labor activities and amplifying the centralization of powers governing labor under the sign of the law. The act banned many of the collective actions labor had taken during the strike period, including threats, violence, and mass picketing (Lipsitz, *Rainbow* 172), while also centralizing the prosecution of labor for these new offenses in the hands of the federal government, since many local governments had supported labor in the strikes (172). Recognizing, as Senator Robert Taft declared, that the labor rank and file was "more radical than their leaders," the act also strengthened labor leaders' power over workers by making the former responsible for controlling wildcat strikes. Finally, for the first time nationally, in the infamous section 9h, the act associated labor agitation with "the Communist menace" and compelled all union members to sign an affidavit claiming they had no affiliation with the Communist Party.[1] "Communism" now became a euphemism for rank-and-file agitation. Strikes could henceforth be attacked not as the eruption of working-class sentiment against the continuing corporate profits of the war and its aftermath but as "political strikes," as attempts to destabilize the country from within (Richter 70).[2]

The law, as represented by the federal government, was now arrayed against labor through a combination of federal agencies and congressional committees. This combination included continual legal and illegal probes by the FBI, "the highest law in the land," which turned its findings over to the congressional committees (Schrecker 139); congressional investigations, including HUAC and McCarthy's Senate committee; Internal Revenue Service audits; deportations by the Immigration and Naturalization Service; National Labor Relations Board procedures that regulated union economic functions; and (anti-Communist) Smith Act indictments (142).[3]

While government agencies often worked behind the scenes to confront labor, the public attack was conducted by congressional committees. Between 1945 and 1956 more than one hundred hearings dealt with the problem of Communists in the labor movement (Schrecker 142). Prior to its investigation of Hollywood, HUAC already had a history of being used as a strikebreaking tool whose hearings in the midst of strikes swayed their outcome. HUAC investigated unions during an Allis Chalmers strike (the strike that served as the rationale for drafting the Taft-Hartley provisions) and during a strike against R.J. Reynolds. There is evidence that in both cases the investigation took place at the instigation of the employers (Schrecker 142), just as it would in HUAC's 1947 investigation of Hollywood sparked by the testimony of Walt Disney and Jack Warner, employers who were recent victims of a strike.

The other layer of law that was invoked against the strikers was their own labor leaders. The strongest evidence of this internal policing was the CIO's expulsion of eleven unions in 1949–50, claiming the unions were "Communist dominated" (Rosswurm 2). In this move the CIO expelled close to 1 million members, almost 20 percent of its membership, including the most radical union, the United Electrical Workers (UE) with almost 500,000 members, and other unions that were for the most part dominated by women and minorities (Rosswurm 2).[4]

Thus militant labor, which had earlier found itself outside the law in a series of strikes that the populace supported, now found its actions officially outlawed and its more radical members criminalized.

Hollywood Postwar Labor: How the Snakes Got Loose

In the noir period, Hollywood was in many ways a privileged site of labor activity, first as an opportunity for a progressive labor movement and subsequently as the trial ground for launching the prototypical counterattack on labor. In this way, Hollywood labor history, more than mirroring that of the nation as a whole, actually established the patterns that were then followed in other industries.

Just as with labor as a whole, a feverish period of union activity began in 1945 and 1946 in Hollywood, only here there are important differences. The strike activity began *before* the war was over (in March 1945), lasted longer (until October 1947), and was led not simply by rank-and-file union members but by a group of dissident union locals formed together under the banner of the Conference of Studio Unions with a strong leader in Herb Sorrell. So the radical activity was more centrally organized. The chance for victory was also more absolute in Hollywood, with the CSU harboring a collaborative vision of craft and creative unions joining together against the studios.

At its height the CSU consisted of ten thousand members of various studio locals, as opposed to sixteen thousand members in the studio-friendly International Association of Theatrical and Stage Employees (IATSE). Sorrell and the CSU led a total of three strikes in two years. In the twenty-five months from March 1945 to March 1947, Hollywood experienced three major strikes and some kind of strike activity in seventeen of those months (Nielsen and Mailes 160). In addition, the strikes were highly combative, "reminiscent of the worst labor-management confrontations of the Thirties in Detroit" as the studios "employed scabs, thugs, tear gas, fire hoses and . . . private police and fire departments to disrupt picket lines and break the strike" (Ceplair and Englund 216).

The apex of the 1945 strike occurred on 8 October, "Bloody Friday" (Nielsen and Mailes 129), with the CSU picketing Warner Brothers and attempting to halt production. Jack Warner watched from the rooftops as his private studio security forces and fire department sprayed the picketers with hoses and tear gas and dropped bolts on them. As he watched his employees being sprayed and gassed, Warner is said to have declared, "I will never again make a film about the Little Man" (Neve 107).

In the second strike, in July 1946, Sorrell demanded and won a contract for the industry as a whole that granted a 50 percent wage increase that would ease the burden of the reduction of hours from the wartime forty-eight to thirty-six hours (Nielsen and Mailes 140). Sorrell's success prompted him also to call for a single crafts and creative union bargaining unit "to unite the motion picture unions for the protection of the autonomy of each" (Cogley 55). In working toward this goal he sought and received the support of both crafts and creative unions and particularly of the Screen Writers Guild. The SWG's Abraham Polonsky called the CSU its natural ally and said that, regarding HUAC's attack on the SWG, "A thriving CSU would have bolstered us tremendously" (Ceplair and Englund 219).

The third strike, which began in September 1946 and continued through 1948, was more in the nature of a studio lockout, "decided after advice from New York executives" (Ceplair and Englund 222) in a move to break the union through studio collusion with the IATSE, the Screen Actors Guild, and the Teamsters (160). The strike featured for the first time the combination of the labeling of militant labor as Communist (Sorrell was investigated by a congressional labor subcommittee charged with rooting out Communists in labor [251]) and the direct intervention of various governmental agencies, including the California state assembly (Nielsen and Mailes 101).

The result was the breaking of the strike and the CSU, with Sorrell's painters local expelled from the international for associating with "organizations and groups which subscribe to the Communist party" (Friedrich 283) and with over thirty-five hundred CSU members blacklisted (Nielsen and Mailes 158) in a far larger and earlier blacklist than the much more highly publicized one of the creative workers.[5]

So, the strike activity was an everyday part of living and working in Hollywood in this period, and though no direct mention of this activity was ever allowed on the Hollywood screen, it would have been difficult for it not to have been represented in an oblique fashion.

How the Guilds Were Lost

Hollywood Ten member Dalton Trumbo identified three reasons for HUAC's investigation of Hollywood: to destroy the trade unions, to paralyze anti-fascist political action, and to remove progressive content from films. As to the first reason, with the CSU demobilized, the main remaining opposition union in Hollywood was the Screen Writers Guild (Schwartz 286).

The writers, actors, and directors guilds, founded in the 1930s under intense opposition from the studios and by the middle of the war finally established as legitimate bargaining agents, were undoubtedly a part of the upper tier of Hollywood labor as opposed to the crafts unions. Nevertheless, despite their more middle-class status, they also—especially the writers, the lowest rung of the guilds—had important similarities with the more straightforwardly working-class crafts unions.

"Hollywood workers [including writers] speak always of the industry, never of the medium. For motion picture workers are purely industrial workers," said Trumbo of their status (qtd. in Horne 83). The SWG represented a group whose average member was barely making a living, with studios designating only about 1 percent of production costs for screenwriting (Buhle and Wagner 279). They were at the same time both white-collar proletarian and new middle class, since the screenwriter "worked with his hands only as much as a bank clerk, social worker, typist or other white collar worker; but he could be dismissed as readily as a nonunion ditchdigger" (Buhle and Wagner 8).[6] In addition, as with labor as a whole, writers' opposition was also a factor in their observation of the increasing profits of the studios as the war ended.

There was also, as with postwar labor in general, a struggle for control of the production process going on in Hollywood, expressed here as a struggle over the content of the products of the culture industry. Although, as Trumbo maintained, "the freedom of the artist to express himself decreases in proportion to the increase in capital investment required for the production of the work" (qtd. in Horne 83), still, with the acceptance of the writers, actors, and directors guilds, as Paul Buhle and Dave Wagner claim, from 1936 to 1946, working-class attitudes and ways of life began to proliferate in Hollywood films, culminating in the film noir (159). The clampdown on content that was a result of HUAC—especially at Warner Brothers, once known as the writer's studio, since its policy was not even to hire a director until after the script was finished (Buhle and Wagner 164)—put an end by the beginning of the 1950s to these working-class assertions on the screen.

The SWG, then, was not only a supporter of the craftsworkers, whom many of its members identified with, but was also immediately critical of the Taft-Hartley Act, and particularly of the anti-Communist loyalty oath. The guild's oppositional membership characterized the oath as "an attempt to divide labor against itself and to destroy trade unions" (Schwartz 264).

The Time of the Toad

The 1947 HUAC hearings were nominally called to investigate Communism in Hollywood. Much of their thrust, though, was not anti-Communist but anti-labor, or rather, their thrust was anti-labor in the guise of being anti-Communist. The first, and in some cases the only, question that several of the witnesses were asked was, "Are you a member of the Screen Writers Guild?" This was often followed by, "Are you a member of the Communist Party?" (Friedrich 323–26), thus illuminating the strategy of the hearings, which was to link the threat of Communism with the threat of labor activism.

Figure 3. John Howard Lawson and *Crossfire*'s producer, Adrian Scott, at a press conference for the Hollywood Ten.

Three of the main witnesses, each of whom had been bruised in the CSU strikes, hammered home this theme. Jack Warner and MGM's Louis B. Mayer, each of whom had had production halted by the CSU, named creative workers who were subsequently blacklisted (Cogley 16) and called for a blacklist, or as Mayer put it, "a national policy regulating employment of Communists in the industry" (qtd. in Friedrich 315). The IATSE's Roy Brewer claimed that the sweetheart studio union had saved Hollywood from "the Communist plan to control the motion picture industry" (318). In his rebuttal, which was never allowed to be read to the committee, screenwriter Lester Cole instead accused HUAC of attempting to "destroy democratic guilds and unions by interference in their internal affairs and through this destruction bring chaos and strife to an industry which seeks only democratic methods with which to solve its problems" (qtd. in Ceplair and Englund 275).

On the same day Congress voted 346-17 to uphold contempt citations for the Hollywood Ten, the studio producers issued the Waldorf Statement, saying they would no longer hire the Ten or any known

Communists, in effect initiating the blacklist. The impetus for their statement came from the "the money men in New York, both the executives at the film corporations and the banks" (Friedrich 335), and coincided with the large-scale strategy of U.S. corporate capital to discipline militant labor by equating it with Communism and to curb overproduction (which was certainly the case in Hollywood, where 1947 was the first of many years of a decline in box office) through blacklisting.

The effects of the HUAC hearings and the Waldorf Statement throughout the later 1940s were to transform the SWG from an oppositional union into more of a sweetheart union along the lines of the IATSE, making it a union that accepted the rationale of the blacklist, did not seriously challenge management (Ceplair and Englund 292), and acceded to a general chilling effect in the industry in terms of activism in post-HUAC Hollywood. As one creative worker described this changed mood, "I came to understand that it is not right for an actor who has enormous influence because of his popularity to campaign actively and take a political position" (Cogley 78). In the crime film this led to the retreat from the social problem crime film into the still oppositional pattern of the sympathetic fugitive.

There was also, following the hearings and the Waldorf Statement, a generalized attack on the content of Hollywood films. Prior to the hearings, an SWG-oppositional group, the Motion Picture Alliance, had called for a return to "films as pure entertainment" and had railed against "the number of times you have seen industrialists portrayed on the screen as slave drivers" (Ceplair and Englund 254). Echoing this sentiment, Motion Picture Association of America head Eric Johnston made his famous declaration about screen content: "We'll have no more *Grapes of Wrath*, we'll have no more *Tobacco Roads*. We'll have no more films that show the seamy side of American life. We'll have no pictures that deal with labor strikes. We'll have no pictures that deal with the banker as villain" (qtd. in May 145). Johnston subsequently enlisted Ayn Rand to write a "Screen Guide for Americans." The guide's dos and don'ts included "Don't Deify the Common Man," and it concluded with this imperative: "It is the moral duty of every decent man in the motion picture industry to throw into the ashcan where it belongs, every story that smears industrialists as such" (qtd. in Cogley 11).

As with labor in general, the attack against Hollywood labor was mounted by a phalanx of federal agencies culminating in 1950 in the jailing of the Hollywood Ten. The period that had begun with such hope, with the surge in power of the CSU and its militant supporters in the SWG, moved to a moment of these activists first feeling themselves together outside the law and then finally feeling themselves alone and isolated in a country where "any opposition to big business was now equated with unpatriotic beliefs" (May 144).

The Postwar Crime Film: Through the Strikes Darkly

This work's characterization of the film noir hero and heroine emphasizes the fugitive outside the law and borrows most strongly from the original French definition of this 1945–50 permutation of the crime film. Borde and Chaumeton, writing in 1955, provide not only the best description of film noir but also the best periodization and delineation of the film noir from the next permutation of the crime film, the police procedural. The remarkable characteristic of the war and postwar crime film, they maintain, was that these film noir consistently looked at crime "from the inside, from the vantage of the criminals involved," while the police procedural viewed crime from the outside, "from the police's legalistic position" (Borde and Chaumeton, "Definition" 60).

Roger Tailleur, writing in the left journal *Positif* in the 1940s, derives his prototypical (or master) noir plot from 1947's *Ride the Pink Horse* and describes that plot as consisting of an investigator outside the law (a private detective) or a petty criminal himself (such as an amateur blackmailer), an "intermediary between the gangster he intends to exploit and the cop whose offer of assistance he rebuffs and whose surveillance he fears," who "makes his way with difficulty through a labyrinth of moral choices passing between the law on one side and crime on the other" (40).

To this description we might add Richard Maltby's concentration on the noir protagonist's "neurotic attitude toward the past." The character "has to account for a period of his life when he was outside the world in which the film is set, and in which things happened to him which set him at a distance from that world and its inhabitants" (67). If we add to this George Lipsitz's more directly allegorical presentation of the noir protagonist as paralleling the wildcat striker, then the repression is not of the distant past but instead of both the recent past and the simultaneous present, the strikes and their aftermath, which the workers are watching being repressed almost in front of them.

In *Rainbow at Midnight*, Lipsitz, following a chapter on the strikes of the 1940s, stresses the strikers' connection to their increasingly hostile environment in describing a noir plot centered on a protagonist, "vulnerable because he is alone," made to look guilty through circumstantial evidence, who longs for the "understanding of neighbors, relatives or friends" but who "meets only strangers who show him hostility and indifference" (285). As these protagonists "break the law and avoid authorities to advance their own interests . . . they expect and fear disapproval and battle enormous guilt . . . but ultimately choose to be true to themselves at the risk of appearing 'illegitimate' to others" (285). At the time, producer Mark Hellinger, active in the genre, also stressed the positive quality of the noir protagonist: "Practically all bad men were really good men who were forced by circumstances to live outside the law" (qtd. in Lipsitz, *Rainbow* 155).

As to the relation of the noir protagonist to the figure of labor, Paul Buhle and Dave Wagner, looking back on the complicated history of the genre and its criticism, describe a situation in which "American filmmakers were required in noir to sink the social allegories so deep in the storyline to avoid political censorship, that in many cases it would be years before critics and film historians would find the submerged meaning" (358).[7]

My own master plot, detailed below using *The Blue Dahlia*, is an amalgam of these definitions with an increased emphasis on the equivalence of the fugitive outsider and the figure of labor, with the law representing the more active force of government in repressing labor in this period and with the criminal kingpin often looking or behaving much like a business leader. In the next chapter I add a topology of film noir types who together constitute a hegemonic bloc of working- and middle-class characters. This master plot with the sympathetic protagonist outside the law characterizes 200 crime films in the 1941–55 period, most falling between 1945 and 1950, making this the dominant pattern of the crime film in the 1945–50 period (see the appendix for a list of titles).

This characterization of film noir refutes the most popular contemporary way of conceiving the genre, the current industry view which also has its supporters in film noir criticism. In this noir master plot, "a fated or hired man, often bitter by life experience, meets an experienced, also bitter, woman to whom he is fatally attracted. Through this attraction, the man does wrong . . . cheats, murders or attempts to murder a second man to whom the woman is . . . [unhappily] attached . . . which then often leads to the woman's betrayal of the protagonist, . . . [causing] the destruction of the woman, the second man and often the protagonist" (D'Amico 101).

This plot, derived most strongly from the James M. Cain–adapted novels *Double Indemnity* and *The Postman Always Rings Twice*, is in my definition subsumed under the outside-the-law plot. This variation of the dominant is the one most often accepted today in the industry and has now come to be the basis of a B-genre in its own right, the "erotic thriller," the staple of a period I later characterize as "faux bohemian noir" (see chapter 5). It is, however, not the way most observers of the classic noir period characterize it, stressing as it does the genre's most misogynist aspects. Its revival and dominance in the present may indicate a propensity to glorify and revive regressive and negative values rather than subversive ones. It also elides the fact (upon which this study focuses) that many of the women in film noir, far from being the femme fatale, were instead class allies of the outside-the-law figure or are fugitives themselves. This study focuses instead on reviving the figure of a sometimes troubled working- and middle-class male-female alliance against both of their corresponding representatives in the upper or business classes.

The Social Problem Noir

After the war, there was a generalized feeling in the industry that Hollywood films would change for the better because of the effects of the war. This feeling was voiced by critics (James Agee: "The time has come for a fully social cinema"; Stead 147), screenwriters (Philip Dunne: "The trend is obviously toward greater realism, toward a more frequent selection of factual American themes, toward the theory that motion pictures should not only entertain and make money, but should also give expression to the American and democratic ideals";

Ceplair and Englund 200), and even Hollywood establishment directors (William Wyler: "American films should reach their belated maturity"; Clarens 193). There was also a rough consensus on what this change for the better meant, a consensus centering on, as Agee put it, films that were "journalistic, semi-documentary and social minded" (Stead 147). *The Best Years of Our Lives* (1946) grandly announces this change, in this case in the form of an exploration of the problems faced by the return of soldiers and the restoration of the economy to a peacetime footing.

The crime film, an established genre that had a history of dealing, if often obliquely, with at least the traces of poverty and working-class problems as they were expressed in the outlet of crime, was a place where writers of the left congregated and a natural place to begin to effect this change. Dorothy Jones, who studied the changes in screen content before and after HUAC, noted the propensity of the Hollywood Ten to make films classed as "murder-mystery, mystery, spy and espionage pictures," films that were often celebrations of "the underdog, the underprivileged and the social outcast" (205). This potential of the crime film to portray the problems of inequality was also noted by a conservative group of exhibitors, the Allied State Organization, who feared that this new combination of "reform themes" and a "documentary style" would effect a change whereby the "motion picture will become class entertainment" (Stead 155). It must be noted, however, that this tendency of filmmakers to express social problems was dialectically met most forcefully with a reverse tendency of the studios to obliterate from the screen *the* social problem most dominant in Hollywood: the union demands for equality and greater control of the mode of production.[8]

The model for both content and mode of production of this kind of film was *Crossfire*, produced at RKO in 1947, its title, in one sense, referentially suggesting the blending of two genres. The film was the brainchild of Dore Schary, who had come over from working with David O. Selznick to head RKO, where he found a studio rich in a heritage of the crime film (with Dmytryk's *Murder My Sweet* and the noir-scented visuals of *Citizen Kane* [1940] and the Val Lewton horror films). Schary, who had won an Academy Award in screenwriting for *Boy's Town* in 1938 and had a history of promoting socially conscious films, envisioned a series of low-budget crime thrillers that would

Figure 4. Another member of the Hollywood Ten, *Crossfire*'s director, Edward Dmytryk.

add social content through their scripts. This content would make the films more profitable, providing additional value without an increase in budget (Kelly and Steinman).

The first of these films, *Crossfire*, deliberately stressed its social content as a film about anti-Semitism and race hatred in general. This "20-day quickie squeezed between two major films on a shoestring budget" cost only $550,000 but grossed $1.27 million, and it was eventually nominated for five Academy Awards, including Edward Dmytryk as best director (Kelly and Steinman 114). Schary followed this success by scheduling a series of films that dealt more and more directly with working-class problems, including *The Window* (1949), about life in the tenements; *They Live by Night* (1948), a *Romeo and Juliet* with Romeo being an escaped con; *The Set-Up* (1949), about the last boxing match of a down-and-out fighter; and Dmytryk and producer Adrian Scott's follow-up to *Crossfire*, *So Well Remembered* (1947), which approached the taboo subject of the strikes in the form of a crusading newspaper editor in favor of workers' rights. The commercial success of *Crossfire* as a model of the social problem film also helped to bring on the blacklist, with producer Scott and director Dmytryk, the only non-writers in the group, being added to the Ten because of their participation in *Crossfire*.

Crossfire also provided a model for how social content could be grafted onto the crime film, as explained by Scott, who with Dmytryk had also pioneered the RKO crime film with *Murder My Sweet*:

> We had made several melodramas and were generally dissatisfied with the emptiness of the format.... Screen melodramas ... were concerned with violence in pursuit of a jade necklace [as in *Murder My Sweet*], a bejeweled falcon. The core of melodrama usually concerned itself with an innocuous object, without concern for reality although dressed in highly realistic trappings. Substituting a search for an anti-Semite instead of a jade necklace, at the same time investigating anti-Semitism, seemed to us to add dimension and meaning to melodrama, at the same time lending outlet for conviction. (Kelly and Steinman 114)

The film also went further than the localized problem of anti-Semitism in suggesting that a history of intolerance that could generate a native fascism was endemic to America. Its famous phrase to describe the belief that in the changeover from Roosevelt to the far more conservative regime of Truman there was a chance of these sentiments taking hold is "the snakes are loose." Late in the film, the Roosevelt-like character, the cop Finlay, relates a story of intolerance to the young soldier who is in danger of succumbing to the race hatred that overcomes the film's villain, played to the hilt by Robert Ryan. At the end of the story, Finlay says, "That's history, Leroy. They don't teach it in school, but it's real American history just the same," reminding the audience that, as Adorno (2005) commented on postwar Germany, behind the bright glow of public opinion lies a dark residue of suffering, what he called "non-public opinion," a political unconscious that is capable of being mobilized by authoritarian regimes as the Nazis had in the 1930s.

If low-budget studio films were one mode of production in which noir flourished, the other mode was independent production, which began in Hollywood in earnest after the war. One of the most successful of these independent producers, and one directly aligned with the working class, was former journalist Mark Hellinger, who had produced *High Sierra, Manpower* (1941) and *They Drive by Night* for Warner Brothers, all of which dealt with the overlap of crime and the working class. Hellinger then signed a deal with Universal International and independently produced *The Killers* (1946), which introduced to the screen the tough working-class persona—here as a world-weary boxer—of Burt Lancaster. Lancaster and Heller's next indie effort, with director Jules Dassin, was *Brute Force* (1947), a prison escape film that deliberately recalled Warner's *I Was a Fugitive from a Chain Gang* (1932), which, with its suggestion of the inequity of prison, was perhaps the most radical film ever made at a Hollywood studio. Similarly, *Brute Force* was to be the sole film of the period that, even if obliquely, depicted the strike period in America and Hollywood and, in that depiction, exceeded the fairly circumscribed bounds of the social problem film.

There are many ways to depict prison life, but *Brute Force* shows it centering on work, with the work organized around an assembly line. Worker-prisoners are shown at a series of factory machines, manning lathes, drills, and blowtorches. The subgroup that will plan the escape, of whom Lancaster is the leader, works on a drainpipe in a tunnel below the prison, and the physical activity of digging with pickaxes, loading the refuse in a railway car, and carting it away resembles the work of miners, one of the more radical unions during and immediately after the war. The activity most often focused on in this assembly line is organizing: initially, the prisoners organize the killing of a stoolie, and later they organize an escape. The film also focuses on the oppressive quality of time, opening with the giant clock that taunts the prisoners—most of whom are there for life—and serves as a reminder that the assembly-line mode was one that functioned on its efficient exploitation of the worker's time. The prisoners' own use of time, passing along the codes "Wilson, 10:30" (the time when the stoolie is to be killed) and later "Tomorrow at 12:15" (the time of the prison break), is a way for them to make time specific and reclaim the endless drudgery of the prison/assembly line.[9]

In the final scene, the prison break, the prisoners not in on the escape are prodded by Lancaster and his cellmates to riot, but when they find out that the brutal, sadistic Captain Munsey has been appointed warden, they riot on their own, with a single unified "Yea" as both black and white prisoners storm the guard tower where Munsey is already lording it over them. Munsey then, à la Jack Warner, orders a machine gun to open fire on the prisoner-strikers in what is the closest screen depiction ever of the pitched battles that took place in Hollywood every day for two years.

The film follows a central proposition of noir in that it sets up an ever stronger structure of sympathy for the prisoners, in this case through the shifting meaning of the title *Brute Force*. At first it seems it is the prisoners who are the brutes, in the killing of the stoolie Wilson by backing him up into a furnace. But that definition changes as we see Munsey's more callous, because unmotivated, driving of another prisoner, Tom, to suicide, with the camera lingering on the shadow of his body hanging in his cell and, later, Munsey's Hitlerian beating, to Wagner's *Tannhäuser*, of the prisoner's messenger, Louie. Given this sadism, with Munsey also presented in *Crossfire* fashion as a sadistic Trumanesque replacement of the former humanitarian Rooseveltian warden, the prisoners' rioting seems justified and Lancaster's sacrificing himself to hurl Munsey off the tower appears heroic. A post-riot coda has one of the prisoners, the Caribbean singer Sir Lancelot (a staple of the Val Lewton films), explaining the riot/strike in terms of perpetual struggle. His answer to the more resigned prison doctor's "NOBODY ESCAPES, NOBODY REALLY ESCAPES" (the studio ending) is the more dialectical "WHENEVER YOU GOT MEN IN PRISON, THEY'RE GONNA WANNA GET OUT."[10]

Noir as Subversive Genre

After the HUAC hearings, left artists retreated into the generic staples already established in what became the mainstream of the crime film in the 1945–50 period, the drama of the fugitive outsider. *The Blue Dahlia*, released in April 1946 at the end of the strike era with the repression looming, is a typical, though early, example of the noir pattern and will be used here to represent the noir master plot. The film's producer, John Houseman, described the protagonist of this and similar films at the time as an "outsider figure, lacking confidence in and alienated from the values and aspirations of mainstream society" (qtd. in Krutnik 89).

Johnny Morrison (Alan Ladd), just back from the war, is still part of a collective with his two pilot buddies, but one that breaks down in the course of the film as Johnny is accused of murder. As with many of the noir heroes, there is a backstory of a past collective memory (equivalent to the workers' immediate memory of the strikes) of Johnny and his buddies sharing dangers in the same plane that is being attacked. It is this collective memory that the accusing of Johnny of murder attempts to erase.

The first act of the film, after establishing the wartime collective, then shows Johnnie's alienation from the more individual and greedier values of the atomized capitalist home front, expressed here as his wife's partying and infidelity. At the midpoint in this film, and much earlier in subsequent noirs, the protagonist is accused of a crime, here the murder of his wife, and must flee to protect himself. The character is often either directly innocent, as is the case here, or innocent through extenuating circumstances, as is the case for Burt Lancaster's angry drifter who kills a man in self-defense in a bar brawl in the opening of *Kiss the Blood Off My Hands* (1948). Johnny is then, as his buddies describe him, "on the dodge like a cheap criminal," the understanding being that he, like the striker, has been falsely labeled a criminal.

In the second act, or middle section, of the noir, which constitutes the main action of the film, the protagonist is pursued by both the police, characterized as either cold or corrupt, and the criminal element, usually portrayed as either direct figures of authority or as gangster-businessmen. To the protagonist, the two forces are somewhat interchangeable, since both are out to get him. "The police are looking for me and if they catch me, they're not going to worry about pinning it on someone else" is the way Johnny describes his relationship to the law. The law is marked by its structural position vis-à-vis the protagonist as working in tandem with the criminal/business element. Thus the structure is a recognition of the position that the government, the law, could and would play in suppressing the strikers and turning them into fugitives.

The criminal/businessman—in this case Harwood, the supposedly respectable club owner whose past conceals a murder—is almost always a figure of authority, in this case of the supreme authority of the club owner in the nightmarish lounge world of noir.[11] Often the figures of the gangster and the businessman are combined, perhaps alluding to the collusion in Hollywood of studio heads and mobsters. The equation of the two by the noir creators is exemplified in *The Blue Dahlia* by writer Raymond Chandler's description of studio executives coming back from lunch: "They looked so exactly like a bunch of top-flight Chicago gangsters. . . . It brought home to me in a flash the strange psychological and spiritual kinship between the operations of big money business and the rackets. Same faces, same expressions, same manners. Same way of dressing and same exaggerated leisure of movement" (qtd. in Friedrich 258).

In fleeing the law, the protagonist often encounters an ally, usually a woman, and in this case Johnny encounters Joyce (Veronica Lake), who is a kind of fugitive herself, refusing at first to identify herself to Johnny and hiding from her ex-husband, Harwood. Here, as is often the case in noir, the woman's social position as outsider inclines her toward viewing the male fugitive as a class ally.[12] The protagonist also encounters class traitors as he or she traverses a landscape where money may take precedence over class loyalty. In *The Blue Dahlia*, the room clerk at first hides Johnny, then attempts to extort money out of him, and finally turns him in for money, a reminder that "public opinion" was being bought off and turned against the strikers.[13]

In the last act, the protagonist shows more resourcefulness and early in the cycle is able to clear himself by forcing the law to administer justice, as here Johnny first exposes Harwood as a murderer, showing that it is the businessman, not Johnny, whose past is built on a crime, then is able to force the police to establish that the murderer of his wife is "Dad," an ex-cop/hotel detective, thus also unconsciously linking cops and crime. The ending changes dramatically in the cycle, with the early noirs featuring the protagonist returned—in this case somewhat unscathed—back into society, but later, as in the next year's *Desperate*, with the character much more mentally scarred as the truck driver walks off into the shadows (see next chapter), and finally, in the latter part of the cycle, as in *Night and the City* (1950), with the protagonist dead (and the corporate gangster triumphant) in the ultimate outside-the-law position.

Noir as Savage Lament

In the latter part of the noir period, crime films such as *Force of Evil* (1948) began to look like the opposite of the social problem films that marked the period's opening. In these films the problem cannot be solved. The structure and mood of the films exhibit the disillusioned sentiment of their directors at the end of the period of the cultural front and of the New Deal, with the attack on the former accelerating after HUAC and the latter after Henry Wallace's loss in his 1948 presidential bid. The hoped-for social change, fueled by the strikes—here, after Taft-Hartley and in the wake of the concerted attack on the radical unionism that provided the mass base for both the New Deal and the cultural front—is replaced by despair.[14] The only hope these films exhibit is in the force of their thoroughgoing critique.[15]

There was also a good deal of despair about a defeat over access to the means of production that was taking place at this time. *Force of Evil* marked the end of the first phase of Hollywood independent production, as company after company began closing in the wake of the industry downturn after 1946. The film was a product of the most radical of the indies, Enterprise Studios, with at that time acknowledged Communist Robert Rossen sitting on its board of directors. The film, directed by Abraham Polonsky, the screenwriter on the studio's biggest hit, *Body and Soul* (1947), was designed as an experimental film both in its style, mixing rapid-fire poetic street language and at times Eisenstein-derived dizzying montage, and in its content, directly conflating gangsters and Wall Street investors. By the time the film was released, though, Enterprise was bankrupt and its distributor, MGM, instead of stressing the film's radical content and form, cut twenty minutes, marketed it as a B crime film, and released it at Christmas, a deliberate swipe at the mood of the film, which was hardly conducive to holiday cheer (Clarens 221).

Force of Evil involves the takeover of a series of small numbers operations by a larger criminal kingpin named Ben Tucker, engineered by Tucker's lawyer, Joe Morse (John Garfield). One of the operations belongs to Joe's brother Leo, who resists the takeover. Joe tries to help Leo, but Tucker's "corporation" becomes increasingly ruthless in enforcing its new regime. Leo gets caught in the crossfire between Tucker and Tucker's old gangster rival Fico, who returns to try to muscle in on the numbers operation, and Leo dies after being kidnapped by Fico. In a shootout to avenge Leo's death, Joe participates in the death of both Tucker and Fico, then goes to reclaim his brother's body, dumped ignominiously on the rocks at the base of the George Washington Bridge.

As director Polansky said, the numbers racket in the film is "a kind of symbol of the capitalist system" (Neve 133), and that system, which was penetrating society at an increasingly deeper level, is portrayed in the film as nothing but predatory gangsterism. The film is set on Wall Street and links the legalized gambling of the stock market with the illegal numbers racket. The syndicate, "the corporation," when it monopolizes the small mom-and-pop numbers rackets, materializes a fear common to the period of a nation of workers and small business-people losing their freedom. Leo's accountant Bauer is told that he can't show up late for work since he is now "working for a big corporation" and later also told that he can never quit the organization.

The film also criticizes the myth of the purity of the small business and shows how that form of capitalism is already imbued with the values of the larger corporation. Joe confronts Leo's supposed small-business morality in treating his workers humanely: "Honest? Respectable? Don't you take the nickels, dimes, and pennies from people who bet just like every other crook, big or little, in this racket? They call this racket 'policy' because people bet their nickels on numbers instead of paying their weekly insurance premium. . . . Tucker wants to make millions, you [to Leo] thousands, and you [to Leo's secretary Doris], you do it for $35 a week."

Leo himself points to the corruption of the petit bourgeoisie in equating their activities to petty crime, as the corporation is equated to organized crime. Before the numbers racket, Leo worked in real estate, "living from mortgage to mortgage, stealing credit like a thief," and then owned a garage, "three cents overcharge on every gallon of gas, two cents for the chauffeur and a penny for me, a penny for one thief, two cents for the other." He presents the corporate takeover as the end point of this systemic corruption: "Now I won't have to steal pennies anymore, I'll have big crooks to steal dollars for me."

A generalized mood of despair hangs over the film and culminates in Joe's finding Leo's body under the George Washington Bridge,[16] "thrown . . . away on the rocks by the river like an old dirty rag nobody wants" in a location sequence that is presented as a descent into hell, one of many symbols of the end of an era that was once filled with hope. The last half of the film is filled with Leo's premonitions of his own death and Joe's watching his capitalist dream go up in smoke as the law closes in on him. Joe's recounting of this change is an apt description of the structure of feeling of the once-energetic radicals of the period, now forced underground: "You don't know what it is to have real fear in you. You don't know what it is to wake up in the morning, to go to sleep at night, to eat your lunch and read the papers and hear the horns blowing in the streets and hear the horns blowing in the clubs and all the time, wherever you are, whatever you're doing, whatever you're seeing, whatever you are, you're afraid in your heart. Is that what life is?"

chapter 3

Noir Part 2

Fugitive Kinds

Perhaps the best way to illustrate the dominance of left ideas in the film noir is by focusing on the additive quality of the various types of fugitives outside the law. Seven main categories of these figures collectively describe a working- and middle-class bloc aligned against corporatism and constitute various ways of considering the immediate past of the war and the strike period and the not-so-distant, more radical past of the Depression.

The working-class section of this bloc consists of three categories of fugitives: working-class characters figured directly; convicts/criminals who are often innocent but whose intransigence against the system allies them with the radicalness of the working class in this period; and Depression-era drifters, wanderers from an earlier era whose presence evokes the great period of labor organizing of the 1930s. The middle-class category consists of middle-class characters figured directly and the war veteran, who usually had attained the equivalent of a middle-class rank in the service. Between these two groups, again exhibiting characteristics of both, is the private detective, now thoroughly outside the law. A final category is the fugitive victim, who, no matter what class, is doomed almost from the start of the film, representing the fallen or non-class status of the blacklistee. If the detective is considered as a boundary figure and split between working and middle class, then the number of films for working- and middle-class characters is roughly even for the period (see appendix).

Each of these categories, and two in particular, establishes a relationship to the immediate or distant past. While the Depression-era drifter recalls a time when class tensions were most acute, the war veteran is often an amnesiac, cursed with forgetting the immediate past. A traumatic experience in the present has caused him to forget, and in this forgetting he is then declared guilty of a crime, as often also is the detective. In the process of the former recovering his memory and the latter discovering what has happened in the moment when often he has blacked out, each finds that the guilty party is instead the criminal businessman. This focus on forgetting the immediate past, equivalent to the time of the strikes, which was traumatically excised from the Hollywood screen, followed by the recovery of this memory, is yet another trace of the vestiges of the strike period that in shattered and fragmented pieces revitalizes the mainstream of the mid- to late 1940s crime film.

The Working-Class Fugitive

The most stunning fact about the working-class fugitive is that, strictly speaking, there isn't one. The outside-the-law fugitive is the crime film dominant in the 1945–50 period, but none of these fugitives work in the industries (mining, manufacturing, etc.) that form the core of those that were on strike in the period. Probably the most solidly working-class film of the period, *The Window* (1949), with its "neo-realist shots of New York tenements and streets" (Neve 169), though "firmly rooted in the sociology of urban working-class life" (Reid and Walker 84), remains pointedly domestic in its setting, focalized through a young boy and never actually stating where his parents work.

The majority of working-class figures belong to two professions, both of which have exceptional status in working-class representation: sports, which as entertainment is necessarily about the mediation of the working-class athlete by the culture industry; and trucking, where workers are often alone and isolated and difficult to organize, though the teamsters were active in supporting strikes in Hollywood and the nation as a whole.[1] Sports, and boxing in particular, though a special case, also functioned—particularly in the Enterprise film written by Polansky, *Body and Soul* (1947), with its corrupt promoters, agents, and mobsters—as a metaphor for life under capitalism, with the crucial question often being the boxer's ability to maintain his integrity and working-class values in the face of a machine that turns all activity into money. Boxing, then, as a form of entertainment, could also be figured as a metaphor for the working-class writer's relationship to the studio.

The movement within the working-class fugitive films parallels that of noir as a whole with the figure of the trucker Steve Randall embracing the American dream at the opening of *Desperate* (1947), proceeding to the more down-and-out actions of the last chance for the trucker losing out to a syndicate in *Thieves Highway* (filmed 1948, released 1949) and the closing gambit of a fighter refusing to take a dive ending beaten in an alley but with his integrity intact in *The Set-Up* (1949), to the final position of an unemployed worker lynched because of a crime he committed over his shame at not having the objects of the consumer society, most particularly a television, in *Try and Get Me* (1950), which Thom Anderson called "the masterpiece of film gris."

Desperate

This prototypical working-class fugitive film was produced at RKO under Dore Schary in 1946 at the time when the backlash against the strikers was gathering momentum. It was directed by Anthony Mann and sets the stage for the later work by Mann and cinematographer John Alton, a duo whose predilection for depicting the dark aspects of working-class life began in *Raw Deal* (see convict section below), reached an orgiastic height in the Mann-directed end sequence of *He*

Walked by Night, which refocalizes a police procedural around the fugitive's desperate plight, and concluded with *Side Street* (which saw the duo reuniting under Schary at MGM, where Schary again attempted to form a low-budget socially conscious crime unit), about a mailman who, with no other way to meet the demands of the new consumer society, steals mail.

In *Desperate*, Steve Randall (Steve Brodie) owns his own truck and trucking business and wants nothing more than to prosper in that business with his pregnant new wife, Ann. This middle-class dream is interrupted almost immediately when Steve, thinking he is going to a job, finds himself instead in the middle of a heist led by a boyhood pal turned mobster, Walt Radak (Raymond Burr). When Steve attempts to foil the robbery, the police seize Walt's younger brother Al, who kills a cop in the shootout. Walt threatens to kill Ann if Steve will not turn himself in to save Al, but Steve escapes and, with Ann, flees from Chicago to her aunt's farm in Minnesota, with both the police and the criminals chasing Steve. Walt catches up with Steve, who then sends Ann and their newborn baby to California, and Steve faces Walt in a final showdown. Though the police intervene, it is Steve who shoots Walt, then disappears into the night, cleared of the crime and on his way to meet his family in California, but, or so his fading into darkness implies, forever marred by this experience.

The fugitive narrative here serves two functions. First, it interrupts Steve's upward mobility and reunites him with his working-class heritage. Second, the arbitrariness of his being outside the law—one minute supposedly rendezvousing for a pick-up, the next running for his life from the police—reminds him that working-class mobility is tenuous and can just as quickly lead downward. Steve is reminded by Walt of their tenement origins, then on his journey outside the law reverts from truck owner to mechanic in order to survive. Steve and Ann's journey leads them to a peasant enclave of Ann's Czech relatives, different from Steve's Chicago origins, "born and raised in the back of a stockyard," and recalling the Old Country reminder that many of the working-class radicals and Hollywood artists' origins were in these enclaves particularly those of the Russian Jewish shtetl, to which this seems more than a veiled reference.

Steve's flight across a landscape that is defined as individualistic and greedy is best exemplified by a used-car salesman, Morgan, who claims he will give Steve a deal on a car if he fixes it; and when he does, Morgan takes Steve's money, jacks up the price, and kicks Steve off the lot. Steve then sneaks back onto the lot at night and "steals" the car, with the crime film now promoting the understanding that, as Brecht says, the crime of robbing a bank is nothing compared to the crime of owning one.

Desperate begins in the warm rays of daylight with Steve at work in his truck and Ann at work at home and, in a typical noir pattern, ends in the grim shadows of night with Steve shooting Walt on the staircase of a tenement building. As they flee Chicago by train in the daytime, Steve and Ann believe they are identified, when in reality the man opposite them mistakes them for a honeymooning couple, an innocent status now no longer granted to them. The visual high point of the film, a scene where Walt and his gang torture Steve in a basement, develops what would become the Mann-Alton arsenal of menacing, off-center, low angles stressing Walt's girth and the broken bottle that threatens Steve, choker close-ups of a sweating Steve, and backlighting with a single light source, here a swinging overhead light bathing different parts of the room in its eerie glow. If Steve is tortured by the gang in their business suits, he receives no better treatment from the police, who at first pursue him though he is innocent, and then, when they do believe him, use him as bait to catch Walt.[2]

The film's mixture of light and dark grows dimmer as a brightly lit wedding sequence with Ann's relatives is contrasted to the gang in the basement discovering Steve's whereabouts. As Ann is in the hospital having her baby, Steve is in the waiting room buying a life insurance policy, now figuring himself worth more dead than alive. From the moment he buys the policy, the film is shrouded in darkness, culminating in Steve's complete entry into Walt's world with the shadowy gun battle on the stairs. Steve shoots Walt and is cleared by the police, but instead of walking into the sun and the bright promise of a new start he skulks away into the night, slouching toward the supposed promised land of California where he has sent his wife and newborn, recalling the endings of both *The Grapes of Wrath* (1940), where Tom Joad, also in California, remains a fugitive trapped in the night, and *I Was a Fugitive from a Chain Gang*, where James Allen's reply to the question "How do you survive?" is hoarsely croaked from the darkness that engulfs him: "I steal."

The Convict Fugitive

If the working-class structure of feeling of this period is somewhat embedded in the (admittedly few) films with working-class figures that Hollywood undertook in the period, these feelings may be even more strongly a part of a series of crime films with the convict as protagonist, films that reached their apogee in the year after Taft-Hartley and the HUAC hearings. In these films the law is a strong presence, since the pursued character is, from the opening, perceived as dangerous, since the character has either escaped from prison (*Dark Passage, Raw Deal*), is a prisoner him- or herself (meaning he or she is in a perpetual state of confinement, a degree worse than pursuit by the law) (*Brute Force*), or has just been released from prison (*I Walk Alone*). The manhunt, then, is a much more palpable and forceful figuring of the now criminalized status of the wildcat striker than in the working-class fugitive films, where the pursued is an ordinary individual suddenly gone afoul of the law. Much of the work of the film is in aligning and engendering allegiance with this criminal figure through stressing either his or her direct innocence of the crime of which he or she is accused or the extenuating circumstances, including an understanding of the character's past, that make the crime understandable. Allegiance is also engendered by a positive presentation of the customs and modes of thought by which these characters survive, relating them to working-class customs and modes of survival.

These films were more daring than the major studios usually attempted; the majority were made by small studios like Eagle-Lion (*Hollow Triumph, Raw Deal*) or independent producers like Hal Wallis (*I Walk Alone*). By 1949 the films had mostly stopped being made, with the transition film perhaps being Nicholas Ray's *In a Lonely Place* (1950), in which the structure of sympathy for the delinquent fugitive is tempered by his confession to a murder at the end, preparing the way for the conversion of the sympathetic fugitive to the post-HUAC psychotic fugitive.[3]

Raw Deal

Raw Deal, the most interesting convict film and perhaps the best crime film of the period, was produced by Eagle-Lion, a small studio noted for crime films that had scored a hit with the Mann-Alton first teaming,

T-Men (1948), an undercover cop film whose expressionist techniques often seemed at war with its police procedural veneer. *Raw Deal*, written by Leopold Atlas and John C. Higgins, both of whom later confessed to being Communists (Neve 164), converted Dennis O'Keefe's undercover treasury agent in *T-Men* to an on-the-lam convict. The film also refused *T-Men*'s objective veneer (authoritarian voice-over, fetishizing of police technology, clipped, proto-documentary pacing) in favor of what would be the fullest development of Mann-Alton expressionism. This style included a highly subjective (female) narrator amplified by appropriately eerie music; use of odd-angle framing and wide-angle lenses that often distorted faces and objects, such that one critic claimed that "there isn't a commonplace camera set-up in the entire film" (Miller 30); and side and back lighting or natural lighting at night, a material manifestation of the trapped feeling in the characters. The overall effect of this style was to extend the metaphor of the prison to the landscape the convict traverses after his or her escape.[4]

The film's protagonist, Joe Sullivan (O'Keefe), is imprisoned for an unspecified crime he did not commit. He has taken the rap for a gangster, Rick Coyle (Raymond Burr), a childhood playmate from a San Francisco slum called Corkscrew Alley. Rick helps Joe's girlfriend, Pat (Claire Trevor), break Joe out of jail, hoping he will be shot as he attempts to escape. Once out, Joe and Pat kidnap Ann (Marsha Hunt), a social worker assigned to Joe's case, and hold her hostage. Joe and Ann argue as the three flee the law, but Ann softens toward Joe when he lets a fellow fugitive seek refuge with him. Rick has arranged another ambush for Joe, but it is thwarted when Ann shoots Rick's henchman, afterward acknowledging her love for Joe. Joe tells her to leave, which she does, but she is then captured by Rick to lure Joe back to Corkscrew Alley where Rick can dispose of him. Pat, who knows she is losing Joe to Ann, finally tells Joe of Rick's plan, and Joe goes to rescue Ann. Joe saves Ann but dies in her arms as Pat, now captured by the police, looks on.

One of the most striking aspects of the film is the emphasis on the modes, customs, and ways of being of Pat and Joe, quite clearly working class and generally presented either favorably or nonjudgmentally, no mean feat for a Hollywood film. Joe and Pat's relationship began when they were kids playing together in the slums of San Francisco, and theirs is a striking moment of a male-female working-class al-

Figure 5. Joe and Pat under the watchful gaze of the law in *Raw Deal*.

liance. Though Joe is the protagonist, Pat's consciousness is also highlighted with a voice-over that, unusual for the period, continues throughout the film. "I have a kind of feeling for the city, even Corkscrew Alley where I grew up, jumped rope, cried, laughed," Pat says in reminiscing about her and Joe's upbringing. Her communication is often nonverbal but always direct. She confronts Ann about making a play for Joe. "Joe means nothing to me," Ann answers. Pat slaps her and says, "Then that's for nothing," and Ann then acknowledges that Pat is correct. Joe's responses are also often nonverbal, as when he smashes a glass at not being able to express his confusion about his love for Ann. And both characters express strong feelings for others, in the way ultimately that Pat tells Joe of Ann's kidnapping, which also grows out of her stated recognition that Pat is also "a dame in love with Joe," and in Joe's willingness to go with Pat to South America because of their past association rather than to return to Ann, whom he now loves.

Raw Deal also highlights the hollowness, or perhaps the impossibility, of the middle-class dream in this moment when the working class is under attack as Joe describes his anticipated life with Pat in Panama in a droning monotone that reflects his disbelief both in its possibility and in its ability to make him happy. He describes in a scene whose shadowy, inert mise-en-scène is as frozen as his voice, a "new place" where they can "get a ranch, start fresh . . . [have a] house, kids, maybe bring 'em up right, scrub 'em all up, send 'em off to school."

The film undertakes a difficult project of allegiance, since Joe is an escaped convict whom an audience might normally disavow. Instead, sympathy is enlisted for Joe through a complex debate with Ann, the middle-class social worker, who might be more an audience identification figure. Ann, the social worker whose family was also poor in the Depression, contrasts her family's working with Joe's life as a convict. Joe's continual answer is that his life was shaped by his social and economic circumstances. Ann tells Joe she is working on his case because "I got interested in a kid I read about in some records. When he was twelve there was a fire and he risked his life to save eight other kids. He got a medal for it. What happened to that kid?" Joe's first answer is a defensive posturing, "How would I know? Maybe there were other fires. Maybe he became a fireman. Maybe he got burned, I wouldn't know." But ultimately he explains his life by referring to social circumstances that differed from hers: "If you want to know what happened to that kid with the medal, he had to hock it at sixteen; he got hungry."[5]

These interactions begin a dialogue between the two, with Joe allowing a fellow convict to enter his hideout after he sees that Ann does not approve of Joe's leaving him out in the cold to face the police alone, and, finally, with Joe risking his life and his freedom to save Ann. On the opposite side, Ann, who at first says that if she had a gun she would shoot Joe, later, when she sees Joe threatened, picks up a gun and instead shoots Rick's henchman, the ultimate proof that when she is placed in the desperate circumstances that mark Joe's life, she will react in the same way he has, her actions conditioned by her need to survive and to help her ally in a desperate world. The film thus takes its middle-class character directly into the life of its working-class protagonist and in so doing makes his actions more understandable and sympathetic.

If *Raw Deal*—and the convict film in general—goes further than most films of the period in enlisting sympathy for working-class figures directly in conflict with the law, the film also presents a hyperbolizing of the other aspects of the fugitive noir. The police are for the most part absent from the film, with the chase instead focalized around the convict Joe. When they do appear in a midpoint sequence in which they track another fugitive to Joe's hideout, their representation is as dark, fascistic forces who gun down the fugitive in a gangland-style execution, with the police captain then coming into the hideout, asking to use the phone, and coldly characterizing this brutal slaughter by telling his office, "There's been a little trouble."

Rick's villainy is likewise hyperbolized. He has risen to be lord of Corkscrew Alley, but his exterior as a smooth businessman keeps breaking down to reveal a sadistic pyromaniac ironically consumed in flames himself by Joe, falsely imprisoned for Rick's crime. Finally, if the landscape is treacherous, it also contains pockets of resistance as Joe encounters the farmhouse couple from his past, Oscar and his wife, who immediately take him in and help him.

The convict films, and particularly *Raw Deal*, represent the strongest positive representation of working-class figures who actively contest representatives of both the law and the business classes for their place in the world, though in the end, as the defeat of the strike era is registered, that fight ends in death, but still a death that points to the possibility of a hard-fought alliance with a middle class to confront an evil which, at an enormous expense, still might be erased, as Joe dies in Ann's arms after destroying Rick.

The Depression-Era Drifter

This small group of films, which includes *The Chase, Fallen Angel, Gilda, The Postman Always Rings Twice*, and *The Strange Love of Martha Ivers* (all 1946), most of which were made during the latter part of the strike era, have as their protagonist a drifter, often a gambler, who wanders into a town, near penniless, but who soon becomes entwined with some part of the power structure of the place. With their protagonist on the outside looking in, these films present highly charged class conflict, since the disparity between the protagonist and his or her wealthy patron or opponent (or patron revealed to be an opponent), whose riches have often been acquired illegally, forms the central and very explicit tension of the film.[6]

The drifter, who recalls the thousands who rode the rails in the early part of the Depression (the parallel made explicit in the opening Depression-era sequence where the protagonist becomes a "wild boy" in the paradigmatic *Strange Love of Martha Ivers*), also usually has a checkered past that may involve a crime out of desperation and which is contrasted to the cold-blooded crime for profit of his or her benefactor/employer.

Thus in these films class conflict is the explicit subject. Critics have noted that they, and the noirs in general, describe "a bleak world of class envy and alienation" (Kemp qtd. in Neve 169) where one character wants another dead because "I work in a drug store and your husband owns hundreds of them" (Neve 165, from *Sorry Wrong Number*). These are films where, as Philip Kemp notes, instead of the lighthearted satire of the 1930s screwball comedies, another genre where class was also an explicit subject, class is more directly "an instrument of oppression" that functions "as a cause of hatred and violence" (269).

The Strange Love of Martha Ivers

The best of the drifter films, *The Strange Love of Martha Ivers*, presents an overarching critique of postwar America and an assessment of how class oppression had hardened since the Depression by contrasting two pairs of star-crossed lovers, each from different classes. *Martha Ivers*, shot during the height of the strike period, was independently produced by Hal Wallis, who had produced *I Was a Fugitive from a Chain Gang* and would go on to produce *Sorry Wrong Number*, an early Lancaster *I Walk Alone*, and *The File on Thelma Jordan* (1950) about a corrupt attorney. The script, with every line oozing with class tension and later cited by the anti-union Motion Picture Alliance as containing "sizable doses of Communist propaganda" (Neve 140), was by *Body and Soul* director Robert Rossen, and the direction was by longtime left activist and director of the antiwar *All Quiet on the Western Front* (1930), Lewis Milestone.

The film's prologue is set on the eve of the Depression in 1928 on the night the teenage Martha Ivers, heir to the fortune of the wealthiest family in the town, is set to run away from Iverstown with her friend Sam. Instead, Martha is captured by the local police and brought back to her aunt who "owns" the town. Sam steals back into the house and offers Martha a chance to leave with him. When she says no, Sam leaves, then Martha pushes her aunt down the staircase to her death. Her story of a mysterious murderer is backed by Walter, the frail boy her age, and his father the family attorney, who sees a chance to corral the Ivers fortune. Years later, the grown Sam (Van Heflin), a gambler, stumbles on Iverstown when his car swerves off the road. Walter (Kirk Douglas) is now an alcoholic district attorney, while Martha (Barbara Stanwyck) runs the factory. Both are consumed not only by the original murder but also by Walter's prosecution and the subsequent execution of an innocent man whom the two had framed as the murderer. Sam falls for a fellow drifter recently released by the police for suspected larceny, Toni Marachek (Lizbeth Scott), but is also courted by Martha. Walter, jealous of Martha and Sam's childhood attraction, threatens to put Toni in jail, forcing her to betray Sam, and then has Sam beaten and dumped outside the town. Sam returns and confronts Martha. She reveals her original crime to him, urging him to kill Walter so they can be together. Sam refuses and leaves the mansion as a despairing Walter and Martha kill each other. Sam and Toni then escape the town.

In the pre-Depression prelude, in a *Citizen Kane*–like shot recalling lightning flashing on the perverse kingdom of Xanadu, lightning here flashes on the "I. P. Ivers" sign that overlooks the town, with the sign's shadow then catching the teenage Sam being pursued by the police. Years later, Sam's car skids off the road because he is shocked to see the sign "Welcome to Iverstown, America's Fastest Growing Industrial City," as once again this oppressive industrial power confronts the working-class figure. The film will detail the inner psychological workings of the way power is maintained in "America's Fastest Growing Industrial City" and after laying bare these mechanisms will in the end compare this supposed economic miracle to Sodom and Gomorrah as Sam tells Toni not to turn around and look, or she will be cursed like Lot's wife, as they flee the town's corruption.

The film makes its point by contrasting the formation of one set of (working-class) lovers with the dissolution of another set (of upper-class lovers). Rossen's script casts a Shakespearean spell over a mid-century, ever more rapidly corporatizing, America. Walter and Martha are compared to Macbeth and Lady Macbeth, with Martha particularly "soaked in and shot through with money and the coolly intricate amorality of money," as James Agee described many of the characters of the noir (qtd. in Neve 147). Martha props up a weakening Walter by telling him coldly, about the two murders, "What's done is done," and Walter answers, "The deed's done but not the thought." Later, Sam's downtrodden lover sums herself up in tones that recall Hamlet's acceptance of his position as "Hamlet, the Dane": "I'm not the best of people, I'm just Toni Marachek." But this is Shakespeare by way of Marx, and in the end the film so powerfully suggests the structural element at play in what Louis Althusser will call the interpolation into class position that Walter can say to Martha, on the verge of their double suicide, "Don't cry, Martha. It's not your fault, nor mine, nor my father's. It isn't anyone's fault. It's just the way things are. It's what people want and how hard they want it, how hard it is for them to get it." This kind of direct concentration on the structure of class inequality and its ability to destroy lives is highly unusual in American cinema and in America in general, where class is so often denied.

The film strives to establish Sam's and Toni's working-class credentials. Both connect most immediately through their backgrounds (both had fathers who were cold) and their shared experience in being kicked around. When Sam encounters Toni, she has been booted out of the boardinghouse he grew up in. Sam later describes this similarity in their background to Martha. "We lived in the same house," he says, indicating the class similarity in their positions, and contrasting the boardinghouse they inhabit with Martha's mansion. Sam then mentions other class markers they share: "taxi cabs, hotels, Bibles, and we don't like some of the same people and places."[7]

The nature of Sam and Toni's relationship also indicates a working-class orientation. Love is here the severely compromised fellow feeling despite adverse conditions. Toni is pointedly neither femme fatale nor redeemer but rather class ally. She does betray Sam, but this is because she is threatened with being imprisoned by Walter, and she is equally irate when she senses Sam's betrayal of her with Martha. Yet each responds to the other with an understanding of the mitigating class circumstances. When Sam learns why Toni betrayed him ("Go ahead and hit me, Sam, I've got it coming"), he replies, "The only thing you have coming, kid, is a break." And when Sam is succumbing to Martha's seduction, Toni reminds him of their mutual struggle against the power structure of the town: "I liked you when you said . . . you didn't like to be pushed around. [After being beaten] you were looking for trouble, but it was a good kind of trouble."

Finally, the film does not accept the "to-be-looked-at-ness," as Laura Mulvey puts it in describing the male gaze upon the female, of an upper class on a lower one. When Martha, clad in an elegant, long-flowing jacket and hood, sees Toni in a two-piece skimpy outfit enter Sam's room, her accusatory look prompts Toni's defensive response: "I give another show at 8:00." Martha's answer seals her characterization of Toni as a tramp: "In your room or here?" But the film with its prior soft-focus treatment of Sam lovingly pulling the covers over a sleeping Toni to Miklós Rózsa's lushly romantic score counters Martha's vulgar characterization of Toni and Sam's relationship.[8]

While the working-class relationship is about the difficulties of loyalty under economic and legal adversity, the upper-class relationship is characterized as decadent and impotent, marred by its formation in the most alienating of crimes, murder for money, the destruction of human life for profit.[9] In the opening, Martha's aunt is trying to wipe away the working-class side of Martha, who is the result of the union of the aunt's daughter with "a nobody, a mill hand."[10] The memory of her father is wiped away by Martha's interpolation into her mother's class by the killing of the aunt on the stairs of the mansion. She then uneasily assumes the role of her aunt in her own stern leadership of the town and then finally assumes the coldness of the aunt's power when, again on the same staircase, she urges Sam to kill Walter, to become co-ruler of Iverstown. Here the symbol of the staircase, a habitual marker in film noir, is explicitly defined as what is usually disguised. It marks a passage from one class to another, as Martha originally passes into the ruling class in the opening on the staircase and then urges Sam to do the same at the conclusion.

While Martha is strong and cold but sexually unfulfilled, her husband, Walter, is weak and impotent. Walter's ascension into power, to the head of the town's political and legal system as town prosecutor and candidate for mayor and eventually governor, was sealed with his prosecution, years after the original murder, of an innocent drifter charged with the crime. Here the direct characterization of the law as corrupt servant of the ruling class reaches its apogee in the film noir

Figure 6. Sam Masterson after a beating from the Iverstown political establishment in *The Strange Love of Martha Ivers*.

as Walter furthers his original crime by using his power to declare Sam a criminal and using the police force to dump him outside the town.

The mutilated quality of Walter and Martha's relationship based on power as mutually concealed crime is illustrated in a scene where Martha strides boldly into the mansion having just delivered a campaign speech for Walter, whom she finds home drunk. When Walter touches her, Martha stiffens and pulls away. His response is to pour another drink. Their relationship is characterized by Martha's dominant role, her sexual refusal, and Walter's seeking refuge in the drink, a fluid that substitutes for what Martha denies him. The circuit of power that regulates the town, with Martha as head of the economy, or base, as the factory owner and Walter as head of the political and legal order, the superstructure, is characterized in private as impotent, the suggestion being that the couple's supposed dynamism in public conceals the inert impotence of an oppression that is more obvious in private.

The last act of the film focuses on the crisscrossing of class relationships. Martha, upon seeing her boyhood "crush" in town, is for a moment reborn as a teenager herself (and in touch with the projection of her factory-worker father that Sam represents). She bounds down the mansion staircase to see Sam and shows him the room she has kept just as it was when he left Iverstown. Martha, then, in biblical fashion, tempts Sam three times to join her, and each time he counters with a highly charged working-class response.

In her office, Martha tells Sam she is chief executive of the factory and gazes wistfully at a mural depicting work in the factory. "Catches it, doesn't it, the feeling of a factory?" she says. "When your aunt owned the place, I couldn't get past the gate," Sam replies. His answer, which focuses on the oppressiveness of having the town's resources being owned by one family, dilutes the romantic quality of her celebration of her ownership. Later, when the two go to an isolated spot overlooking the city, Sam admires the scenery while Martha declares that "Up here it's very real, it gives you a sense of power." Sam has an ability to admire the collective quality of nature and human society, but Martha sees this only as the expression of personal authority. In his dingy hotel room, in the third of these moments of direct class conflict, Martha exoticizes Sam's poverty, "I've never been in a hotel room like this before," to which Sam replies, "I've been in too many." In each of these cases, the film noir tough-guy language, which is often read as simply the protagonist's cynicism, is explicitly presented as a contesting of the sentimentality of the ruling class, a way of maintaining the integrity of a working-class position when confronted with the raw power of an opposing class.

Although his language constructs a defense, Sam still begins to fall under Martha's spell, until finally he finds himself in the place she was years before when he instead left the town. A drunken Walter has fallen on the stairs of the mansion, and Martha urges Sam to finish him off, as she did her aunt. "You've killed," she screams at him. "It says on your record." Sam admits that as a gambler he has strayed outside the law, but his "crime" is different from Martha's. It was in self-defense. His final answer to her last temptation suggests an unbridgeable gap between them: "I've never murdered." He will not turn his back on his fellows to enter the world of the rich. Sam refuses the interpolation that consumes Walter and Martha. Yet even in her death there is a surreal moment, which Buñuel borrows five years later in *Los Olvidados*,[11] where Martha hears the voice of her aunt commanding "Ivers, Ivers" and answers in her teenage voice, "No, Martha

Smith," indicating the power of this process to destroy lives, but also indicating that it is always an unfinished process, as the voices continually struggle within Martha. The film also ultimately points to the fact that the process can be resisted, as Sam and Toni flee "America's Fastest Growing Industrial City," their happiness and their humanity intact.

The Criminal Detective

The detective is a dominant character in the postwar film noir as well, but the change in that character signals again the change in the crime film as a whole. In contrast to Sam Spade's licensed private detective, who is initially suspected of the murder in *The Maltese Falcon*, the ur-detective text of the period, detectives in the postwar, strike, and post-strike era are themselves wanted for a crime, either ordinary people who must become detectives to clear their name or quasi-representatives of the law who have gone afoul of it. The generic pattern is set in *The Dark Corner*, where the detective is also a falsely framed convict with a working-class orientation who in the course of the film is pursued by the police for a murder.[12]

Out of the Past

This film, with its fractured half-flashback structure explaining the detective's quasi-criminal past, was produced in late 1946 and early 1947 as the Republican Congress debated how to repress the strikes. It opened, as Richard Maltby points out, on the same day (25 November 1947) and just a few blocks away from where the studio producers released the Waldorf Statement, which effectively started the blacklist.

The script was adapted by Daniel Mainwaring from his novel *Build My Gallows High*, the title taken from a slave poem about lynching, with the novel deliberately putting the detective in the outsider position often occupied by African Americans (Mainwaring, 44).[13] Visually, the trapped aspect of the lead character was highlighted by the team of director Jacques Tourneur and RKO's most astute noir cameraman, Nicholas Musuraca. The pair had previously worked together on two of Val Lewton's outsider films during the war, *Cat People* (1943) and *I Walked with a Zombie* (1943).

Jeff Bailey (Robert Mitchum), a garage owner, is discovered in a small California town by a gangster in black trench coat who tells him his old client Whit wants to see him. On the way to Whit's Lake Tahoe ranch, Bailey, who reveals his real name is Jeff Markham, tells Ann (Rhonda Fleming), a woman from the town who wants a future with him, about being hired by Whit to find his girlfriend, Kathy Moffitt (Jane Greer), finding her in Mexico, falling in love with her, watching her kill his detective partner, and then covering up the murder. The flashback ends as Jeff reaches the ranch, where Whit hires him again for a job in San Francisco. The job, though, is a setup, engineered by Whit and Kathy, now returned to Whit, with Jeff to be blamed for the murder of Whit's accountant. The setup succeeds, and with the police looking for Jeff he returns to Whit's ranch and has Whit agree to turn Kathy over to the police. She kills Whit and flees the police, whom Jeff has called, in a car with Jeff where both are shot dead. In a coda, a deaf boy who had worked for Jeff points to Jeff's name, itself a pseudonym, on the gas station sign, the only trace left of his existence.

The differences between *Out of the Past* and *The Maltese Falcon*, which this film rewrites, are instructive. Spade's name signifies his ability to spot the truth; Markham's name signals his fate as being duped. The opening scene in the former film is told in a flashback in the latter which begins with the cynical intonation "We called ourselves detectives." While Spade doggedly works for his client, Brigid, and covertly avenges the death of his partner, ultimately turning his client over to the police, Markham abandons his client, Whit, falling in love with Kathy, and ultimately participates in covering up her murder of his partner.[14]

On a moonlit beach in Mexico, Jeff asks Kathy if she stole Whit's money. She snuggles up next to him and coos, "I didn't. Won't you believe me?" He replies, "Baby, I don't care," and kisses her. Here, the detective chooses desire over the law, and the law eventually destroys him for this choice. Spade, on the other hand, sacrifices even love for the law. Jeff's choice of Kathy, relayed in flashback, is a part of a just-completed past that in the present has returned to haunt him, as the desire of the workers in the strike era is now returning to haunt them as the law moves to repress them and the story of their struggle.

There is a difference also in the use of the tough-guy language and attitude, visible also in the personas of Bogart and Mitchum. Bogart eventually triumphs with his language, outwitting the thieves, while Mitchum's language and hesitantly defiant body posture signal that the best he can do is survive, the combination marking the internalization of a defeat expressed as cynicism. "Is there a way to win?" Kathy asks Jeff. "There's a way to lose more slowly" is the best he can muster in response. Later she says, "I don't want to die." "Neither do I baby," he replies, "but if I have to I want to die last."[15]

The death sequence, where the fugitives Kathy and Jeff flee and are gunned down in a police roadblock, deliberately evokes the couple caught in the coolly arrogant police sniper fire of Fritz Lang's *You Only Live Once*. It suggests the length the detective, initially a working-class-aligned figure whose support of the law echoed the working-class support of the war and the society, has moved outside that notion of the law to a defiant, irreconcilable position.

The final scene, with the deaf boy pointing to the sign on the garage that is the last trace of Jeff, and which is a false name under which he was hiding, is a metaphorical reminder of a moment when members of militant labor were "trying to live a normal life as . . . well-adjusted American[s]—but propelled to justify [their] citizenship by accounting for . . . past dubious connections with people and organizations working against the social order" (Maltby 52). The image of the deaf boy as the sole repository of Jeff's story points to how any memory of the triumph of working-class consciousness immediately after the war was now being obliterated.

Middle-Class Protagonists: The Middle-Class Fugitive and the Amnesiac War Veteran

While films featuring the working-class fugitive figured the strike-era structure of feeling of the militant working class, the middle-class films (see appendix) figured two sources of middle-class struggle. First, several of the films featured writers who were forced to hide out (*Sunset Boulevard, House by the River*) or blacklisted (*In a Lonely Place, Underworld Story*) (all 1950), with, as Mike Davis put it, noir itself becoming "a conduit for the resentment of writers in the velvet trap of the studio system" (38). Second, the fugitive outsider figured a specifically middle-class area of resentment, the increasing corporatization with its resultant control of the society in the war and postwar years. In 1900 the United States was overwhelmingly (90 percent) a nation of independent businesspeople and small farmers, with only 10 percent of its population employed in factories and in larger businesses. By 1990 that situation had exactly reversed, with 90 percent of the country employed by corporations or in factories, or in factories owned by corporations, and only 10 percent self-employed (Vanneman and Cannon 84). This trend toward corporate employment, which included a changeover from smaller firms to larger, monopolistic ones (Mandel 85), vastly accelerated in the postwar at the midpoint in this changeover. The middle-class fugitive films registered the fear of this takeover where "resistance to the moral-legal authority of corporatism is tantamount to criminal behavior" (85).

The Big Clock

This film, shot during the HUAC investigation of Hollywood and released one year later, is based on a book of the same title by a 1930s poet known for his critical, anti-capitalist politics, Kenneth Fearing. The book is based on his experiences at *Time* working for Henry Luce (Neve 158), who in 1942 had coined the term "American Century" to promote an age of American imperial expansion and to counter the New Deal's "Age of the Common Man." The screenplay was by Jonathan Latimer, principal auteur of the middle-class fugitive film, who went on to script *The Accused* (1949), in which a fugitive psychoanalyst (Loretta Young) accidentally kills an upper-class student who sexually assaults her.

The Big Clock is helped enormously by the gargantuan presence, in both size and conviction, of Charles Laughton as the Luce-like publisher. The next year Laughton was to star in a stage version of Brecht's *Galileo*, rewritten by Brecht to stress the parallel between the sixteenth-century church's inquisition of scientific truth and HUAC's persecution of those outside the cold war "consensus."

George Stroud, a high-powered editor at *Crimeways*, the lead magazine in the publishing empire of Earl Janoth, has had no time off in his seven years with the firm. On the day he is about to begin his belated honeymoon, Janoth fires George for leaving. George goes on a drunken spree with Janoth's mistress, Pauline Delos, which ends with her being murdered by Janoth, who sees George's shadow as he leaves her apartment. George is called back from his vacation to lead the manhunt for a man whom Janoth and his next-in-command, Steve Hagen, say is the murderer, a man who fits George's description. As George attempts to foil this manhunt for himself, the noose tightens as more and more witnesses are brought into the Janoth building to identify George. With the building sealed, George accuses Hagen of killing Pauline. When Janoth threatens to turn Hagen over to the police, Hagen identifies Janoth as the killer and is then shot by Janoth. Attempting to flee the building, Janoth plunges to his death in his own elevator shaft, and George embraces his wife in the shadowy boardroom.

The Big Clock is the middle-class film that most explicitly combines that class's fear of the loss of freedom that a much more managed corporate life was bringing with the specific threat of the curtailing of political freedom through the blacklist. In language that is not in Fearing's book, written before HUAC, Janoth explicitly uses that threat to keep George at work: "You'll see this through or you're finished with Janoth Publications . . . and I'll have you blacklisted all over the country. You'll never work on another magazine." Janoth's threat suggests that Luce's imperial vision of America began at home with a vision of control of his own company.

The film stresses Janoth's attempt to master space and time. The spaces of the film are entirely corporate spaces, from the opening shot of the Janoth skyscraper where most of the action takes place, to the cold, impersonal offices of Janoth and Hagen, to the bar where employees meet for after hours, a space for relaxation that is instead as rigid a space as that of the office. Here, a bartender gasps at George's order of a drink other than the usual Manhattan. The corporate spaces so dominate the imagination of the film that George and his wife's original space of West Virginia, site of their seven-year-belated honeymoon, is never seen except as an interior in one shot. Janoth's control of the space and his parceling it up is emphasized in George's opening journey up the elevator, where each floor is, à la *Time* magazine, a compartmentalized chunk of commodified reality: *Smartways, Artways, Styleways, Newsways, Crimeways* (Silver and Ursini, "Farrow" 148).

If the spatial symbol of Janoth's tyranny is the skyscraper that eventually traps George, the temporal symbol is the mammoth clock that overlooks the building's lobby, the clock that Janoth puts his workers on and which never stops ticking. Janoth is introduced popping out of the elevator under a giant cuckoo clock, as if he were the cuckoo, and immediately complaining about the editorial board's inefficiency: "There are 2,081,376,000 seconds in the average man's life. Each tick of the clock, a beat of the heart. Yet you sit here useless, ticking your lives away." Later he extends this total control beyond the boardroom to the bedroom, telling his mistress to be gone because he is "six minutes behind my schedule." He closes the door on her with a curt summons to their next sexual liaison: "I'll see you tomorrow night, 10:55."

Janoth is then attempting to eliminate the distinction between the working class, rigidly bound to a clock, and the middle class, supposedly enjoying more "freedom," with his ultimate capitalist attempt to quantify the human heartbeat and parcel it into work time. Indeed, George, the middle-class manager, complains that he works "twenty-six hours a day, Christmases, Fourth of Julys, Mother's Day."

In the specific conjunctural moment of the postwar, the film describes this drive to control time as fascist. George Lipsitz notes that the American worker is the most managed of any worker in the industrialized Western countries (*Rainbow*), and Janoth's bid for ultimate control of his workers recalls Hitler-supporter Henry Ford, as Janoth attempts to extend Ford's assembly-line control from manual to mental labor, that is, to the intellectual work of the magazine.[16] Janoth's use of the law also summons up a kind of corporate fascism. There are no police in the film; instead, the building is sealed off, protected by Janoth's own "security force," which is ordered to shoot to kill when they find the supposed murderer. Within the building, then, Janoth is the ultimate law. George also participates in this fascistic control. His specialty for *Crimeways* is locating criminals before the police by using his system of "irrelevant clues"; that is, he studies the personal psychology of the fugitive, "his character, his mind, his emotions" and functions as a far more intrusive force than the police. His punishment is to be caught in his own fascistic web.

In this context, George's journey outside the law, starting the day as a "decent, respectable, law-abiding citizen" and finding himself hounded and harassed a scant day later, represents the structure of feeling not only of the fugitive worker in the late 1940s but also of the harried middle-class employee, under the gun to finish one assignment and begin another. George's flight to the basement, the bowels of Janoth's empire, and his stopping Janoth's clock for the first time is also a frantic attempt to end this control, a control that, in a utopian ending, stops with Janoth falling victim to his own structure, plunging down the elevator shaft of his building.

The alternative spaces in this film are not those of a working-class community but rather those of the world of art, in a way that suggests Adorno's notion of autonomous art as critique of the capitalist commodification process. Louise Patterson, whose paintings George collects and who finally enlists on George's side against Janoth, is working on a painting called *Avarice*, and when asked to do a representation of the murderer for Janoth she instead draws an abstract symbol Janoth labels "decadent." The other anti-corporate space is Burt's Place, where the bartender, like an alchemist, claims he can create anything that the customers name. One of Burt's customers is the radio actor (his real name is never actually given) who calls himself Jefferson Davis and who impersonates a police officer for George as he does on the radio.

These spaces pose the free imagination against Janoth's attempt to harness all human activity for money. Ultimately, though, the film ends with a false happiness, eliding the point that, as Barton Palmer ("Continuum") suggests, a now-chastened George will take over and become a kinder, gentler Janoth. The book has no such illusions, and it ends with George in awe of the relentless drive toward capital accumulation: "The big silent, invisible clock was moving along as usual. But it had forgotten all about me. Tonight it was looking for someone else. Its arms and levers and steel springs were wound up poised in search of some other person in the same blind, impersonal way it had been reaching for me on the night before. And it has missed me, somehow. That time. But I had no doubt it would get around to me again" (Fearing 144).

Amnesiac War Veteran: *Somewhere in the Night*

Films featuring World War II veterans as a whole portrayed "a frustrated search for community" as "people who learned to work purposely with each other in military, community or industrial projects now faced the future alone" (Lipsitz, *Rainbow* 283). The noir variant featured a veteran who, through the trauma of the war (*Somewhere in the Night*, 1946) or the trauma of returning to the greedy, atomized home front where the class war was still raging (*The High Wall*, 1947), loses his memory and is accused of a crime in the blacked-out time.

Somewhere in the Night, produced at Darryl Zanuck's Fox—the last of the major studios to promote liberal content after HUAC—and written by 1930s Group Theater director Lee Strasberg, concerns a Purple Heart–decorated veteran who wakes in a hospital with no memory. His only clue, a letter, identifies him as George Taylor and points to a Los Angeles club called The Cellar run by Mel Phillips. Through the help of a singer in the club, Christy, Taylor learns he is actually Larry Cravat, a seedy detective who before the war was suspected of killing his partner in pursuit of loot from the German war machine. The killing was actually done by Phillips, who is killed by the police as Taylor/Cravat then declares himself through with detective work.

Taylor describes himself as being "born in a hospital," with the subjective camera in the opening through the eyes of the patient and the natural sounds of the hospital indeed suggesting a kind of birth. Throughout, the film builds sympathy for this reborn character who declares that "three years of war can change a man." While the collective experience of the war has changed George for the better, the club owner, who initially seems respectable in contrast to George's shady past, is revealed instead as the actual killer. It is he who collaborated with the Germans to steal war loot and then killed their mutual partner.

The terrain George returns to is one of women waiting to prostitute themselves, sanitariums, and shady nightclubs. In this landscape he is repeatedly attacked, experiencing the class war at home as reduplicating the battlefield. The middle-class protagonists of the amnesiac veteran films find themselves under siege with the strings being pulled by the owner in the shadows who uses their trauma to cover his own class crimes. Their solace and strength is the still recollected collective experience of the war, which counters the now painful dawning recollection of the embattled life they left at home.

Coda: *Night and the City*'s Fugitive Victim

Though the element of doom surrounds the crime film of this period, only a few films foreground this doom as an overwhelming principle of their composition, with the character, often in flashback, trying to understand what has led to his or her destruction, which is either imminent (*Detour*'s lead character awaits the police) or has already happened (*Sunset Boulevard*'s writer narrates from beyond the grave). One of the starkest, Edgar Ulmer's *Detour* (1945), appears at the beginning of the noir period with its doomed murderer representing the distance Ulmer experienced from the "dignity and drama in the vitality of working-class communities in the thirties" in his Yiddish films of that period to the "guilt, frustration and hopelessness by 1945" (Lipsitz, *Rainbow*, 296). Ulmer's prescient feeling of defeat was amplified in the crushing defeats of the Popular Front at the end of the period and in the films that bear the stamp of that defeat, including *Crisscross* (1949), *D.O.A.* (1950), and most markedly *Night and the City* (1950).

The production circumstances suggest that *Night and the City*'s director, *Brute Force*'s Jules Dassin, was undergoing in his career a process similar to the lead character's of being hounded and harassed by the law. Because of HUAC pressure on Dassin, Darryl Zanuck, the head of Fox, canceled the plans to shoot the film in Hollywood and instead sent Dassin to London "to do the last picture you may ever do," instructing him to "start with the most expensive scenes, then they may not stop you" (Dassin interview). Indeed, when Dassin returned to the United States he found his name had been mentioned (by former noir director Edward Dmytryk) in HUAC testimony and that he could no longer get work, and he exiled himself to Europe.

Night and the City tracks the momentary rise and immediate fall of Harry Fabian (Richard Widmark), an expatriate in London who scams to bring in tourists to a seedy club, the Silver Fox, but longs to make a big score as a boxing promoter. His promotion of an old boxer named Gregorius (Anthony Quinn) goes awry when another boxer, the Strangler, is hired by the club owner to destroy Gregorius. Gregorius wins the bout but dies in the ring, and his son, the gangster promoter who controls boxing in London, Kristo, then swears "You're a dead man, Harry Fabian." The last act features Harry running frantically, being betrayed by his former friends in the underworld, and finally having his neck broken by the Strangler and being dumped in the Thames as the gangster businessman watches and then strides magnanimously over the bridge.

Two immediate devices establish the context of the film. In the opening, before his rise and fall, Harry is running frantically through the streets of London, hiding out, having welshed on a bet. The opening sense of being hounded and pursued is so powerful that it functions almost as an unacknowledged *Detour*-like flashback, with the narrative then recounting how Harry came to be in the predicament that opens the last act. Second, Harry's last name, Fabian, recalling the nineteenth-century British socialist movement, suggests in 1950s America the end of the line for the possibility of any vestige of socialism being realized because of the social and political repression.

Harry describes himself as "an artist without an art." He is a promoter, a popular artist who wants nothing more than to be successful but finds all legitimate routes to success cut off. Not only is his ability to practice his art of promotion degraded by Kristo's fixing of the fight industry, but he operates in a milieu that is itself a degraded form of thievery at the outskirts of the working-class world. This urban space is a *Three Penny Opera*–like world of counterfeiters, beggars army, and petty crooks, with the bombed-out locations of postwar London functioning as a kind of landscape that maps a working class turned in on itself ("How much you selling me for?" Harry asks Figgler, the head of the beggars army) in the wake of a defeat.

The ending of the film is a crowning lament for a failed revolution. Harry "testifies" against himself, turns himself in, to get the bounty put on his head by Kristo in order to give the money to Mary, an ally at the club. The Strangler, the working-class wrestler, now commanded by the businessman Kristo, snaps Harry's head dispassionately and throws him into the river. The police appear below Kristo's perch on the London Bridge to lead off the Strangler, as Kristo, visually presented as the gangster businessman pulling the strings, smiles at their movements.

Here, in 1950, with the second HUAC hearing looming, with radical labor excised from the unions and being blacklisted from its industries, Harry's story is erased, and this time not even a deaf-mute, as was the case with Jeff Markham, remains to tell the story. Kristo walks confidently and supremely across the bridge in a moment that can be taken as expressing the agony of the defeat of the Popular Front and its underpinning in militant labor.

chapter 4

The McCarthyite Crime Film

The Time of the (Quasi-Scientific) Toad (Criminal/Informer/Vigilante Cops versus Psychotic Fugitives)

> The triumph of McCarthyism was in effect the cutting off of a generalized social movement that had begun before the war and that had identified itself with the objectives of the war.... The loss of progressive unionism allowed McCarthy to operate.
>
> Abraham Polonsky

The 1950–55 period consisted of an increasingly docile labor movement, now shorn of its radical members, being enlisted as junior partner in U.S. global corporate expansion under the guise of the cold war, where its chief role was to contain or "police" more radical labor movements both in the United States and in the world at large. In Hollywood labor, with the militant crafts unions broken, the reactionary studio and government forces turned to an all-out attack on the creative guilds, which resulted in not only the elimination of many of the cultural front writers, actors, and directors but also in a virtual exclusion from the screen of working-class concerns and attitudes previously allowed utterance under the discourse of "the common man."

In the crime film, one of the bastions of working-class expression, the terms of the previous era were reversed. The protagonists of the now dominant police procedural were often working-class cops who surveyed and policed the neighborhoods that had previously hidden the sympathetic fugitive. There was a rough progression whereby the cop-hero at first reverted back into a fugitive (*Where the Sidewalk Ends*, 1950), then moved inside the law (*Detective Story*, 1951), and finally journeyed outside the law, this time not as lawbreaker but as vigilante, as supra-representative of the forces of order (*Big Heat*, 1953). The sympathetic fugitive, now transformed into a psychotic criminal (*Niagara*, 1953) who threatened the fabric of the society, was pursued by an array of federal and local agencies who enforced the rigid boundaries of a society that feared the violent return of what it had repressed.

Let the Sleepwalking Begin

At the 1947 American Federation of Labor convention, following passage of the Section 9h loyalty test in the Taft-Hartley Act, United Mine Workers president John L. Lewis compared this moment to the onset of fascism in Italy and Germany, warning the members that "if you don't resist, the power of the state, the central government will be used against you that much more quickly, because they won't lose any sleep at night worrying about a labor movement that is fleeing before the storm" (qtd. in Boyer and Morais 355).

His words proved prophetic. Federal and state legislative committees, either HUAC or modeled on HUAC, called subpoenaed activist labor leaders and rank-and-file agitators. The result, as many refused to testify, was loss of jobs, blacklisting from the industry, and, in some cases, jail. The subpoenas and trials interrupted strikes and union election campaigns, immobilizing the more radical unions and their leaders, who by the mid-1950s were "involved almost full time in staying out of prison" (Schrecker 156).

An array of federal and local agencies aligned with HUAC to terrorize union activists. The FBI pursued those who did not testify, even approaching employers in different industries and having blacklistees fired again. The fear engendered by this pursuit could only have been heightened when, just prior to the Korean War, FBI director J. Edgar Hoover proposed before Congress imprisoning 500,000 "unfriendly"

Americans along the model of the Japanese internments in World War II (Boyer and Morais 369). In addition, the Justice Department used the 9h affidavits to attempt to obtain conspiracy indictments against unionists, and the Immigration and Naturalization Service (INS) investigated naturalized citizens, threatening them with deportation if they were found to be Communist. In the most obvious case of union harassment, the INS spirited a leader of the transport workers off to Ellis Island for eventual deportation in the middle of a strike (Boyer and Morais 369).

Shorn of its radical members, labor was enlisted as junior partner in domestic and international corporate expansion through its support for, first, the Marshall Plan and, when that did not solve the crisis of overproduction, the cold war. That support often took the form of domestic policing of its own members and foreign policing of more radical labor unions. The federal government, the epitome of the law, took the lead in promoting this corporate expansion, becoming in this period "the prime accumulator for US capital" (Lipsitz, *Rainbow* 190), attacking opposition to this program both at home and abroad and enlisting labor under the sign of the law to further this process.

When the Marshall Plan failed to solve the problems of overproduction and underemployment,[1] the government sought refuge in what had worked during World War II, creating what was to be in Seymour Melman's words a "permanent war economy"[2] with the coming of the cold war and its particular embodiment in Korea.[3] This involvement, which contributed greatly to a 12 percent rise in the GNP from 1950 to 1953, resulted in the creation of 11.5 million jobs in heavily unionized industries such as aviation, electronics, motor manufacturing, and steel (Renshaw 136). Thus labor, offered a choice between "a class-conscious but thoroughly defeated radical movement and a conservative AFL [and CIO] that promised much less but at least was permitted some successes" (Vanneman and Cannon 15), chose the latter, becoming in the assessment of one labor commentator "*the* most significant supporters of these policies" (Renshaw 127).

Labor's role in the postwar consensus, in its foreign and domestic capacity, was to act as a cop, patrolling its own and enforcing business unionism with the support of U.S. government agencies. In France, Italy, the Netherlands, and Germany, AFL representatives, often directly funded by the State Department and the CIA, attempted to duplicate the U.S. domestic attack on militant labor under the rubric of anti-Communism (Renshaw 123),[4] fracturing unions and destroying the left's idea of labor unity.[5] The identification of U.S. labor with the U.S. government was so strong that *Labor's Untold Story* characterizes organized labor's policy as "largely directed by the State Department" (Boyer and Morais 353). AFL and CIO labor leaders worked hand in hand with the CIA, which they regarded as "simply another institution which financed the extension of American-style corporate unionism overseas" (353). The effectiveness of this policing was acknowledged by *Fortune*, which declared in 1952 that "on the whole the present governments of Western Europe are—and ought to be—to America's liking" (Van Der Pijl 177).

Labor policing at home began in earnest with the CIO's expulsion in 1949 and 1950 of eleven of the most militant unions, constituting between 17 and 20 percent of its membership (Rosswurm 2). The expelled unions, many with large numbers of women and blacks in leadership positions,[6] were critical of the Marshall Plan,[7] the defense buildup, and a business unionism that kept workers silent on all issues except wages. The expelled unions were the driving force behind organizing the unorganized, and with their expulsion both Project Dixie (the CIO's plan to organize workers in the South) and the period of CIO organizing in general came to an end (Moody, *Injury* 39).

Accompanying these expulsions was the institution in the remaining CIO unions of a less democratized, more centralized leadership that "represented and became part of a corporate elite" (Renshaw 147) and acted the role of "industrial police officers" (Lipsitz, *Rainbow* 246). This conformity meant workers also gave up their right to control over the assembly line. This change initially (1949–50) was met with a series of strikes[8] that tapered off through the 1950s as a labor movement shorn of its radical members began a long period of, in labor historian Sidney Lens's famous phrase, "sleepwalking through the corridors of history" (Moody, *Injury* 45).

Both the quietism and the role of industrial cop was sealed at the end of the period in 1955 with the merger of the once more radicalized, semi-skilled CIO with the more conservative, craft-union-based AFL. The merger contained language that validated both the union position as corporate junior partner and the policing roles. Both groups pledged to protect their members from "the undermining efforts of the Communist agencies and all others who are opposed to the basic principles of our democracy and of free and democratic unionism" (Renshaw 150). The AFL's George Meany, a stalwart of foreign and domestic policing, became the head of the combined group.

This abrogation of militant struggle on the part of the unions was accompanied by a cultural offensive to eliminate or devalue the position of the working class and its customs and traditions that had blossomed in the 1930s and 1940s in the "Age of the CIO," traditions that emphasized a society built on the collective rather than the individual. This offensive took the form of a discourse on America being a society in which, as CIO president Phillip Murray declared in 1948, "there are no classes. . . . We are all workers here. And in the final analysis the interests of farmers, factory hands, business and professional people, and white collar workers prove to be the same" (qtd. in Boyer and Morais 351). Or, as the still radicalized and now ostracized unions saw it, "all facets of American life were rapidly becoming instruments of Wall Street's national policy—industry, banking, farming, the press, the movies, television, education and science" (353).[9]

Policing Hollywood

Just as Hollywood from 1945 to 1950 was at the forefront of radical labor organizing with the stridency of the craftsworkers in the CSU and the newfound power of the creative unions, so too from 1950 to 1955 Hollywood was in the forefront and a model of how to repress union struggles under the guise of anti-Communism.[10] HUAC, supported in Hollywood by the studios, the sweetheart union IATSE, and some prominent members of the creative unions, in particular Ronald Reagan and other past and future presidents of the Screen Actors Guild, systematically undertook between 1951 and 1953 the demolition of the radical, militant members of the creative unions who had supported the CSU and who on the screen had promoted the values of the cultural front.

HUAC had far-reaching effects not only in Hollywood but also in society as a whole. Throughout the country, 13 million workers, more than 20 percent of the workforce, were subject to loyalty oaths and risked investigation if they refused the oath. The committee compiled over 1 million dossiers on 60,000 employees, with over 15,000 losing their jobs (Walsh 17). In Hollywood, David Caute's conservative estimate was that more than 350 creative artists lost their jobs, while the total number in radio and television by 1954 reached 1,500 (Pells 110).

The rules of the second HUAC incursion, after the 1947 investigation, were that the studios themselves would not be called into question, only individuals. Screen content, instead of being attacked directly, would be remade by removing those who had championed progressive positions.

This was also a concerted attack on labor activists (of the 324 names on the HUAC list, two-thirds were active union and guild members [Cogley 110]), an attempt to discipline the guilds which had consolidated their power in the early 1940s and were becoming a major force in studio negotiations. Actor and SAG activist Larry Parks, on the verge of stardom, was the first witness called in HUAC's second coming. Parks named names, but his career was publicly ruined by his appearance before the committee, with a *Los Angeles Examiner* newspaper headline the next day screaming "Larry Parks Loses $74,000 Screen Role." Parks appeared in only three more roles until his death in 1975 (Cogley 372). Another worker was asked to explain why he was engaged in "active trade union work after having been at the studio for only six months" (161), a clear attempt, like so much of the investigation, to curtail the workers union activity.

The committee's power was enhanced by the array of federal, state, and local government agencies that assisted it in its work, agencies that became lionized in the McCarthyite police procedural. These included the FBI, which hounded those who refused to name names at home and at the workplace, pursuing them even if they left the film industry (see Navasky; Ceplair and Englund); the State Department and the INS, which revoked passports so that blacklistees could not go abroad for work; and the Internal Revenue Service, which threatened the financial solvency of progressives including Dashiell Hammett, Charlie Chaplin, and Orson Welles (Ceplair and Englund 365).

Besides HUAC, the most visible enforcer of the purge was the leading union figure in Hollywood, IATSE president Roy Brewer, perhaps the prototype for the tough, working-class cop of the period. Brewer had already helped engineer the destruction of the rival militant crafts organization, the CSU, and was then entrusted by the studios with disciplining the creative guilds by supervising the clearance procedure by which those accused could repent and go back to work (Cogley 159). Brewer's (and the studio's) "vision" of a corporate Hollywood was fulfilled with the formation of the Motion Picture Industry Council, a joint studio-union group whose purpose was to publicize the efforts of the film industry to purge itself of "subversives," "clearing penitent Communists and demonizing unfriendly HUAC witnesses" (Ceplair and Englund 358). Brewer's chief aid and alter ego in the creative unions was SAG's Ronald Reagan, who, like former and future SAG presidents Robert Montgomery and George Murphy, "played" to the hilt the "tough" union enforcer of the blacklist.

Behind all of this, of course, were the studios, which handed out the subpoenas, refused the blacklistees work, and had their own investigators compile dossiers against potential "Communists" or union troublemakers (Cogley 109). In addition to curbing union activism, the blacklist functioned as a way to curtail independent production, which had bloomed after the war, with many of the producers, directors, and actors—especially in the crime film indies—named by the committee. The blacklist was also a convenient cover for downsizing as attendance at Hollywood films dropped almost 50 percent in the years surrounding the HUAC investigations (Cogley 92). The model was Howard Hughes at RKO, who in 1948 effected a 33 percent reduction in the workforce and in later years justified additional cutbacks by claiming the employees were subversives (Bartlett and Steele 168).

The blacklistees, drummed out of work and hounded even if they changed professions, described themselves as beginning to feel guilty and behaving like criminals "even though they had done no crime" (Navasky 351). The crime film itself would complete this process of converting paranoia into guilt and fear into aggression by remaking the noir sympathetic fugitive into the police procedural's psychotic killer whose underground life menaced society.

Again, 1955, a year often identified as the end of the classic noir era, and as we have seen, the year of the unification of the AFL and CIO, is crucial in the remaking of Hollywood as well. In that year, Roy Brewer, "the straw boss of the purge," the "master of the inquisition," left Hollywood and accepted a job in the New York executive offices of Allied Artists, moving seamlessly from chief union leader of Hollywood to the front office of a studio, the move itself signifying the completion of the destruction of what was once the most militant union movement in the country.

The Screen Police They Are inside Our Heads

In the 1950s, Hollywood production, and indeed American cultural production in general, shifted away from working-class concerns and reality; it was no longer interested in, as Parker Tyler put it, "industrial America." Novelist James T. Farrell noted at the center of this cultural shift—which often included films that either celebrated corporate culture directly or genres such as the Western or the epic that validated empire building—"an inner emptiness," the mark of a commercial culture that had developed as a "a kind of substitute for a genuinely popular, a genuinely democratic, culture" (qtd. in Stead 170–72). Hollywood Ten member John Howard Lawson went further, characterizing the cultural shift as class war by a cultural industry whose subtext in glorifying "conspicuous consumption" was that "working-class life is to be despised," that workers ought to dispense with "the values by which they live and emulate the values of their enemies" (168).

Hollywood attempted to compensate for the loss of its audience by introducing a range of technological innovations, including the wide screen (Cinemascope, Panavision, VistaVision), which, in its "celebration of the large scale" (Izod 141), again validated the burgeoning American empire. These innovations failed to counter the loss of the relevant social content that the now-blacklisted Popular Front artists had brought to the screen in the 1930s and that had flowered in the wake of the war and its aftermath. The movies suffered, as Robert Sklar notes, not simply from the incursion of competitors like television, but also from "an apparent and troubling fact: American movies were not as good as they used to be" (*Movie-Made America* 279).

In this period, the outstanding feature of the crime film, which accounted for one-fifth of Hollywood production (Jones 229) and thus was a key to effecting this cultural shift, was its focalization of the audience through the perspective of the cop. Just as the empire Western (John Ford's *Fort Apache (1948)*, *She Wore a Yellow Ribbon (1949)*, *Rio Grande (1950)*) positioned the spectator behind the barrel of a rifle firing at the Native American (and metaphorically taking aim at the budding anticolonial movements) (Stam 120), so too the crime film positioned its viewer behind the wheel of the squad car responding to an all-points bulletin in a working-class neighborhood.

French left-wing critics of the time noted this "historical liquidation" of the "noir detective film" (*Positif*'s Pierre Kast qtd. in Palmer, introduction 48), with the crime film previously presented "from the vantage of the criminals involved" giving way to "a documentary dedicated to glorifying the police" (Borde and Chaumeton, *Panorama* 60). And so, as Philip Kemp says, "Doubt, dissatisfaction, the left-wing habit of healthy skepticism were declared un-American and equated with treason" (18). With socialism—that is, the possibility of actual social change—"deleted from the national curriculum" (18), the crime film, its social content now evacuated, celebrated the multifarious agencies that were in practice hunting down the elements of militant labor and the Popular Front.[11]

Unlike the immediate postwar period, when the typology consisted entirely of figures outside the law, here four of the five figures (and 70 percent of the films) of the period feature cops as the protagonist. The dominant (50 percent) figure is the often working-class and informer cop who upholds the law, or the plainclothes detective, where the trench coat, once signifying the private detective's ambivalence to the law, now marks a forced nonchalance that only barely conceals the rigidity underneath. However, the transformation of the sympathetic fugitive into the conformist cop did not proceed without impediment, and the earliest figure in the period is the criminal cop (10 percent of the films) who goes outside the law either for personal profit (*The Prowler*, 1951) or because he is unable to conform (*Where the Sidewalk Ends*). The second-largest group of films, approximately 30 percent, are those with the psychotic fugitive, where the sympathetic fugitive becomes a public menace. These films provide the rationale for the last change in the period, the Mickey Spillane–inspired vigilante cops (*I the Jury*, *The Big Heat*, both 1953), approximately 10 percent of the films, who go outside the law to more strongly enforce it (see appendix). These films signal the end of the line for the noir period as Dashiell Hammett's resistant detective transforms into Spillane's fascistic enforcer of the law.

The Police Procedural: Mapping the Naked City

Surveillance, investigation, order, control: these were the new watchwords of the country as a whole and of the crime film. In the Eighty-third Congress (1953–54) alone there were fifty-one anti-Communist investigations, almost one-fifth of the total number of investigations from the birth of the republic in 1789 to 1925 (Englehardt 126). The deputizing of the legislature included a range of positions from "government investigator of subversive activities," to the "HUAC counsel who prepared witnesses to testify," to the "congressional representative whose investigative committee rooted out un-Americans" (123).[12] This broad scope is echoed in the crime film in the range of its investigators (and agencies): from treasury agents (*T-Men*, 1948), to FBI undercover drifters (*Street with No Name*, 1948), to the Secret Service (*Trapped*, 1949), to the IRS (*Undercover Man*, 1949), and even to the daring exploits of the post office (*Post Office Investigator*, 1949; *Appointment with Danger*, 1951), extending on the municipal level beyond the police even to the arson squad of a city fire department (*Flaming Fury*, 1949), which in those desperate times was required not only to fight fire but to infiltrate crime as well.[13]

The crime film in its documentary turn was influenced directly by the FBI, the main enforcer, next to HUAC, of the blacklist. J. Edgar Hoover, whose stated goal during the war was to "fingerprint every adult American in the name of National Security" (Clarens 185), was looking for a vehicle in which to propagandize. He found it in director Henry Hathaway and producer Louis de Rochemont's *House on 92nd Street* (1945), often credited as the prototype police procedural.[14] The writers had access to the FBI files that they used to form the basis of the screenplay; the film was shot with cameras hidden in specially designed cars and trucks supplied by the bureau; actors and technicians were investigated before being allowed to be part of the project; and lead actor Lloyd Nolan underwent a two-week indoctrination course at the bureau before starring as an FBI agent in the film. It was noted at the time that *House*'s Nazis with their secret cells behaved similarly to the then-beginning-to-circulate image of Communists (or for that matter of labor unions) with their collective patterns of organization. The bureau also assisted on *Street with No Name* (1948), with Lloyd Nolan this time going undercover to fight juvenile delinquency. Thus the FBI played a major role in establishing the two main currents of the procedural: the profiling of the surveillance unit and the narrative of the undercover cop.

The police procedural substituted an "objective" truth whose guarantor was the use of documentary techniques for the more subjectivized experience of the detective and the noir protagonist (Arthur, *Shadows*). The "machinery of official detection" replaced the "intuitive action of the private eye" (Jon Tuska qtd. in Krutnik 279) and, as screenwriter Michael Wilson characterized it at the time, the "romantic protagonist" of the film noir was replaced with the "fascist personality" of the procedural's hard-nosed but otherwise anonymous cop (qtd. in Ceplair and Englund 413).

The shared features of this style included story sources that, instead of being fictional, were fictionalized accounts of stories drawn from government or police files or newspaper articles; location shooting often also with the cooperation and assistance of the police or the federal agency; inclusion of nonprofessional actors to form the background of the action; emphasis on direct, diagetic sound over orchestral accompaniment; an iconography of surveillance devices that included "tape recorders, a lie-detector, information processors, ballistics and other kinds of laboratory equipment, and to a lesser degree, movie cameras" (Arthur, *Shadows* 209); and, finally, the signature opening and closing law enforcement narration or a "voice of God" stentorian narrator through the entire film (Clarens 182; Krutnik 208).

In part, these techniques, which entered the Hollywood film in the late 1940s, were borrowed from Italian neorealism. It was in the crime film that this documentary realism applied to the fiction film was most stridently realized in the American film. However, here the techniques were not, as in the Italian context, used as reportage on social problems but instead as a means of enforcing control on the same working-class neighborhoods that are lovingly represented in the Italian films. "The breakthrough into realism had come in the form of a tribute to and eulogy of the police" (Stead 164).

The Naked City (1948), a key film in the fashioning of the procedural, is a divided text that begins in the mode of the city symphony, invoking, in its attempt to show the breadth and class depth of life in the city, 1930s films like *Berlin, Symphony of a City* (1927), and, closer to home, Jay Leyda's *Bronx Morning* (1931) (MacDonald). However, the

Figure 7. Working day and night in the opening city symphony section of *The Naked City*.

film's narrative thrust drives instead toward a different type of documentary, the *Crime Does Not Pay* MGM series of the early 1940s.[15]

Over the city-symphony-like narration ("There is a pulse to a city and it never stops beating"), we see night shots of a woman scrubbing a floor, a factory worker alone on his shift, a newspaper writer, an overnight disc jockey, and finally a society party with men and women in formal evening dress, the sequence organized not at random but to call attention to the class hierarchy where the working and middle classes continue to labor to support the extravagant leisure time of the rich.

But the iterative, as Gérard Genette says, that is, the repeating quality (in this case of class oppression) gives way to the singular, that is, the singular moment of the crime, the murder of the socialite, and the subsequent hunt for the murderer. As the narrative thrust tightens, the narrator's voice moves from third-person objective, analytical statements about the city to a second-person stance that is most often involved in cheering on the manhunt. As *Variety* noted at the time (21 January 1948), the voice took on the sensationalist quality of narrator and producer Mark Hellinger's crime columns to the point where the famous closing narration—"There are 8 million stories in the naked city—this has been one of them"—is over a montage not of social classes but of the characters involved in the murder and the manhunt.

As the narrative shifts from a view of the totality of the city to a particular location in it, the location shooting attains a heightened quality, mapping Manhattan's Lower East Side, perhaps *the* central working-class enclave of the 1930s and 1940s, showing Chinatown, the Jewish section, and the Polish section, focusing on scenes of ethnic working-class life as the manhunt focuses on the killer, the boxer Willie Garzah.[16]

The manhunt itself moves from the single detective Halloran out walking the streets to a group surveillance of the murderer ("two men will follow you, two men in six shifts, that makes six men all together") to the ultimate collective moment in the procedural of the all-points bulletin ("All cars in Lower Manhattan block off and surround both sides of the street"). Here the location camera begins to function like Foucault's panopticon, an apparatus that allows jailers to perpetually gaze on prisoners and "whose major, if not exclusive function, is to assure that discipline reigns over society as a whole" (Foucault 206). In the police procedural the camera becomes an instrument of the law itself, a law whose purpose is the "regular extension [of] the infinitely minute web of panoptic techniques" (213).

A class difference the film exploits is that between the chief protagonist, the suburban cop Halloran, and his antagonist, the boxer Garzah. Halloran, as working-class cop in the new pluralistic, classless society, is the epitome of the now remade working class, patrolling Manhattan but living in Queens, defined as a suburban paradise, with house, lawn, family, and picket fence.[17] In contrast, Garzah's Lower East Side is visually defined as a tenement district, densely populated, congested, garbage ridden, an area the police must approach cautiously.[18] It is the clean-cut Halloran, now with a more substantial stake in society, who must protect his various forms of property (wife, house, children) from the likes of the mangy Garzah. The lone wolf Garzah's defiant last stand (in the end, he is shot off the top of the Brooklyn Bridge) would serve as the model for the ultimate psychotic fugitive, Cagney's Cody Jarrett in *White Heat* (1949), whose "Top of the world, Ma" just before blowing himself up marks the Rubicon mo-

Figure 8. The psychotic fugitive pursued in Manhattan's ethnic and labor-intensive Lower East Side in *The Naked City*.

ment in the conversion of the real paranoia of the blacklisted fugitives into the psychosis of the mad-dog killer. Alternately, the film suggests, Halloran, who needs a promotion to support his lifestyle, will, because of his leading the manhunt, move further along the accommodationist path and further from his working-class roots.[19]

Criminal Cops

Will Straw identifies "a series of film noirs which undertake the psychologization of policemen as bearers of class resentment or disgust at urban degradation" (119), while Frank Krutnik discusses a group of films whose "heroes are overtly corrupt," abusing their "positions of responsibility in order to gain either money or a woman" (192). This is the criminal-cop moment of the McCarthyite crime film. In these films, generally made in the earlier part of the 1950–55 period, the cop goes outside the law, committing a crime either for profit (as in *The Prowler*, where the now-bitter high school golden boy cop attempts to realize the American consumerist dream by killing a suburban dweller and stealing his wife and home) or for vengeance. If the crime is committed for vengeance, though, in these early films, either the film's narration acts to question the cop's motivation (*On Dangerous Ground*, 1952) or the film's narrative thrust is not about the vengeance but rather about the cop as fugitive, returning to the film noir tropes (*Where the Sidewalk Ends*). In these films the corporate consensus that has assigned these working-class cops the role of enforcer of the law does not satisfy them, and they move outside the law, outside that consensus, either to advance materially or to assert their own morality.

Where the Sidewalk Ends starts in full procedural mode with officer Mark Dixon (Dana Andrews)[20] and his partner sitting stone-faced in their car listening to the omnipresent call coming over the police radio summoning them to headquarters. Then, suddenly, in the midst of this hard-nosed cop film, the entire mood shifts and all the film noir types and tropes return. Dixon inadvertently kills Ken Paine, a down-on-his-luck gambler, and must conceal his actions. Dixon, now the fugitive, is forced to impersonate Paine, who was both a writer and war hero, dressing in his trench coat and slouch hat and leaving Paine's apartment in order to provide himself with an alibi. He later—almost literally, as he describes it—"walks a mile in his shoes," hoisting Paine's inert body on his shoulders and carrying it out into the lobby, where he waits beside it as someone comes to the room. Dixon continues this "impersonation" by then falling in love with Paine's wife, Morgan Taylor, in a direct substitution of one man for another, and a reversion of Dixon to the sympathetic fugitive. He even tells Paine's wife that she's a "sucker for wrong guys like Ken and me." He continues his journey through the film noir types later when he shows up at Morgan's house, groggy and forgetful, after having been beaten by the Scalise gang, which he is trying to arrest. Here he becomes the amnesiac (a favorite Cornell Woolrich gimmick and a story motif in a whole branch of the war veteran films), unable to remember why he came to her house.

This middle section of the film visually and subjectively aligns the audience with Dixon as he attempts to thwart the manhunt, much like George Stroud in *The Big Clock*. When Dixon is alone in the room with the dead man, the military hum of the music of the procedural shifts to an eerie, high-pitched sound, the aural equivalent of the film noir subjective camera. Later, in voice-over, Dixon reads the letter he has written explaining his role in Paine's death, just before he is about to go into battle with the Scalise gang, the letter a poignant "confession" of his inability to shake off the violence of his mobster father. This laying open of the inner life of the cop is very far from, say, Sterling Hayden's monosyllabic, rigid, sadistic cop in *Crime Wave* (1954).

Dixon's language also changes in this section of the film, from the take-charge language of the cop to the trapped language of the fugitive. "Innocent people can get into terrible fixes too—one false move and you're in over your head," Dixon says, echoing Bradford Gault's "I'm backed into a dark corner and I don't know who's hitting me." This reversion reminds us of the emotional vulnerability and complexity behind the tough patter of the film noir protagonist, while the alternate reduction of the procedural cop's language to monosyllabic grunts is part of the subhuman portrayal of working-class culture in general in the period.

This section of the film also briefly overturns the 1950s representation of what Will Straw calls the "lurid city," the abstracted city of cop and criminal, brimming with vice. An old woman sitting at the window of her basement apartment in a tenement realizes that Dixon is an impersonator because the dead man, Paine, always waved to her as he left. This moment of community is disappearing, as Paine is dead and will not be waving to her again.

The long middle section of the film is recouped, though, because in the last third, the resolution, Dixon returns to the role of the cop, first risking his life to capture Scalise and his gang, then confessing to his crime. Unlike the film noir protagonist, whose innocence is either affirmed or denied by the society but who always believes himself innocent, especially against the power of the ruling-class figure, Dixon confesses and may even go to jail in order to reconcile himself to the society and, ultimately, make himself a better cop.

Working-Class/Informer Cops: A Snitch in Time Saves Nine

The crime film with the law enforcement officer installed unproblematically in the lead forms the core of the genre in the 1950–55 period, constituting ninety-five films, or 48 percent of the genre as a whole. There are three main branches, with the large majority simply being the documentary of the police. These ranged from 1950's *Panic in the Streets*, which extended police surveillance to all corners of the city under the rationale of protecting the metropolis from a deadly plague, to the television show and film *Dragnet* (1954), a no-holds-barred celebration of the Los Angeles Police Department, one the most corrupt and racist police departments in the country, which viewed "the public" as either quirky nuisances or criminals.[21]

A second branch featured the informer cop. Initially, these films validated HUAC activity by figuring domestic repression directly, as in *I Was a Communist for the FBI* (1951), in which a labor informer goes undercover to fight illegal Communist activity in a Pittsburgh steel union. That film was both a failure at the box office and perhaps a too direct representation of union repression. More effective was the still on point *Finger Man* (1955), in which the former gang member infiltrates his gang or "cell" (or local union affiliate) as a kind of "clearance" for his past criminal activity. The point was that the security state was better served by figuring the opposition not directly as union members or Communists but as criminals whose secret activity could be read as Communist or union activity.

The third branch was the narrative of the ordinary individual tempted by or attempting to avoid crime. This plot could no longer be focalized through the individual but now needed the intercession of the cop. *Crime Wave*, initially about an ex-con named Steve who hides two former members of his gang, gives way to the efforts of Sterling Hayden's surly cop to catch the psychopathic armed robbers and return Steve to "all the everyday problems of families, groceries, schools," warning him, and the American worker, that getting involved in any organized activity beyond that needed for daily subsistence was dangerous.

One of the most prestigious of the procedurals was Paramount's A-budget production of the equally successful Sidney Kingsley Broadway play *Detective Story*, directed by William Wyler. Kirk Douglas, who had almost exclusively played sleazy gangsters in the 1940s, here moves inside the law to play a troubled police detective, Jim MacLeod, who goes too far: he refuses to give a young embezzler, Arthur, a break; beats an abortion doctor; spurns his wife when he finds out she is one of the doctor's clients; and, ultimately, suicidally and fatally walks into a bullet to make the station house safe by subduing a psychotic three-time loser, Charlie.

Detective Story is important for codifying three key patterns in the McCarthyite procedural: first, it refocalizes the working-class characters of the sympathetic fugitive crime film into an array of suspects; second, it cements the station house as the central location of working-class life, with the primary positive representation of that life being the working-class cop; and third, it models the permissible parameters of a (cold war) liberal/critical intervention within the now strictly regulated contours of the crime film.

The film features an array of working-class characters drawn from two sources: the crime film, with actors like William Demarest as a forgiving cop, and the Broadway stage, with its Damyon Runyon types like Lee Grant as a shoplifter. The suspect-characters are arranged (arraigned?) hierarchically with audience sympathy and relative innocence in inverse proportion to the degree of their overt working-class mannerisms. Arthur, the demure clerk who cheated his boss to facilitate his marriage to Susan, is judged as innocent and is ultimately released in the wake of MacLeod's death. The nameless female shoplifter, called "Girlie" by the officer who books her, performs nasally Judy Holiday–like monologues (about, e.g., "wantin' to get mare-ied") before being led away—not for the last time, it is implied—to night court. The suspects most identified as working class are the burglars Louis and Charlie. Charlie's Italian street mannerisms and Sid Caesarish facial expressions and hand gestures, laughing hysterically as he is carted away, convince his partner to inform on him, leading to Charlie's psychotic breakdown where he grabs a gun and threatens everyone in the station.

The precinct itself is located uptown on the edge of Harlem, certainly an area of working-class discontent needing to be patrolled, but represented in the film only by two silent black uniformed cops. The white ethnic police types are "ordinary Joes" with their own working-class grievances. "Why is it every time we drag in one of you mugs, you got $1,400 in your pockets and I only got $11? I'm in the wrong kind of work," one of them complains. The film focuses also on the deliberate and often mundane work of the station house, the routines of booking a suspect, rolling fingerprints, typing up reports, arranging a lineup, and notifying victims that stolen property has been recovered, with Wyler's trademark long take and moving camera integrating the working-class cops and suspects into the station-house setting.[22] However, the "work" in this environment is repression, a far cry from the use of the moving camera to capture the unemployed worker Ricci's walk with his wife amid the poverty of the Roman suburbs in *Bicycle Thief* (1948).

For cold war liberals like the playwright Kingsley, who was concerned in the 1930s with documenting the process of ordinary work in plays like *Men in White*, and the director Wyler, whose Depression-era *Wild Boys of the Road* lionized working-class survival techniques, this film, in questioning MacLeod's "blind self-righteousness," has been read as suggesting a way to attack "the right-wing red-hunters then plaguing the film community" (Leff and Simmons 167). However, as Hollywood Ten member Adrian Scott pointed out, it might more clearly be seen as a betrayal by both artists of their formerly more cognizant view of social causes and ideological uses of crime (Navasky 337). Douglas's character "goes too far," but ultimately his recklessness is needed to combat the far more dangerous homicidal insanity of Charlie, and it is Douglas's star turn that dynamically animates the film. At the end of the film, when MacLeod's partner Lou lets Arthur go, he tells him, "If I see you up here again I'll kick the guts out of you." This is meant to be hard-nosed compassion, but it more clearly bespeaks the same authoritarianism that has now supposedly been eliminated with the death of MacLeod. Rather than critique, the film and its coda point to the fact that the minimal critique permissible under the corporate cold war consensus is easily recouped by the security state.

Maniac on the Lam: The Psychotic Fugitive

If in the previous period, as James Naremore says, "many leftist filmmakers were treated as outlaws, and it is not surprising that they made some of their best pictures from the point of view of criminals" (*More Than Night*, 128), here, with the majority of those leftist filmmakers in retreat or ostracized, if the film is arranged around the criminal, that criminal is now seen as a menace. The second-largest category of McCarthyite crime films (fifty-one films, 30 percent of the total) was those in which, though the audience is visually aligned with the fugitive, the narration works to arrange an alliance against these (as Raymond Durgnat terms them) "psychopaths," "morally responsible mad dogs deserving to be put down" (49). Thus, as Richard Maltby says of an earlier period of the crime film, "a tool of liberal analysis" is "displaced and perverted into an instrument of political repression" (71).

The series begins with a divided text, *He Walked by Night* (1949), most apparent in the final scene, directed by Anthony Mann, called in to finish the film, which cuts between a sympathetic view of the hounded fugitive and a view of the cold-blooded efficiency of police hunting a cop killer.[23] Cagney's psychotic gangsters who begged to be put to sleep in 1949's *White Heat* and the next year's *Kiss Tomorrow Goodbye* functioned as ways of maintaining his "street credibility" while at the same time denying his past association with left-wing causes. The genre culminated in Bogart's thug turn in Wyler's *Desperate Hours* (1955), where, unlike the tragic deaths in the Depression-era gangster films, the destruction of the public menace in a hail of bullets guarantees the safety of the middle-class family he had threatened (Sklar, *City Boys* 63).

Niagara, one of the first big-budget color crime films, was directed by police procedural cofounder, via *House on 92nd Street*, Henry Hathaway. The film was shot on location at Niagara Falls and ends with the protagonist's plunge over the falls. The color and location shooting of the falls create an image of sexual and societal potency, since the falls is the place where the new bourgeois couple consummate their marriage, an image that stands in sharp contrast to the social and sexual impotence of the protagonist, George Loomis, whose eradication is proposed as necessary for society to progress.

The narrative works initially to introduce Loomis (Joseph Cotton) as the typical protagonist of the film noir, replete with subjective voice-over narration, but then slowly to pull back from him, refocalizing instead through the bourgeois wife, Polly, who understands George but whom he also menaces, and ultimately to distance him to the point where his death is seen as necessary to return bourgeois life to normal.

Loomis, a man out of place in the bright consumer society of the corporate couple, Ray and Polly, is a character rich in associations to the cultural front period. He is a war veteran, unable to adjust to contemporary society, only his dis-ease, instead of being seen as nausea at the betrayal of the collective vision of the war, is described by the corporate executive on the rise, Ray, as the result of George's stint at an army medical hospital whose inmates are "mostly psycho." George's gloom, initially linked to his "checkered work history," contrasts sharply with the effervescence of Ray's boss, the breakfast cereal executive, caricatured by *The Jack Benny Show*'s Don Wilson as buffoonish but ultimately harmless. In contrast to Ray's corporate verve, George spends his time brooding over his miniature model cars (a reminder of the auto strikes in the 1930s which began the era the CIO?).

This despondency is presented in the film's terms as impotence. The falls are a social symbol of sexual potency, but as the water gushes down in front of him in the opening scene, George's voice-over, noting his own inadequacy, asks, "Why should the falls drag me down here at 5:00 clock in the morning? To show me how big they are and how small I am?" In the next scene, his wife, Rose (Marilyn Monroe), wide awake and puffing seductively on a cigarette, hears George approaching and turns over in bed, resisting his attempts to wake her. The psychological impotence that is infecting his life, which will be converted into homicidal rage as he later kills Rose, is literalized in his marriage.

Rose, who likewise becomes a fugitive after her failed plot to murder George, is also an outsider. Polly notes Rose's blatant sexuality and its open threat to the bounds of the bourgeois marriage when she replies to Ray's wish that she buy a dress like the one Rose is wearing: "For a dress like that you've got to start laying plans when you're thirteen."

At the beginning of the film, George and Rose are living isolated in a cabin at the falls, unsure of their next move, having overstayed their announced date of departure, ensconced in a life analogous to that of the blacklistee, trying to get work at whatever they can and having to move in the dark corners of the society. George makes this nearly explicit when he later secretly appears to Polly after the police think he is dead, the supposed victim of Rose's plot. George asks Polly to keep his secret, or in HUAC terms, not to expose him: "I put on his shoes [of Rose's lover, whom she sent to kill him] and walked out of there officially dead. [That] Meant I could get a job, go somewhere and get organized.... Let me stay dead."

The fugitive couple is presented in sharp contrast to Ray and Polly, the rising young corporate couple from Toledo, Ohio, "the place where breakfast food became a national institution." To Ray, whose goal on his vacation is to spend time with his boss and move up the corporate ladder, George and Rose are invisible. He, like George Stroud in *The Big Clock*, has been waiting "three years for our honeymoon" and does not want to "spend it with a couple of spooks," but unlike Stroud, he is not upset over his delayed honeymoon and does not protest against this creeping corporatism.

In the end, though, George does not go quietly. He kills Rose, and in the final sequence he steals the boat owned by Ray's boss and tries to make his escape with Polly aboard. Here he directly menaces the corporate property of both Ray's boss and Ray—the boat and the wife, respectively—and the police pursue George as Ray and his boss cheer them on. George sets Polly free and then, to this cheering, goes over the falls, entombed in a watery grave. The falls, whose power at the beginning was diffused by the despondency of the memories of the past and infused with dangerously unfathomable sexuality, now stand in their proper place as the consecration of the appropriately harnessed energy of consumer capitalism and its personal equivalent, legally bounded monogamy.

Vigilante Cops: Hammering the Revenge-o-Meter

The majority of the vigilante cop films, those in which the cop goes outside the law not as fugitive but in order to better enforce the law, were released in the second half of the 1950–55 period. The earlier criminal cops were transmuted to a form where the cop, rather than wanting a personal payoff for defending society, simply wants revenge. The intuitive investigation of the hard-boiled detective and the scientific deduction of the procedural are replaced here by an investigative technique that "consists of beating up the suspects to force confessions, and this violence is described with a detail and intensity that leaves no doubt of the great emotional catharsis it brings to the hero" (Cawelti 188). The hyperbolic violence suggests that the vigilante cop also absorbs the fury of the psychotic fugitive, but here it is rationalized by the cop's righteous indignation. The violence might be read as an unacknowledged rage by a now immobile working class that has traded its right to contest both its role in the process of production and the larger direction in which the society is moving for a few pieces of silver in the form of more commodities and a more affluent lifestyle.

The chief adaptee in this cycle is Mickey Spillane (*I, the Jury* and *The Long Wait*, 1954; *My Gun Is Quick*, 1957), whose Mike Hammer is warned by the police not against breaking the law, as with Hammett's and Chandler's detectives, but against enforcing it himself against the city's "scum." Hammer is the ultimate enforcer of the corporate consensus against the remaining pockets of urban resistance, and in the novel *One Lonely Night* he presents his "vision" of the classless society: "I ought to get out of it. I ought to take Velda [his secretary] and my office and start up in real estate in some small community where murder and guns and dames didn't happen.... No more crazy mad hatred that tied my insides into knots. No more hunting the scum that stood behind a trigger and shot at the world" (qtd. in Cawelti 190). "Scum" also refers to women (i.e., women who are not his property as is his secretary, whom he can move as easily as he can move his office), and at the end of the film *I, the Jury* he inhabits the title role by leaving the female villain to die, perhaps reminding us of the fate of the women who constituted a majority and the leadership of many of the outlawed unions.[24]

Perhaps the prime example of the vigilante cop is Dave Bannion in Fritz Lang's *The Big Heat*. Much fine auteurist criticism has concentrated on the ways in which Lang questions Bannion's "movement from policeman to avenger" (MacArthur 78), similarly also questioning the thin veneer that separates Bannion's companion on his underground quest, Debbie, from the respectable policewoman's wife, Bertha, her "sister under the mink": "I work at being a B-girl and she has a wedding ring and a marriage certificate." Although Lang's film does question Bannion's motivation, it also in the end affirms it; the film cannot escape its cultural moment, and this reading attempts to show in what ways the film conforms to the dominant social discourse.

The first half of the narrative concentrates on justifying Bannion's vigilantism both in collective terms (because even the police force is on the take, corrupted by Mike Lagana, the gangster who controls the town) and in individual terms (to avenge the murder of his wife). Lagana, at the apex of the pyramid of quietism that surrounds the town, surveys the city and says, "Never get the people steamed up. They start doing things, grand juries, election investigations, deportation proceedings." However, the modes of collective action he identifies were at the time not means of popular expression but rather the devices of McCarthyite repression. Indeed, the spontaneous organization of "the people" in the film is a group of ex-servicemen who come together to protect Bannion's daughter. Bannion himself confuses them with Lagana's gangsters, though they more accurately resemble the fascist ex-GIs of *Best Years of Our Lives* and (Hollywood Ten members Dmytryk and Scott's) *'Til the End of Time* (both from 1946).

The Big Heat might be read in one sense as the eulogy of a great noir actress, Gloria Graham, as gangster's moll Debbie Vance and the end point of an experimentation with the woman as class ally. In contrast to Debbie's seedy life with her sadistic boyfriend Vince Stone (Lee Marvin), which results in her being scalded, the equally suburban household of the stone-faced Bannion (Glenn Ford) is held up as (Spillane's) utopian refuge from the city's "garbage." (Bannion will later descend into lounges, junkyards, and a fleabag hotel that Debbie refers to as "early nothing.") Bannion's reading to his daughter of the "three little kittens who lost their mittens" is interrupted by a bomb, and the next moment he tearfully pulls his wife's charred body from the car's wreckage on his front lawn.

Thus begins an alliance between Bannion and Debbie, but it is an alliance that benefits only one member. Ultimately, Debbie saves Bannion from enacting the retributive violence that would forever alienate him from society. Then, after "humanizing" him, she is erased so that Bannion may be returned as legal custodian of a restored social order. Bannion does "execute" Larry Gordon, his wife's killer, but he does it in a less direct way by putting out on the street that Gordon has talked to him and watching as the gangsters then eliminate the killer. Debbie, though, does her killing directly, eliminating Bertha, the wife of a corrupt cop, securing a letter that leads to Lagana's demise, and scalding Vince Stone, in all three cases saving Bannion from having to cross the line into deadly force himself. As Debbie lies dying from Vince's bullet, Bannion begins for the first time since the murder to talk about his wife in a way that suggests he has been "rehumanized."

As Debbie dies in his arms, Bannion in effect effaces her, staring out into the distance and droning on about his suburban existence, no less coldhearted here than earlier in the hotel when he had pushed aside her invitation to help him.

The final scene shows Bannion, gun now holstered, back in the squad room, responding to a call for help in the now recuperated town. When he left the force Bannion had turned in his badge but kept his gun, claiming he had bought it himself, and thus pointing to his vigilante tendencies well before the murder of his wife. The now peaceful Bannion, has, in the film's terms, exorcised his vengeance and is again ready for duty. But it could equally be argued that, now having absorbed and integrated Stone's and Lagana's use of violence, having practiced it himself but having not been implicated in its use because of Debbie, he becomes the quintessential protector of suburban privilege against the remaining working-class enclaves from which Debbie had materialized and then been extinguished.

chapter 5

The Neo-noirers

Fugitives, Surrealists, and the Return of the Degenerate Detective

The sympathetic film noir fugitive of the cultural front and the stone-faced, scientific working-class cop of the McCarthyite cold war were defined in their respective historically contingent moments, but once defined they then existed as tropes, with each subsequently reinvoked in successive periods of the crime film and television series, adding these past associations—what George Lipsitz calls "material memories"—to the moment in which they re-materialized. This chapter examines three of those moments. The first is a duel that took place on television for four decades between two of that medium's foremost producer-auteurs, each of whom was formed in the twin crucibles of the classic crime film period: Roy Huggins, creator of *The Fugitive* (1963–67), who identified himself with the cultural front and called the motif of the innocent fugitive pursued by an authoritarian government "the American theme"; and Jack Webb, who introduced and codified the HUAC-era police procedural on television in

Dragnet (1952–59). *The Fugitive* brought the bohemian/beatnik ethos to the American mainstream and helped lay the foundation for more widespread protests, come, while *Dragnet* extended the quietism engendered by the Hollywood HUAC hearings as the everyday "Joe," officer Friday, reduced the populace to quirky, reluctant witnesses and criminals.

The noir themes and style returned, in an instantiation that might be termed "neo-noir," amid the blatant repression—that is, blatant to working-class people and minorities—of the Reagan and Bush eras. The term "neo-noir" is sometimes applied to all noir after the classic 1941–55 period (see Silver and Ward's *Film Noir*), but it might be better used to describe the 1986–92 period. A majority of the films that constitute neo-noir were made in that period, and its periodization in this way grounds the term and links film noir, through its reappearance in a time of political repression and its use by directors to tell harsh truths, to the classic 1945–50 period. Here, especially in the work of the surrealist auteur David Lynch, particularly *Blue Velvet* (1986) and *Twin Peaks* (1990–92), the style was deployed to emphasize the two Americas, as the country in proto-Victorian fashion had split into a bright, decaled surface and an invisible and grimmer underbelly.

Finally, post-9/11, the launching of a new cold war with "terrorism" replacing "Communism" (with lowercase "communism" indicating the characterization of the new enemy as more global than the contained and more specific earlier menace) has featured on television an almost programmatic return and rerun of the police procedural (including a brief revival of *Dragnet* in 2003). There are almost no counter-narratives in the crime film and television series, but the noir spirit is being kept alive in detective fiction so that, just as the 1930s authors paved the way for 1940s cinematic noir, so too, as the current "permanent war" consensus dissolves, these authors may find themselves spearheading a more openly antagonistic moment.

Dueling Discourses: "Just the Facts, Ma'am" versus the Twitch of Innocence

B-film production, in which both film noir and the procedural flourished, had effectively ceased in Hollywood by 1955. The most obvious immediate formal companion to the low-budget film with its working-class audience was the television series, with a short shooting schedule for each weekly episode and an audience of those who, with the lowering of the price of the television by the mid-1950s, now found series television cheaper entertainment than the movies. Thus it is no surprise that the themes of the B-crime film migrated also and propelled the careers of two of the medium's most successful auteurs, with each constantly promoting one discourse over the other and consistently rewriting each other from the 1950s to the 1980s. Both are still primarily identified with the series that most directly appropriated each discourse. Webb's *Dragnet*, "the most successful police series in the history of television" (Brooks and Marsh 217), was also the one that proved the viability of series television, while Huggins's *The Fugitive*, "the most self-consciously noir series and undoubtedly the most successful one" (Ursini 284), was voted best dramatic series of the 1960s by *TV Guide*, with the finale being the most watched program on television up to its time, commandeering 44 percent of America's television households.

Huggins's work before coming to television, consisting of both pulp novels and film scripts, like that of many of the noir auteurs, stressed working- and middle-class dissatisfaction with the system and often had the lead character running afoul of the law. His 1949 novel *Lovely Lady, Pity Me*, about an innocent man framed by a southern California aristocrat whose mansion is "like the great wall in China" (106), contains a critique of the emerging cold war order and a longing for a return to the more radical days of the Depression: "A siren wailed from the direction of Wilshire and I thought how the siren more than anything else was the sound of our day. From somewhere off to the south came the sharp yet distant shock of boxcars being coupled" (28).[1] Another novel, *Too Late for Tears*, describes a woman who kills two husbands because she "wanted to move out of the ranks of the middle-class poor" (Silver and Ward 293). His best-known film before coming to television was the criminal cop entry *Pushover* (1954), which had *Double Indemnity*'s Fred MacMurray as a cop outside the law who shoots his partner to, like *Double Indemnity*'s Walter Neff, get "the money and the girl" and ends up with neither. Huggins was also directly involved in the politics of the period. He was an active member of the Communist Party until 1939, and when called to testify before HUAC he "reeled off about twenty names" (Gordon 53). Later, though, he renounced his testimony, often hiring blacklisted actors, writers, and technicians (Marc and Thompson 142), and in his television work he remained remarkably true to the ideals of the Popular Front period.

Webb's career in the crime genre displayed the schizophrenic quality of the genre as a whole. In his film career prior to the show, the stoic, impassive quality that was such an integral part of the Joe Friday television character was interpreted as having a brutally sadistic underside. Webb was cast as the killer without remorse in *Appointment with Danger* (1951), cold-bloodedly strangling his future *Dragnet* partner, Harry Morgan, and as a cheap, small-time hood in *Dark City* (1950). He also appeared in one of the most crucial crossover films in the transition between the cultural front fugitive and the cold war cop, *He Walked by Night* (1949). Here he played a police technician, and it was the suggestion of that film's technical adviser, police chief William H. Parker, that Webb create a series detailing the day-to-day practices of real-life cops that led to *Dragnet*. Four years after this transition film, then, as HUAC was at its peak, Webb took the techniques of the then-dominant police documentary, in an atmosphere in which all kinds of investigations were being validated, and applied them to television, where the bit actor as psychotic is reborn as the lawman supreme.

The duel, from the 1950s to the 1980s, began with Webb's assertion of *Dragnet*'s stolid, no-nonsense lawman, which begat an onslaught of police dramas that included *Highway Patrol* (1955–59), *M Squad* (1957–60), and (adapted from the prototype film procedural) *Naked City* (1958–63). Huggins countered this trend in a first cold war thaw with *77 Sunset Strip* (1958–64), which featured "debonair, martini-sipping" detectives and a "hipster parking lot attendant," Kookie Burns (Marc and Thompson 146), in a location, Los Angeles's glamorous Sunset Strip, opposite *Dragnet*'s commercial downtown Los Angeles, which suggested that detecting could be about pleasure rather than punishment.[2] Webb attempted to participate in this opening, which also included the more overtly anti-authoritarian *Johnny Staccato* (1959–60), with John Cassavetes as a beat jazz pianist turned detective, and *The Fugitive*'s David Janssen as *Richard Diamond, Private Eye* (1957–60), and proved himself particularly inept at conveying pleasure. He took over the last season of *77 Sunset Strip*, making the detectives world travelers against Communism in a move that resulted in such strong audience rejection that the formerly hit series was canceled before its season ended.

In the meantime, Huggins was busy remaking the other dominant television dramatic genre, the Western. His *Maverick* (1957–62) countered the series-dominant lawman (*Wyatt Earp*, 1955–61; *Gunsmoke*, 1955–75) with an anti-authoritarian hedonist gambler, often on the wrong side of the law. Huggins claimed that the creators "set out to see how many rules we could break" (Marc and Thompson 145). Indeed, three points in Huggins's "Ten Point Guide to Writing *Maverick*" reflected the film noir, anti-corporate stance: (1) "Bret's goal was to make 'easy money' rather than to do the right things"; (2) he was a "disorganization man" at a time when popular sociology talked about the conformity of "the organization man"; and (3) "heavies in the show were to be treated with sympathy rather than pure contempt" (145). This same ethos, minus *Maverick*'s humor, was applied to *The Fugitive*, the first show to feature a convicted criminal in the lead. The show was entirely focalized around a character who was irrevocably outside the law and at the same time the most sympathetic character Huggins was ever to create.

Again, Webb attempted to counter this series with a return of *Dragnet* in 1967, the last year of *The Fugitive*. This time Webb stressed the whimsy of the quirky civilians Friday interviewed, allowing him to mock the youth culture of the time. In his next series, *Adam-12* (1968–75), Webb, in his own way, embraced this new outsider culture with a series that featured two young "street" cops patrolling Los Angeles neighborhoods in a squad car. Huggins's answer was to return *Maverick*'s James Garner to television as an ex-con private detective, "a guy who didn't like to put himself in danger," "didn't like to work hard," had a "wry sense of humor," and was "somewhat cowardly" (Marc and Thompson 150) in again a different Los Angeles that this time consisted of an outlying trailer culture peopled by Rockford's fellow ex-cons and grifters. *Rockford Files* (1974–80) was one of television's most popular series, and one of the first to present the lead character's constant obligation to scam as the structure of feeling of a casino capitalism in which scamming at all levels was part and parcel of survival.

This Is Richard Kimble and This Is How It Is with Him

Huggins described how allegiance was to be fostered for the convicted wife-murderer, Richard Kimble, in his magnum opus, *The Fugitive*: "Kimble is pursued and in the eyes of the law he is guilty. But no American of any persuasion will find him so. The idea of natural law is too deeply embedded in the American spirit for anyone to question Kimble's right, after all recourse to law has been exhausted, to preserve his own life. Even Hobbes, the great philosopher of authoritarianism, acknowledged one circumstance in which a man has a right to resist Leviathan; when an attempt is made to take his life on mistaken grounds" (Robertson 29).

Given the active repression in the country, Huggins, who called this sentiment "the American theme," was wrong. Just before the series aired, ABC studio executives called it "a slap in the face of the American judicial system" (Robertson 13) and "the most repulsive concept in history" (17). Indeed, the concept as it played out in the series had more far-ranging implications about the nature of cold war American law versus justice.[3]

Kimble's innocence was not proved until the end of the series. However, it was demonstrated each week, not by "the facts" but by his own actions toward others (very often in his literally healing someone, since his profession was the humanitarian one of a doctor, a pediatrician); through his actions he "proved" to another character that he could not be guilty of this crime.[4] The audacity of the script, though, centered on the secondary protagonist. The prototypical plot of the series, laid out in the pilot, involved persons whom Kimble encountered and helped to challenge authority in their own lives. In the process, they realize their kinship with Kimble, intuitively grasp his innocence, and then defy the law themselves by helping him to escape.[5]

In the pilot, a Tucson nightclub singer, Monica Welles, herself a fugitive from her husband, a wealthy businessman who abuses her, is befriended by Kimble, who confronts her husband when he attempts to grab her. She then responds to Kimble's story of being convicted and then pursued by the sadistic Lieutenant Gerard with "I don't want him to find you," as if she were also a stand-in for the audience, also hearing Kimble's story for the first time. After Kimble exposes her husband's violence to the disbelieving police, who then shoot him, Monica helps Kimble escape, and in the epilogue, over her husband's grave as she is finally free of him, she tells Kimble's pursuer Lieutenant Gerard, "He's innocent." "The law says guilty," Gerard replies coldly. But the last word belongs to Monica, "The law isn't perfect. Wherever he is, he knows I believe him. I always will."

There are several advances here even over the classic noir period, as week after week a convicted killer not only remains free but is actually *set* free by characters who defy the law based not only on their knowledge of Kimble's character but also on their own experience with authority. These secondary protagonists contest the power of the law as state, economic, or patriarchal authority to hold power over them in their own lives. In addition, the conversion of the American populace to lawbreakers because of their rejection of the individual, capitalist-limited notion of the law and their embracing of the more collective notion of justice challenges the *Dragnet* notion of a quietist populace preoccupied only with their own concerns, a population of potential informers.

Allegiance is also fostered by the contrasting coldness of those pursuing Kimble. He describes the effects of this pursuit to Monica: "I keep running and they keep hunting. One man in particular, Lieutenant Gerard. [As the camera moves in on his contorting face] Sometimes I feel like I've known him all my life. Some nights I can't sleep I feel his footsteps on the stairs. See his face outside my door—[screaming] Gerard!" In addition, the show deploys the film noir visual and subjective alignment repertoire to foster sympathy, primarily, of course, through Kimble's physical presence in most of the scenes.

Whereas *Dragnet* was supposedly drawn from actual police cases (a marker of authenticity which merely means that "the facts" are seen entirely from the police's perspective) and paid a great deal of attention to daily police detail ("It was 3:55, we were working the day shift out of homicide"), *The Fugitive*, particularly in the opening sequence, emphasized noir subjectivity.[6] Kimble, accused in the daylight, in the deep darkness of the night is washed out of the water near the trainwreck that frees him, melding into the undergrowth in the shadowy existence that is to define him after his encounter with the law.

A key difference between the two series is the use of narration. Webb's narration at the beginning and end of *Dragnet* deploys the stentorian "voice of God," announcing at the beginning that "The story you are about to see is true" and at the end intoning the sentence of the criminal corralled during the show. (The show neatly elides the trial of the defendant and thus substitutes the police investigation for judge and jury, reaffirming the power of the police to always arrest the correct suspect.)[7] As the show progresses, the narration takes on the quality of the singular voice of Detective Joe Friday, wryly accusing suspects in the case.

Narration in *The Fugitive* has two modes also. The first is an intense second-person linking of Kimble with the average person in the audience through the booming baritone of actor William Conrad. The series opens with Kimble in a bus station and the voice announcing: "Another journey. Another place. Walk neither too fast nor too slow. Beware the eyes of strangers. Keep moving." And later as Kimble finds solace, "In a low-rent hotel. In a side door. You're safe for now." At the end of each episode, the narration has a more omniscient aspect, used not, as in *Dragnet*, to convict the suspect, but rather to summarize the desperateness of his situation. (And, slyly, to celebrate his ingenuity at once again escaping, that is, at not becoming one of Joe Friday's prisoners in profile.) In the pilot, as Kimble disappears into the night hidden by fog at a railroad crossing,[8] this magisterial voice drives home Kimble's plight vis-à-vis a cold and merciless law that, unlike Joe Friday's cop, spends its time pursing the wrong man: "Now six months, two weeks and another thousand miles a fugitive. This is Richard Kimble and *this* is how it is with him."

The Fugitive not only returned the noir modes of alignment and allegiance to a mainstream audience in the 1960s but also returned the milieu and the preoccupation with working-class employment of the 1930s and 1940s cultural front at a moment (1963–67) concurrent with the emergence of new modes of protest and challenge to authority. Kimble, forced to "toil at many jobs," was, as Stephen King pointed out, one of the few series characters to be shown performing everyday work (Robertson 22), especially at a time when cop and sheriff were the predominant occupations on television. The jobs Kimble occupied comprise a veritable litany of the professions of the CIO in the 1930s and 1940s: handyman, janitor, longshoreman, warehouse worker, construction worker, truck driver, gas station attendant, dishwasher, teacher, and grocery store clerk (190–92).

The milieu Kimble inhabited was that of a world left behind, the world of the CIO-aligned film noir protagonist. He traveled by bus or hitchhiked through small towns, rural patches of the country, or, if in the cities, working-class neighborhoods.[9] The names of the towns he surfaced in bear the imprint of the industrial mode of production that defined them: Hempstead Mills, West Virginia; Clay City, Oklahoma; Weber's Landing, Florida. In the early 1960s this wandering accumulated the additional connotation of the itinerant bohemian drawn from the beat generation's seminal work, Kerouac's *On the Road*, adding another level of resistance defined by an emerging counterculture.

Sympathy for Kimble was also generated by the characterization of both the law that pursued him and of authority in general as obsessive and heartless. Almost as daring as a series that fostered active approval for the actions of a convicted murderer in eluding the law was the opposite feeling of antipathy generated for the Joe Friday-type trench-coat detective, Lieutenant Gerard. Patterned after Hugo's Javert from *Les Misérables*, the most ruthless cop in literature, Gerard, whom Stephen King described as "completely nuts" (Robertson xi), in the pilot outlined his unwavering devotion to blind obedience-and the ethos of the McCarthy era—in pursuing Kimble: "Whether the law is right or wrong is not my concern. Let others debate and conclude. I obey."

As the series progressed, Gerard became isolated in this pursuit. In the third season, Kimble saves Gerard's temporarily blinded wife, who then lets Kimble go free. Later in the season, Kimble saves Gerard's life in a migrant workers camp, though there is in this case no conversion of the secondary protagonist. Instead, Gerard bellows, more insanely than *Moby-Dick*'s Ahab, at the itinerant workers as they let Kimble go, "You're obstructing justice. I'm in search of a fugitive. I'll arrest all of you."[10]

The Fugitive also portrayed the law in general as menacing, cruel, and corrupt, a portrayal that tended to position Gerard as the epitome of this insane authority rather than as a "rogue" cop. In the pilot, in a scene that echoes the false arrest in Hitchcock's *The Wrong Man* (1954) two plainclothes cops sadistically taunt Kimble, taking their orders from the businessman Ed Welles. As to the reason for this humiliation, one of the officers says, "I was born here, I'll die here, I like to keep Tucson clean as its air—I don't like strangers," thus rendering the lawman not as upholder of a universal law but as petty enforcer of a rigid and parochial conformism.

The critique of authority extended beyond the law to the political and economic power behind it. Ed Welles (played by a bloated Brian Keith), the wife-beater in the pilot, is a pillar of the community. "He owns 250,000 acres of Arizona, contributes to charity, belongs to the proper social associations. He has even been mentioned as a possible political candidate," Monica tells Kimble in explaining why she is afraid of him. In this rewriting of the McCarthyite psychotic fugitive, it is Welles who, wound ever more tightly as his control over his wife dissipates, finally pulls out a gun and starts firing, and it is he who dies in a hail of police gunfire.

The Fugitive rewrote *Dragnet* and in its revival of the cultural front film noir tropes helped prepare the way for a wider-ranging questioning of authority that was erupting in society at the time of its departure from television.[11]

A Thousand Points of Dark: Noir under Reagan and Bush I

> If there was ever a hell on earth, it's Dallas County.
> The falsely convicted inmate in *The Thin Blue Line*

Film noir "returned" again as a style deployed to critique the conservative turn of the Reagan and Bush era (1980–92) in what is generally termed "neo-noir." Countering Reagan's bright world of decals, which he suggested should be put up in the South Bronx to hide the devastation of the neighborhood, the sea of smiling white faces that marked Reagan's second-term convention movie *A New Beginning* and its title song, "It's Morning in America," and the "kinder, gentler" ex-CIA chief Bush's "Thousand Points of Light," neo-noir mocked this imagery and revealed its sordid underbelly, particularly the work of David Lynch on film (*Blue Velvet*, 1986) and television (*Twin Peaks*, 1990–91).

Reagan's "politics of imperial nostalgia" promised "growth without pain" (Krieger 155).[12] His appeal to a mythical middle America of white houses and picket fences superimposed the 1950s onto the 1980s and was designed to evoke a time when living standards were high and

America was unqualifiedly, both militarily and economically, "number 1." Along with this went what Andrew Britton and Robin Wood dubbed "Reaganite entertainment": innocuous adolescent cinema (*Star Wars, Indiana Jones, Back to the Future*) that evoked the nostalgic familiarity of 1940s serials.

But Reagan's and Hollywood's reassurance was being performed in the face of a declining dollar, wage, and living standard and the mass exodus of heavy industry from the heartland, most notably in the auto industry of Detroit and the steel industry of Pittsburgh. Just below the surface of the supposed imperial peace to be guaranteed by his Hollywood weapons system ("Star Wars") were both rising international tensions, fueled by a huge increase in the U.S. defense budget and by deploying first-strike weapons in Europe, and, domestically, an open declaration of war on American labor, signaling the end of the thirty-year labor-employer pact, with Reagan's first official act being the announcement of the abrogation of this pact by breaking the Professional Air Traffic Controllers Organization (PATCO) strike.[13]

Neo-noir, a bounded period of noir that flourished during the Reagan-Bush years, brought its dark style and violent themes to Reagan's America—to places like the Sun Belt (*After Dark My Sweet*, 1990) and the ravaged heartland (*At Close Range*, 1986)—indicating all was not perfection with those regional economies. James Foley's *After Dark My Sweet* was the best of a cycle of Jim Thompson adaptations updating ex-Communist Thompson's bleak view of the 1950s American economic miracle, which had focused on the decay lying beneath 1950s consumer society, to here critique the equally harsh underbelly of Reagan's decaled America.[14] Set in the Arizona Sun Belt, "Reagan's spiritual home" and the epicenter of the high-tech explosion that was propelling this new economic miracle for the few, the film contrasts a faded and decaying hacienda with the bright pastels of the local country club as Bruce Dern's Reaganesque alcoholic patriarch, hands shaking, confesses, just prior to his last-ditch attempt to buy his way into this economy by kidnapping a rich man's child, "I'm not the man you think I am."

Neo-noir delineated the corruption that lurked behind the "can do" spirit of Reagan-era optimism and located this critique at the heart of the law enforcement agencies waging Bush's "War on Drugs" (*Bad

Lieutenant, 1992; *Internal Affairs*, 1990; *Unlawful Entry*, 1992; *Q and A*, 1990). *Bad Lieutenant* presented a "day in the life" of the anti–Joe Friday as Harvey Keitel's New York police officer used his powers for bookmaking and cheating his fellow officers, smoking crack while selling a petty drug dealer cocaine, and forcing two young female traffic offenders to have sex with him.[15]

Perhaps the endgame of the corrupt cop films, and maybe the concluding moment of neo-noir, was 1992's *Unlawful Entry*, which reworked Joseph Losey's cop-outside-the-law film *The Prowler* (1951) with Ray Liotta as a sadistic Los Angeles working-class cop who plots to disturb the yuppie serenity of a gated middle-class couple by killing the husband (Kurt Russell) in order to be with the wife (Madeleine Stowe). Though far more sympathetic to and focalized through the middle-class couple than Losey's more critical film—in the neo-noir version, the husband, shot in the beginning in Losey's version, survives to best the cop and restore the nuclear family—*Unlawful Entry*, shot just before the Rodney King arrest and the subsequent Los Angeles riots, presented such a scathing portrait of a corrupt Los Angeles cop, shown in the opening beating street kids, that its message was viewed as incendiary and its release had to be delayed until the city had calmed down. Here the noir critique spills off the screen and ignites with the reality of the oppressed.

In addition, noir occasionally returned the trope of the innocent fugitive as a prism through which to highlight the systemic violence of a criminal justice system, dubbed the "prison-industrial complex," whose race and class repression gained in importance as unemployment, due to industrial flight, rose. *The Thin Blue Line* (1988), Errol Morris's unconventional noir in the form of a documentary, recalled the prototype noir *Detour* (1945) in its detailing how "fate" had tightened the noose on an innocent man, only here "fate" was defined as Dallas County cops, prosecutor, trial judge, and court psychologists acting in concert to condemn an innocent drifter to death row. In one of the film's grisliest moments, the prosecutor blatantly proclaims to Morris's unwavering cinema verité camera his philosophy of jurisprudence in the Reagan-Bush era: "Anybody can convict a guilty man. It takes talent to convict an innocent man."[16]

Lynch's Landing

The quintessential statement on the layers of darkness that lie beneath Reagan's bright-shining America came from David Lynch, who in *Blue Velvet* crossed the themes and concerns of noir with those of cinematic surrealism (and in particular of Luis Buñuel) to both expose the mechanism of repression that for Lynch defined Reagan's America and, at a deeper psychological level than noir often penetrated, to undertake an exploration, later elaborated in *Twin Peaks*, of *what was being repressed*. Lynch frames this exploration in *Blue Velvet* with opening and closing shots of a (too) perfect Norman Rockwell America; an azure sky illuminates red roses against a white picket fence and then gives way to a fire truck with waving fireman and friendly crossing guard guiding schoolchildren across a suburban street.[17] The slow-motion, low-angle sequence suggests childhood recollection, the same innocence Reagan and the Republicans evoked in their 1984 campaign film *A New Beginning* with a boy riding a bicycle through his hometown delivering newspapers and a traffic cop assisting construction workers crossing a street.

Lynch points to the delusional quality of the images in the opening sequence through the saturation of color and the slow motion, then interrupts the idyllic shot of an old man watering his lawn with his sudden collapse and the surreal shot of a dog gutturally yelping as the hose sprays the man's inert body. The camera then penetrates under the lawn's grass to reveal predatory ants tearing a beetle to pieces. The shot introduces the notion of a concealed underworld, a motif that takes over the narrative when the protagonist, Jeffrey Beaumont, the inert man's son, finds a severed ear in a field and the camera travels into the ear. These moments suggest an allusion to Buñuel's surrealist explorations of the libidinal and aggressive impulses that he felt underlie the hypocrisy of bourgeois life. The severed ear as symbol of this journey through the underworld suggests the severed eye in the opening of *Un chien andalou* (1929), which initiates Buñuel's screen career and suggests the necessity of a new way of seeing. The predatory ants suggest the scorpion in the opening of *L'Âge d'Or* (1930), where the scorpion becomes the symbol of the innate aggression that bourgeois "civilization" denies and in its denial perpetuates.

The descent into the ear begins a journey Jeffrey undertakes into the dark side of this all-American town. The striking feature of this journey in the middle section of the film is the use of doubling to continually emphasize how the two sides, so strikingly different as to be almost two different worlds, are flip sides of one another, separated through the process of repression.

Thus, Jeffrey's father, hospitalized and breathing through a respirator, has his "other" in the overt id figure of the child kidnapper, drug-dealing, sexually abusive Frank Booth (Dennis Hopper), who breathes nitrous oxide through a nose mask to keep his id energy flowing. Jeffrey's ineffectual mother (Hope Lang), who spends her time near catatonia watching violent gangster films on television, has her otherworldly echo in Isabella Rossellini's Dorothy, the fetishized nightclub singer who follows Frank's every degraded command in order to save her son. The link is made though Jeffrey's "primal scene" moment of concealing himself in Dorothy's closet and, childlike, watching his surrogate mother and father having sex, which he perceives, as in Freud's dictum, as pure violence, as violation of Dorothy by Frank. Jeffrey's surrogate father in the superego Reaganite world, Detective Williams, who attempts to give Jeffrey "a little fatherly advice" and is a staunch upholder of the law, has his flip side in "the man in the yellow suit," his police force partner who is one of the ringleaders of Frank's gang and who matter-of-factly kills a rival drug dealer in cold blood. Finally, and most controversially, Jeffrey's all-American girlfriend, Sandy (Laura Dern), Detective Williams's daughter, whose name and blond, innocent demeanor evoke suburban-style teen heroines of the 1950s played by the likes of Sandra Dee, is associated with daytime and has a beautiful dream, accompanied by church music, of robins chirping. She is the teen girlfriend in contrast to Jeffrey's underworld "lover" Dorothy, who also doubles as his mother. She is dark haired with a foreign accent, continually associated with nighttime, and introduces Jeffrey to the acting out of violent sexual fantasies.[18]

The concluding act of the film is about how these two worlds intersect, with Sandy telling Jeffrey just before he begins his most thorough immersion into the dark world, "I don't know if you're a detective or a pervert," and Frank telling him at the end of a violent car ride, "You're like me." For Jeffrey, mother and lover also become confused. As one critic noted, in Lynch's "landscape of a terror-stricken child," Dorothy initially occupies the place of mother in his witnessing of the primal scene with her and Frank, then later seduces Jeffrey, and finally, when she appears nude on Sandy's lawn, intruding on Jeffrey and Sandy's date, tells him, in what is generally regarded as the language of emotional incest, "You're my special friend." Lynch, in merging these two worlds, suggests not only the crime, corruption, and violence underneath Reagan's perfect world of bourgeois repression but also hints, in perhaps less stark terms, that incest and abuse lie at the heart of the middle-class American family. (In presenting himself as father of the nation, Reagan often referred to Nancy in public as "Mommy.")

Ultimately, Jeffrey's oedipal and literal killing of Frank restores Dorothy to her role as mother, with Jeffrey himself returning, supposedly unscathed, in the final scene, to Dorothy, Detective Williams, and his own parents. The picture postcard ending, evoking the earlier Norman Rockwell symbology, is called into question by the appearance of the robin from Sandy's dream, who holds a beetle in his beak. The beetle suggests that the world of sex and violence does not disappear by Reagan-style repression but only continually reappears.[19]

Lynch's next masterful presentation of this theme, the television series *Twin Peaks*, appeared midway in the presidency of the "kinder, gentler" George Bush. *Twin Peaks*, a savage rewriting of the soaps that marked Reaganite entertainment on television (*Dallas*, *Dynasty*, *Knot's Landing*), constitutes Lynch's fullest statement and most integral linking of the American bourgeoisie and its power with incest and sexual abuse, and it accuses that class of this complicity in a medium that enters the average American home, with the series attempting to locate this crime in that home.

Critics complained that the series "ran out of steam" midway through the second season, but that claim misunderstands the nature of Lynch's project and reads the series as if it were a typical commercial venture, planned to run one hundred episodes so it could go into syndication, where television series recoup their initial losses and can reap huge rewards. *Twin Peaks* is instead so thoroughly focused around the death of the all-American high school cheerleader Laura Palmer, whose body is discovered in the first scene of the pilot, and the explanation of who killed her, revealed in episode fifteen, that when that explanation is revealed the series is effectively over, and attempts to extend its length did appear gratuitous.

The series pilot begins with the discovery of Laura's body and introduces its characters as radiating out from that discovery, which seems to traumatize the whole town. Likewise, episode fifteen, in which the murderer is revealed through a second murder that imitates the first, centers around that revelation, again with a range of characters, though they are not privy directly to the information, seemingly traumatized by this new revelation. Laura's murderer is her father, Leland Palmer, though this is somewhat confused by his cohabitation with the demon "Bob," and the murder is revealed not only as murder but also as incest, as Leland, this time in the Palmer living room, beats to death Laura's look-alike, her cousin Maddy, played by the actress who played Laura. Leland and his real estate partner, Ben Horne, represent the town's economic power structure, which is attempting to destroy the town's economic base in the sawmill and replace it with a country club. In the murder scene, his secret crimes of the bedroom incest of his daughter, called attention to in the eerie conclusion of the pilot as Mrs. Palmer conjures up the horror in that room, is brought, as Diane Stevenson says, out into the open, into the living room, when Leland murders Maddy. Family violence merges with economic violence, and through the medium of television, both are brought out of the secret space of the bedroom into the public space of the (American) living room.

Doubling here repeats the pattern from *Blue Velvet* of highlighting the way Reagan- and Bush-style America represses its violent and sexual side (seen in the town name and the series title, which is also a "dirty joke" about cleavage, and in the *Blue Velvet*–like postcard town with the whorehouse, One-Eyed Jacks, hidden at the outskirts). The doubling here is also, as Stevenson says, a splitting of personalities because of the original trauma of sexual abuse.[20] There are, for example, two Lauras (Laura and Maddy) and two totemic fathers (father figures who believe it is their right to seduce all women), Leland and his partner, Ben Horne, who also comes on to his own daughter-in-disguise, Audrey, at One-Eyed Jacks, where she is "disguised" as a waitress-prostitute, and who also loved Laura Palmer. Season one, in addition, ends with a number of the characters in comas, as if preparing the way for the fateful announcement to come.

Figure 9. Agent Cooper conversing with the wind in typical anarcho-surrealist fashion in *Twin Peaks*.

Episode fifteen begins with a man whom Laura had cared for found hanged, his suicide note reading, "I am a lonely soul." Meanwhile, in the Palmer home, Leland, Mrs. Palmer, and Maddy sit in the living room as the perfect family unit while the Motorola plays Satchmo's "Wonderful World." Audrey then, in a moment that anticipates the later moment of incest, confronts her father, Ben Horne, who had tried to sleep with her, not realizing her disguise at his house of prostitution, One-Eyed Jacks, and who admits that he did sleep with Laura.[21]

Mrs. Palmer, nearly beaten to death, crawls down the staircase and sees a white stallion in the living room as Julie Cruise in the roadhouse, where many of the characters have gathered, sings "I want you right back inside my heart." A giant then appears to the surrealist detective Agent Cooper, who often uses his dreams to fathom the truth, and says, "It's happening again." In the Palmer living room, the white stallion is replaced by the white-haired Leland, who reenacts the killing of Laura, this time killing her cousin and as he is beating her crying alternately "Laura" and "My Baby." The alternation between sexual object and daughter echoes *Chinatown*'s moment of revelation of the incestuous evil of the developer Noah Cross as his victim tells the detective Jake Gittes, who beats her, that the girl upstairs is "My sister/My daughter."

The Neo-noirers ··· 121

After Maddy's death, back at the roadhouse, the giant now appears as a withered old man and says to Cooper, "I'm so sorry," while the teen friends of Laura look forlorn and cry. They are discussing the man hanging himself, and Laura's classmate Donna says, "He was hurt inside and I couldn't figure it out." To this, Laura's friend James replies, "Everybody's hurt inside." The episode then is completely oriented around the sexual trauma and the pain it bequeaths. Here Lynch uses the surrealist idea of synchronicity—that in the unconscious there is no linear sense of time, but rather time constructed around various traumatic events—to make his most explicit critique of the effects of the violence that lurked at the center of Reagan's and Bush's America.

Running the Sympathetic Fugitive to Ground: Post-9/11 Detective Film and Fiction

If the heyday of neo-noir was the Reagan and Bush mid-1980s to early 1990s, in film this moment was replaced by a noncritical, non-working-class-inflected moment that might be called faux bohemian noir, noir for stockbrokers, or, probably most appropriately, suburban noir. The prime symbol of this moment is Brad Pitt. His smarmy fugitive "outsideness" signified mere hipness. In films like *Kalifornia* (1993) and *Fight Club* (1999) his anti-authoritarian tics hid only affluence in performances that allow an audience which exudes privilege to indulge its fantasies of being outside the society when in fact they are merely impatient about having to wait their turn to take it over.[22]

The outsider, anti-authoritarian impulse instead relocated to television, where *The X-Files* (1993–2002) initiated, post-Iran/Contra, the "paranoid government" series. The government, ruled by a secret cabal of shadow operatives who have infiltrated every aspect of the state, was depicted as a ruthless band of power-hungry men symbolized by their number-one operative, the cynical, chain-smoking, unemotional killer whose nom de plume signified his own death drive, Cancer Man. The protagonist agents, Mulder and Scully, were perennial outsiders whose jobs and lives were often threatened because of their investigation of their superiors. Mulder especially was distinguished by his distrust of authority and his belief both in the existence of unknowable forces outside science and in a conspiracy of the secret government.[23]

However, the theme of the secret government as menace was thoroughly rewritten after 9/11. If the national security state intruded into every aspect of domestic life after this event, it positively dominated network television. The rhetorical 1950s substitution of "terrorism" for "Communism" in this new cold war elicited in the networks a return to the 1950s police procedural (Broe, "Genre Regression"). Again, as in the 1950s, this militarization was not primarily represented through "terrorism" plots and series but rather through a return to law and order. However, especially in the counter-terror series 24, the difference between domestic and foreign policing was obliterated, and America became fair game for all kinds of torture and dirty tricks at the hands of "saviors" like 24's blatant violator of legal rights, Jack Bauer.

In the 9/11 television season (2001–2), *ER*, a hospital melodrama where science is used to save lives, was replaced as the number one series by *CSI*, a procedural about the forensics unit of the Las Vegas police force in which science in the hands of the police becomes a tool of surveillance after the fact of the crime. Forensic science likewise becomes the absolute arbiter of guilt or innocence and, as in the old *Dragnet*, replaces the need for a trial by jury. Series critical of the power structure were consciously rewritten. *Buffy the Vampire Slayer* (1997–2003), with a strong female heroine without a father who battled vampires such as "The Master," a parasitic eternal patriarch, was countered after 9/11 by *Alias* (2001–5), whose grad-student heroine secretly worked for the CIA (campus recruitment returns with a vengeance) and was endlessly fascinated with her father, a cold-blooded CIA killer with a heart of gold. That season also featured the appearance of *The Agency* (2001–2), a CIA procedural that boasted about its liaison with the actual CIA and which premiered with the CIA *saving* Castro. The 9/11 season also saw the expansion of the *Law and Order* and *CSI* franchises, and in case there was any doubt of the overlaying of 1950s ideology, the next season saw the return of *Dragnet*. By the end of the 2002–3 season, one-third of all network series and 85 percent of all hour dramas fell into some form of police or intelligence procedural.[24]

24: All Terror, All the Time

Perhaps the most dramatic post-9/11 change was the remodeling on the fly of Rupert Murdoch's Fox Network's flagship entry for the 2001 season, 24. The series began in full "paranoid government" mode, presenting the Counter-Terrorism Unit's main troubleshooter, Jack Bauer, as an outsider who had in the past investigated agents for corruption and who initially suspects his own agency of aiding and abetting what appears to be a right-wing assassination plot against the first black major party nominee for president. This is the arc of the first eight episodes. However, after a hasty post-9/11 rewrite, Bauer, instead of being pursued as a traitor to his own agency, increasingly assumed the mantle of chief torturer and lawbreaker in the name of national security. (The assassination plot was instead the work of "Serbian" terrorists, and the secret government inside the agency was reduced for much of the season to a lone Latina.) Bauer was quickly converted from the sympathetic fugitive to the vigilante cop to serve the new security state as a super-agent of the law, one who broke all laws in the name of the war on terrorism, becoming the ultimate fascist enforcer of this pseudo war.

Much has been written about the groundbreaking techniques 24 employed to engender suspense (see Peacock), a form of suspense whose purpose is quite different from that generated in the classic noir. Noir "internal suspense" is based primarily on the Hitchcock technique of the audience and a character or characters understanding something that other characters do not (S. Smith), as when in *Notorious* (1946) we watch the American agent Alicia discover that the Nazi Alex and his mother are poisoning her. This form of suspense is often used to generate sympathy for a fugitive or character outside the power structure, as in *Notorious* we watch the pressure put on Alicia and the American agent Devlin by both the (emerging) American security state and the (residual) Nazi regime not to acknowledge their love since their desire questions the basic tenets of both of those states.

In contrast, 24 adds to the traditional character-based "internal suspense" a host of techniques that are "external" to the plot and the characters and which in part account for the unrelenting aspect of the show, often described as "addictive." The elements of this "external

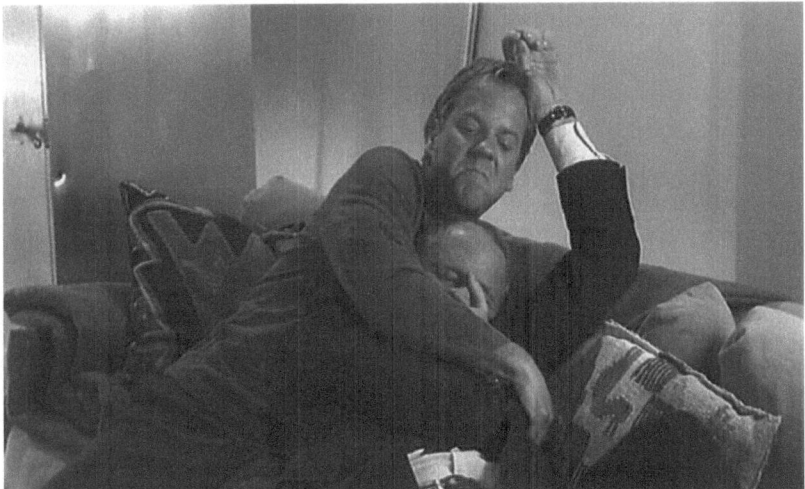

Figure 10. Jack Bauer "bending" the law in the post–9/11 television series *24*.

suspense" include the use of real time as story time, so that the plot events of each show take place in one hour over a twenty-four-hour period that constitutes the time of the twenty-four episodes; running the clock over the commercial advertisements as well, so that that time also is included in the time of the show; constant use of a digital clock showing hours, minutes, and seconds to announce the ticking away of this time; and repeated use of a four-part split screen to detail the multiple stories as each reaches a critical suspense level. The purpose of these techniques, though, is simply to raise the level of anxiety in watching the show. When combined with the constant internal suspense generated by the various plots to attack the country, the net result is an attempt to replace all possibility of reflection about the show with the consistent *feeling* of what it is like to live in terror twenty-four hours a day, the actual meaning of the show. At the end of the first season, when Jack Bauer has saved the presidential candidate and most series would be pausing to catch their breath, the series has Jack discover that his wife has been murdered, slumping to the ground with her dead body—the idea being that the off season should be spent in terror as well. Here, structure of feeling, rather than being the on-screen representation of a class position, is a feeling artificially created by the structure of the series, a feeling whose point is to reproduce and mirror the security state's message post 9/11: Be afraid, be very afraid, and never ask why.

It took five years for television to counter this security-state programming in any meaningful way as finally in the 2006–7 season the medical melodrama *Grey's Anatomy* (2005–), going head-to-head with *CSI*, consistently beat it. In perhaps another expression of Bush II polarization, that season often broke into blue-state versus red-state television with ABC taking the lead in counter-programming with such shows as the pro-immigration *Ugly Betty* (2006–) and a disguised multicultural "multitude" versus scientific security-state plotline in the *Survivor* drama *Lost* (2005–). Yet, as of the 2007–8 season there was still no counter-programming within the detective-suspense-thriller genre constellation.[25]

Instead, where the noir impulse survives and thrives is in detective fiction—not necessarily a surprise, since with the post-9/11 mainstream representation lockdown, alternative modes such as documentary (Michael Moore's *Fahrenheit 9/11*, 2004), political tell-all nonfiction, and internet blogs have thrived as alternative information sources. The first tradition that is being kept alive in desperate times is that of the working-class detective. Perhaps best among writers in this tradition is Grace F. Edwards, whose Harlem-based series sleuth, Mali Anderson, was forced to leave the New York Police Department to maintain her integrity and instead becomes a kind of people's detective in her community. Through Mali's narration, Edwards celebrates the rhythms of black working-class life and most especially *female* working-class life in an era where the most prominent representatives of the global working class are third world women: "I waited, watching the whirl of activity on the avenue: folks rushing from the subway, swirling around a cadaverous crackhead holding a dingy paper cup; lines of vendors moving fast, pushing shopping carts filled with flowers, fruits, cakes and pies and coconut-flavored ices" (235).

A Kiss before Dying concerns the carnage wreaked by a black woman who, in an era in which the civil rights movement has supposedly triumphed, must still "pass" as white in order to marry a Wall Street banker. Edwards documents the racism that persists, now obscured by the 9/11 diversion: "Miss Adele fixed me with a stare, and from her silence I came to understand that it wasn't real laughter at all [she made] but the sounds we make to keep from crying, what we do when we realize race has poisoned the core of this country, and the sound we make is the distraction that keeps us from killing somebody" (179).

Perhaps even more prescient in attacking the "war on terrorism" as simply a means of waging an ever more active domestic war on the poor is Michael Simon's project of exploring through the cases of Austin Police sergeant Dan Reles how Texas in the late 1980s and early 1990s became a laboratory for conservative social experiments rolled out into the country as a whole under Bush II. In the opening novel, *Dirty Sally*, Reles, who takes on the Austin power structure, is already an outsider on the force, a Jew in Texas whose deceased best friend was a Latino cop and who is in love with the friend's wife, Rachel, whose French descent also marks her as different in a South that is supposedly part of a "new" multicultural America, but in practice an America where racial harmony "exists only on the sides of libraries" (Simon 15).[26]

Austin, as Reles sees it, in 1987, as the boom of the Reagan era goes bust with that year's stock market crash, is a place where the flip side of Reagan's "entrepreneurial revolution" is the urban crack epidemic. The city is full of "Southern gentility, high windows, crack dens, trailer parks, whorehouses, six-month summers, dead cops, beautiful wives, fat lawyers, powerbrokers, future governor and fully lawful plans to take over the world. They're not out to get you folks say, it's just how they do business. A new breed of power is gestating in the Lone Star state, the world's biggest lab of trial and error, and you're the guinea pig" (2).

The personal level of the plot, centering on the brutal rape and murder of a prostitute, is linked to the public laying waste to the city by a developer with presidential aspirations (hint, hint). Reles confronts the developer, who exposes to him his plans for Bush II–type privatization through means such as tax breaks for the rich as a way of shielding the business class from the contingencies of the market. "Americans prove in every election that they love millionaires. They want more power and more money in fewer hands, they just keep thinking their own hands will be among the lucky few" (253), the developer boasts to a Reles who, alone in possession of the truth, like *Chinatown*'s Jake Gittes, is unable to usurp the rich man's power.[27] Ultimately, the ending points to the limits of the detective form, where the truth may be unearthed by a lone crusader but the situation can only be changed by mass action.

And so we have come full circle. Just as the detective *literature* of the 1930s established the working-class-aligned conventions that were then brought to the screen a decade later, so too, today, the detective novel keeps alive the "materials memory" of both the anti-authoritarian tradition and the capitalist critique of the film noir fugitive outsider, a memory that, as the sordid reasons behind the endless "war on terror" become more starkly clear, will inevitably lead once again to the emergence of protagonists who, as they become more convinced of the law's inequities, substitute their working-class values for those of a society that is becoming more unequal as it becomes more rigid and rule-bound.

Appendix

Crime Films of Each Film Noir Period

Reference Sources

Langman, Larry, and Daniel Finn. *A Guide to American Crime Films of the Forties and Fifties*. Westport, Conn.: Greenwood Press, 1995.

Silver, Alain, and Elizabeth Ward, eds. *Film Noir: An Encyclopedic Reference to the American Style*. 3rd ed. Woodstock, N.Y.: Overlook Press, 1992.

Personal film viewing

Period One: 1940–1944

This section lists detective films and films evolving out of the detective series that most prominently feature either a detective, a criminal, or someone in between (reporters were common) investigating a crime and in contention with the law because of the investigation. There were in the period also many holdovers from the prior period of the dapper detective, where there is no such movement outside the law, but the films here constitute a powerful trend that was seized upon and magnified in the postwar period. Films following the model of the harassed detective continued to be made after the war, and several are listed here. At the same time, though, in a parallel series of films cataloged in period two, the detective moved fully outside the law and became a suspect and a fugitive him or herself.

Note: Films that are cross-listed (i.e., those that fall prominently into more than one period or type) have a "D" (for Double) following any but their primary listing.

Total: 57 films

1940 *Am I Guilty; Slightly Honorable; Stranger on the Third Floor*
1941 *Among the Living; Face behind the Mask; High Sierra; Maltese Falcon; Meet Boston Blackie; San Francisco Docks; Strange Alibi*
1942 *Dr. Broadway; Glass Key; I Wake Up Screaming; Moontide; No Place for a Lady; Street of Chance; This Gun for Hire; Time to Kill; Today I Hang*
1943 *Chance of a Lifetime; Eyes of the Underworld; Fallen Sparrow; Find the Blackmailer; One Dangerous Night; Shadow of a Doubt; Unknown Guest*
1944 *Crime by Night; Dark Waters; Dead Man's Eyes; Double Exposure; End of the Road; Last Ride; Laura; Murder My Sweet; Phantom Lady; Power of the Press; Seven Doors to Death; When Strangers Marry*

Several postwar films, in a period marked by the protagonist being more directly outside the law, featured the residual formation of the private detective still harassed by the law.

1945 *Johnny Angel*
1946 *The Big Sleep; Crime of the Century; Invisible Informer; Mysterious Intruder*
1947 *The Brasher Doubloon; Calcutta; Crimson Key; Danger Street; Exposed; Gangster; Johnny O'Clock; I Love Trouble; Lady in the Lake; Three on a Ticket*
1948 *Argyle Secrets; Bungalow 13; Mystery in Mexico*
1954 *World for Ransom*

Period Two: 1945–1950

Films of this period are divided into three groups (social problem, retreat into genre, radical disillusionment); the second group is further divided according to the type of protagonist.

Social Problem	16
Retreat into Genre[1]	
Working-Class Fugitive	28
Criminal/Convict	34
Depression-Era Drifter	8
Middle-Class Fugitive	57
Detective Outside the Law	34
War Veteran	16
Victim	3
Subtotal	196
Radical Disillusionment	3
Total	199

SOCIAL PROBLEM

1945 *Cloak and Dagger*; *Cornered*; *Ministry of Fear*
1946 *The Stranger*
1947 *Body and Soul*; *Brute Force*; *Crossfire*; *Dark Horse*
1948 *Berlin Express*; *Border Incident*; *Call Northside 777*; *Open Secret*
1949 *Jigsaw*
1950 *Caged*
1952 *Talk About a Stranger*
1958 *I Want to Live*

RETREAT INTO GENRE

Working-Class Fugitive

1946 *Crack-Up*; *Deadline at Dawn*; *The Killers*
1947 *Big Fix*; *Body and Soul* (D)—also Social Problem; *Desperate*
1948 *The Big Punch*; *Caught*; *Highway 13*; *Lady from Shanghai*; *Out of the Storm*

---

[1] Relevant social problem and radical disillusionment films are listed in the retreat into genre category, preceded by a "D" (Double).

1949 *Alias the Champ; Chicago Deadline; Criss Cross; Manhandled; The Set-Up; Thieves Highway; The Window*
1950 *The Breaking Point; The Damned Don't Cry; Gun Crazy; Side Street; Try and Get Me; Under My Skin*
1953 *Angel Face; 99 River Street*
1954 *Drive a Crooked Road; Fast and the Furious*
1955 *Killer's Kiss*

Criminal/Convict

1945 *Ministry of Fear* (D)—also Social Problem; *My Name Is Julia Ross; Within These Walls*
1946 *Decoy; Inside Job; Thieves Holiday*
1947 *Brute Force* (D)—also Social Problem; *Dark Passage; Key Witness; The Locket*
1948 *Angel in Exile; Hollow Triumph; I Walk Alone; Kiss the Blood Off My Hands; Larceny; Raw Deal; They Live by Night*
1949 *Arctic Manhunt; House of Strangers; Knock on Any Door; Moonrise; Shockproof*
1950 *Asphalt Jungle; Convicted; Gambling House; Hi-Jacked; State Penitentiary; The Sun Sets at Dawn; Walk Softly Stranger*
1951 *Cry Danger; The Scarf*
1953 *Blue Gardenia*
1954 *Fast and Furious; Riot in Cell Block 11*
1955 *Naked Dawn*
1956 *The Killing*

Depression-Era Drifter

1946 *The Chase; Fallen Angel; Gilda; The Postman Always Rings Twice; Strange Love of Martha Ivers*
1947 *Invisible Wall*
1950 *Dark City*
1951 *His Kind of Woman*

Middle-Class Fugitive

1944 *Double Indemnity*
1945 *Apology for Murder; Crimson Canary; Road to Alcatraz; Spellbound; Three's a Crowd; The Unseen*

1946 *Criminal Court; Dark Mirror; Fear; French Key; Girl on the Spot; They Made Me a Killer*
1947 *Backlash; Blind Spot; Born to Kill; Dishonored Lady; Double Life; Framed; The Pretender; They Won't Believe Me; 13th Hour; The Unsuspected*
1948 *The Big Clock; Disaster; Force of Evil* (D)—also Radical Disillusionment; *Gentleman from Nowhere; Impact; Million Dollar Weekend; The Pitfall; Road House; Ruthless; Shed No Tears; Sleep My Love; Sorry Wrong Number*
1949 *The Accused; Reckless Moment; Strange Bargain; Too Late for Tears*
1950 *D.O.A.; The File on Thelma Jordan; House by the River; In a Lonely Place; Shadow on the Wall; Sleeping City; Sunset Boulevard; The Underworld Story; Where Danger Lives; Whirlpool*
1951 *Cause for Alarm; The Scarf; The Second Woman; Secrets of Monte Carlo; The Strip*
1953 *Inferno*
1954 *Witness to Murder*
1955 *Double Jeopardy*
1956 *The Wrong Man*

Detective Outside the Law

These films form a special unit emphasizing the breakdown of the detective as a quasi-legal figure. Films adapted from Cornell Woolrich sources are listed first (since Woolrich's detective protagonists foster this breakdown), followed by films that trace the mainline development of the detective outside the law.

One characteristic of the detective film in this period is the emergence of the female detective, who is often not a private detective but an ordinary person who investigates and who is frequently disbelieved by the law. These films are noted with an "FD" following the title.

Woolrich Adaptations

1942 *Street of Chance* (D)—see period one
1944 *Phantom Lady* (D)—see period one
1946 *Black Angel* (FD); *The Chase* (D)—also Depression-Era Drifter; *Deadline at Dawn* (D)—also Working-Class Fugitive

1947 *Fall Guy; Fear in the Night; The Guilty*
1948 *I Wouldn't Be in Your Shoes* (FD); *Night Has a Thousand Eyes* (D)—also Victim.
1949 *The Window* (D)—also Working-Class Fugitive
1950 *No Man of Her Own*
1954 *Rear Window*
1956 *Nightmare*
1958 *Nightfall* (David Goodis's adaptation, but very Woolrich-like)

Mainline Detective Outside the Law

1945 *Johnny Angel; Lady on a Train; Strange Illusion; Two O'Clock Courage*
1946 *Accomplice; Blonde Alibi* (FD); *The Dark Corner; Inner Circle; Night Editor; Nocturne; So Dark the Night*
1947 *Bury Me Dead; Out of the Past; Railroaded*
1948 *Behind Locked Doors; Bodyguard*
1949 *Cover-Up; Manhandled* (D)—also Working-Class Fugitive
1950 *Destination Murder; Guilty Bystander; Woman on the Run* (FD)
1951 *Danger Zone*
1953 *No Escape*
1954 *Blackout*
1955 *Hell's Island; Mr. Arkadin*

War Veteran

These films detail the vet whose experience in the war, a collective experience akin perhaps to the experience of the rank-and-file member in the strikes after the war, causes him to more acutely feel the greedy postwar landscape.

A subgroup of these films features an amnesiac war vet, whose trauma—because of the dissolving of the bonds of the wartime collective and integration into an atomized homefront—induces forgetfulness of a possible criminal past before the war, in the same way the strikers were being told their recent past collective activity, that of the strikes after the war, was criminal. The amnesiac, though, finally clears himself and remembers that what he did in the past is not the crime that the law accuses him of committing. These films are indicated with an "A."

1946 *Blue Dahlia*; *Nobody Lives Forever*; *Somewhere in the Night* (A); *Step by Step*

1947 *Crossfire* (A) (D)—also Social Problem; *Dead Reckoning*; *High Wall* (A); *The Long Night*; *Ride the Pink Horse*

1948 *Fighting Back* (A); *Key Largo*

1949 *Act of Violence*; *Big Steal*; *Clay Pigeon*; *The Crooked Way*; *Undertow*

1950 *Backfire*

Victim

1945 *Detour*

1948 *Night Has a Thousand Eyes*

1949 *Criss Cross* (D)—also Working-Class Fugitive

1950 *D.O.A.* (D)—also Middle-Class Fugitive; *Sunset Boulevard* (D)—also Middle-Class Fugitive; *Night and the City*

RADICAL DISILLUSIONMENT

1946 *Woman on the Beach*

1948 *Force of Evil*

1951 *The Big Night*

Period Three: 1950–1955

Films of this period are divided into four categories of protagonist (A fifth category, pre-period documentary procedurals, traces the beginnings of the police procedural, the mainline of the period, in the second half of the 1940s). Three of these categories validate the law in an increasingly unproblematic way as the period proceeds, beginning with the criminal cop struggling to stay inside the law, moving to the mainline protagonist of the period in the cop/law enforcement agency/informer procedural, and then evolving to the vigilante cop as supra-agent of the law. Throughout the period a parallel series of films features the psychotic fugitive, in which the protagonist is a fugitive but, unlike the films of period two, which views the fugitive sympathetically, here that fugitive is viewed as a villain, one who becomes more dangerous and less rational as the period progresses.

Pre–Period Documentary Procedural	6
Criminal Cop	17
Mainline Procedural: Cop, Law Enforcement Agency Official, or Undercover Informer	95
Psychotic Fugitive	50
Vigilante Cop	14
Total	182

PRE–PERIOD DOCUMENTARY PROCEDURALS

These films established the procedural and its protagonist, the cop, law enforcement agent, or undercover informer.

1944 *Main Street after Dark*
1945 *House on 92nd Street*
1947 *Kiss of Death*
1948 *Canon City*; *Naked City*; *T-Men*

CRIMINAL COP

1949 *Scene of the Crime*
1950 *Between Midnight and Dawn*; *Man Who Cheated Himself*; *Where the Sidewalk Ends*
1951 *The Prowler*; *The Racket*; *Roadblock*; *Rogue River*
1952 *Kansas City Confidential*; *On Dangerous Ground*; *Scandal Sheet*
1953 *City That Never Sleeps*; *Vicki*
1954 *Private Hell 36*; *Pushover*; *Shield for Murder*
1958 *Vertigo*

MAINLINE PROCEDURAL: COP, LAW ENFORCEMENT AGENCY OFFICIAL, OR UNDERCOVER INFORMER

1948 *Assigned to Danger*; *Dark Past*; *The Street with No Name*
1949 *Abandoned*; *Arson, Inc.*; *C-Man*; *Dangerous Profession*; *Devil's Henchmen*; *Flaming Fury*; *Follow Me Quietly*; *He Walked by Night* (D)—also Psychotic Fugitive; *Homicide*; *Illegal Entry*; *Johnny Allegro*; *Johnny Stool Pigeon*; *Port of New York*; *Post Office Investigator*; *Prison Warden*; *Trapped*; *The Undercover Man*
1950 *Armored Car Robbery*; *Borderline*; *Bunco Squad*; *Customs Agent*; *Deported*; *Federal Agent At Large*; *Federal Man*; *Lady Without*

Passport; *Mystery Street*; *Panic in the Streets*; *Revenue Agent*; *Sideshow*; *Sleeping City*; *Southside 1–1000*; *Tattooed Stranger*; *Tension*; *Undercover Girl*; *Union Station*; *Woman from Headquarters*

1951   *Appointment with Danger*; *Detective Story*; *The Enforcer*; *FBI Girl*; *Fingerprints Don't Lie*; *I Was a Communist for the FBI*; *Insurance Investigator*; *M*; *The Mob*; *People against O'Hara*; *The Sellout*; *Smuggler's Gold*; *Unknown Man*

1952   *Affair in Trinidad*; *Carbine Williams*; *Captain Black Jack*; *Captive City*; *Loan Shark*; *Macao*; *My Six Convicts*; *The Narrow Margin*; *The Turning Point*

1953   *Blueprint for Murder*; *City That Never Sleeps*; *Code 2*; *Cry of the Hunted*; *Inside the Walls of Folsom Prison*; *Murder without Tears*; *Pickup on South Street*; *The System*; *Vice Squad*; *Violated*

1954   *The Big Chase*; *A Bullet Is Waiting*; *Crime Wave*; *Dangerous Mission*; *Down Three Dark Streets*; *Dragnet*; *Duffy of San Quentin*; *Miami Story*

1955   *Big Combo*; *Bobby Ware Is Missing*; *Finger Man*; *House of Bamboo*; *I Cover the Underworld*; *Inside Detroit*; *Murder Is My Beat*; *New Orleans Uncensored*; *Phenix City Story*; *Running Wild*; *Tight Spot*; *Toughest Man Alive*

1956   *Outside the Law*; *Swamp Women*; *Wetbacks*

1958   *The Lineup*; *The Mugger*

PSYCHOTIC FUGITIVE

1948   *Beyond the Forest*; *Cry of the City*; *A Double Life*

1949   *Chinatown at Midnight*; *He Walked by Night*; *The Threat*; *White Heat*

1950   *Dial 119*; *Edge of Doom*; *Experiment Alcatraz*; *Kiss Tomorrow Goodbye*; *711 Ocean Drive*; *Shakedown*

1951   *He Ran All the Way*; *The Hoodlum*; *The Killer That Stalked New York*; *Never Trust a Gambler*; *Strangers on a Train*; *Under the Gun*

1952   *Beware My Lovely*; *Confidence Girl*; *Models, Inc.*; *The Sniper*; *The Steel Trap*; *The Thief*; *Without Warning*

1953   *The Hitch-Hiker*; *Man in the Attic*; *Niagara*; *Split Second*

1954   *Human Desire*; *Loophole*; *Make Haste to Live*; *The Other Woman*; *Suddenly*

1955   *Black Tuesday; Big House; The Big Knife; Crashout; Dial Red O; Desperate Hours; I Died a Thousand Times; Life in the Balance; The Night Holds Terror; Storm Fear*
1956   *The Killer Is Loose; Ransom*
1957   *Man on the Prowl; The Night Runner*
1959   *Odds against Tomorrow*

VIGILANTE COP

1953   *Big Heat; I, The Jury*
1954   *Human Jungle; The Long Wait; Naked Alibi; Ring of Fear; Rogue Cop*
1955   *Crooked Web; Kiss Me Deadly*
1956   *Female Jungle*
1957   *The Midnight Story; My Gun Is Quick; Street of Sinners*
1958   *Touch of Evil*

Notes

Introduction: Let a Thousand Fetish Objects Bloom

1. While Americans were busy creating the form, the French were naming and defining it. The earliest reference to film noir is by Nino Frank in 1946 in the French journal *Positif*, with the form then codified in Borde and Chaumeton's *Panorama du Film Noir* in 1955, in much the same way perhaps, in Marx's formulation, the French had promulgated in 1789 a political revolution that the Germans then theorized.

2. Freud lived through a period in which vague middle- and working-class fears were expressed in the somber shadows of the German expressionist cinema and, earlier, in Vienna, in the brooding drama and literature of writers such as Arthur Schnitzler and Stefan Zweig and in Germany in the tortured novels of Joseph Roth.

3. Hobsbawm also distinguishes the social bandit from the gangster, the representative of the professional underworld for whom breaking the law is part of the normal way of life. Gerald Horne in *Class Struggle in Hollywood* points out the centrality of the mob to Hollywood in the 1940s and 1950s, in its encroaching on studio power and its use by the studios to discipline recalcitrant unions. Horne characterizes the crime film in that period as full of gangsters who validate the ugly antics of the mob. However, the gangster is not central to the immediate postwar film noir period. The gangster, who

had dominated the Hollywood screen in the early 1930s, returns as a force in the 1950s era of the police procedural, portrayed as either a psychotic menace who justifies a preponderant use of force (the Lee Marvin sadistic enforcer in *The Big Heat*, 1953) or a part of an organized underground that rationalizes an extreme emphasis on surveillance and interrogating of working-class neighborhoods (the post–Kefauver Hearings gangsters of *The Big Combo*, 1955, and the citywide corruption nearing anarchy of the Sodom and Gomorrah–like Alabama town in *The Phenix City Story*, 1955). The gangster is still a prominent figure in Hollywood, and his representation on the Hollywood screen is mostly romanticized, though ironically in a hard-edged way through the toughness of a Tony Soprano in *The Sopranos*, who nevertheless is in the end struggling for a better life. Two contemporary films that undercut this image and recognize the centrality of the gangster to Hollywood studio relations are *Death to Smoochy* (2002), with its shady "charity head" calling the shots in an Ice Capade spinoff of a children's television show, and *Mulholland Drive* (2001), where the gangsters dictate the choice of lead character in the film-within-the-film that is part of the actress Betty's dream.

4. This structuralist approach to genre developed through the adaptation of Lévi-Strauss's concept of myths as meditations on and mediations of deep conflicts in a society (see *Structural Anthropology*). Applied to Hollywood genres, this approach has tended to see the various genres as relegated to mediating different realms of experience and conflict in advanced capitalist society. See the work of Steve Neale and Frank Krutnik, especially Neale's *Genre*.

5. These strikes never made it onto the Hollywood screen. For the lack of union representation in this era, see the very few titles listed in the period in Tom Zaniello's compendium of working-class films in *Working Stiffs, Union Maids, Reds, and Riffraff: An Organized Guide to Films about Labor*.

6. These statistics are primarily compiled from Silver and Ward's *Film Noir: An Encyclopedic Reference to the American Style*, Langman and Finn's *A Guide to American Crime Films of the Forties and Fifties*, and my own viewing.

7. The form is often seen as conformist rather than resistant. In his discussion of *The Big Clock*, Barton Palmer describes how "the more radical aspects of Fearing's book are eliminated and the novel is reproduced as a thriller," whose boundaries he claims contain the critique of the book and testify to "the continuing power of socially conservative genre forms even in the heyday of noir filmmaking" ("Continuum" 56). David Bordwell, Janet Staiger, and Kristin Thompson make much the same argument for the formal transgressive aspects of film noir, saying that the form bends but does not break the stylistic boundaries of the classical Hollywood film. In contrast, Krutnik's

In a Lonely Street focuses more on the resistant quality of the film noir protagonist.

8. For example, in *The Country and the City*, Williams finds present in the "literary modalities of the pastoral" the voice of the "otherwise mute and inglorious agricultural workers" whose presence made this pastoral possible (Simpson 45).

9. On the third-period relation of labor to HUAC, see Schroeder 131, 145–46.

10. There is in addition an interesting use of homology in the third period to examine the displaced connection between two instances, a device often used by Adorno and the Frankfurt School. This form depends initially on the observer's describing an initial homological relationship and then being able to determine in the instance under consideration that the relationship has been altered or replaced by some other relationship. The observer then points out in the present instance the absence of that relationship and then elucidates the meaning of that transformation. It is this form which is invoked in the third-period crime film where the second-period sympathetic fugitive is displaced by both the cop and the third-period psychotic fugitive. The sympathetic fugitive appeared in a majority of second-period crime films, then disappeared to be replaced (or displaced) in the third period by the cop, whose working-class characteristics are now stressed, or by the menacing (psychotic) fugitive.

11. As Green points out, postmodern criticism that has taken up the position of the subaltern has subsequently dropped Gramsci's concentration on the working class as part of this grouping.

12. For working-class film in the 1910s and 1920s see S. Ross, *Working-Class Hollywood*. For the attempt to appeal to a more middle-class audience and the elimination of more direct working-class concerns through such means as the Hollywood Production Code see Shindler, *Hollywood in Crisis: Cinema and American Society, 1929–39*.

13. Gramsci termed this more gradual winning of political power a "war of position." At the moment of the cementing of these alliances, the subaltern group would be able to more radically alter the state and civil society in a revolutionary "war of maneuver."

14. One of Hitler's first official acts was to outlaw unions. For details see Bracher.

15. For a detailed description of the trials and tribulations of establishing the writers guild see Schwartz.

16. This study also contradicts the other major direction in noir criticism, best expressed in Marc Vernet's *"Film Noir* on the Edge of Doom," a strict

Foucauldian reading that imprisons noir within a discursive loop wherein it becomes, at least for Vernet, a way for French critics to validate American culture at a time when they were critical of American foreign policy. (Thomas Elsaesser constructs a similar argument about noir's German cousin, expressionism, as being resuscitated by Lotte Eisner after the war as a way of finding a "resistant" Germany.) The idea here is not to deny Vernet's characterization but to contend that the moment also has a grounding in material and class conditions that move it beyond the discursive loop, or perhaps locate it as well in the discourse of labor.

17. Gérard Genette uses the term "narrative discourse" to describe literary devices that operate in the text. As applied to the cinema, the term is understood to take into account processes such as lighting, camera angle, and shot selection.

18. Murray Smith points out that these devices, and especially the point-of-view shot, need not align or ally the audience with the character whose point of view we share, giving the example of the now-standard horror film shot, most strikingly deployed in *Halloween (1978)*, of the creature's point of view as it approaches its unsuspecting victims ("Altered States" 41).

19. The traits and the ideological system the (cinematic) text validates tend to be in agreement with the dominant values of the society. In this regard it is even more remarkable, and an indication of a hegemonic moment, that between 1945 and 1950 the crime film consistently constructed sympathy for the character fleeing the law and accused of a crime. Conversely, the return of the lawman and the allegiance engendered for him, as well as the new antipathy for the fugitive he pursued, indicated a sharp swing rightward in the early to mid-1950s.

20. In this case, however, the "positive" attribute of truth telling conveys an added connotation of racial discourse, of separating white from black, illustrating the cultural context in which allegiance is constructed.

21. The most comprehensive examination of the vicissitudes of this category is Richard Dyer's *Stars*.

Chapter 1: The Home-front Detective as Dissident Lawman (and -woman): Hammett, Chandler, Woolrich, and 1940s Hollywood

1. In this schema, the legalization of collective bargaining, the right to strike, was viewed more as a means to ensure labor peace than as a firm government commitment to legitimize the right to strike. There is strong evidence for this position in the negative way government reacted to the postwar strikes.

2. This change signified the end of the New Deal compromise that had promoted the incorporation of labor as a junior partner (Van Der Pijl 114.)

3. After its inception, Wilson declared that the cold war had two targets: "the American labor movement at home and the Soviet Union abroad" (Boyer and Morais 344).

4. These changes "turned union leaders into agents of social peace forcing workers to go outside the system . . . [and] create their own instruments of direct democracy and political power" (Lipsitz, *Rainbow* 11).

5. Strikes at the UAW, for example, were directed against the central (international) union leadership, the plant management, and the War Board (Lichtenstein, 119).

6. The constant revelations of the machinations of the Browne-Bioff trials during the war gave an immediate impetus for the postwar crime film trend of organized crime as standing for the centralization that seemed so prominent in the labor situation, especially in films such as *The Big Combo* (1955) where the mob is omnipresent. As in Brecht's gangster fascists in *The Irresistible Rise of Arturo Ui* (1940), the gangster stands for a certain kind of centralization that is perceived as thuggish rather than as beneficent as in the early 1930s gangster films.

7. This open support for anti-fascism contrasted sharply with the *pro*-fascist attitude of one studio head, Walt Disney. Disney dined with Nazi filmmaker Leni Riefenstahl on a Nazi filmmakers tour of the United States, was entertained by Mussolini while in Italy making *Snow White*, and featured swastikas in his cartoons (Horne 123, 136).

8. Because of his militancy, Sorrell was often accused of being a Communist (he was not). Nevertheless, he claimed that "Mr. Disney created more Communists [than the party ever did] with his substandard wage scales and the way he handled people" (Horne 137). For a detailed treatment of this pivotal moment in Hollywood militancy, see Denning.

9. On the Hollywood gangster's rise and fall, see Sarris and Sacks. For the onset of the production code, see Leff and Simmons.

10. For a full description of the 1935-40 period, see Clarens.

11. Phillip Dunne notes in describing the period that there was a trend "towards greater realism, towards a more frequent selection of factual American themes, towards the theory that motion pictures should not only entertain and make money but should also give expression to the American and democratic ideals" (qtd. in Stead 144).

12. For a description of the tropes of the platoon film see Bassinger, *Combat Film*.

13. The other series of films critical of the wartime consensus was the eleven films Val Lewton produced for RKO from 1942 to 1946. They ranged

from a negative reading of the American middle class as callous and racist in its handling of outsiders in the way the architect couple treat the Serbian Irena in *Cat People* to the implied accusation that elements of the American ruling class were fascist collaborators in Lewton's adaptation of two Guy de Maupassant stories about French upper-class collaboration with the Germans at the time of Bismarck's invasion of France in 1870–71 in *Mademoiselle Fifi* (1944).

14. For an excellent description of this experimental moment in the detective genre see Flynn, "Three Faces of Film Noir."

15. For a synopsis and reading of *Among the Living*, see Silver and Ward. I am indebted to William Everson for introducing the film to me.

16. Greene's reputation was as a politically committed thriller writer. His most famous novel at that time was 1932's *Stamboul Train* (later sanitized by Hollywood as *Murder on the Orient Express*), which followed passengers across Europe as they confronted the changes wrought by the Russian Revolution. His inclusion for adaptation by the wartime gangster film points to a desire to directly invest that genre with progressive political content.

17. For a more expansive description of the proletarian novel see Foley.

18. Ernest Mandel notes a similar occurrence in the detective story, where, with the multiplication of different types of detectives, still "the only type we have not encountered is normal industrial workers or farmers"; he suggests that this is "largely because these people do not have the leisure time to be detectives" (77).

19. Dick Powell's persona coming into *Murder My Sweet* was as a song-and-dance man (with the title of the novel *Farewell My Lovely* changed so that audiences would not think this was another Powell musical [Luhr, *Chandler* 120]), but even he benefited from the tougher, working-class-aligned stigma of the detective film that Bogart had helped create. This role began a successful transformation of his persona into a more hardened character that continued in the anti-fascist war veteran in *Cornered* (1945) and made him a noir staple.

20. See, e.g., Higham on the Bank of England's support of the German central bank into and during the war (7). There have also been numerous films on the British upper-class support for fascism, including *Remains of the Day* (1993) and *Tea with Mussolini* (1999).

21. The fascist connection is made more explicit the next year in *Across the Pacific* when Huston again casts Greenstreet to play opposite Bogart and Astor, this time as a Japanese sympathizer enamored with the fascist aspects of Japanese culture.

22. For a similar portrayal of the intersection of gangsterism and fascism, see Brecht's *The Resistible Rise of Arturo Ui*.

23. The word "thuggish" has taken its place in contemporary discourse, used by the forces of law and order to describe unions (in New York mayor Bloomberg's description of the head of the Transport Workers in the 2005 strike) and the disenfranchised (in French interior minister Sarkozy's description of the unemployed rebelling in the Parisian *banlieues*). In the noir world, the word more accurately describes the forces of law and order.

24. The lack of first-person narration in *The Maltese Falcon* has a darker effect, though, than simply not allowing the audience access to Spade's thoughts. In the opening of the film, we do not see Spade's face when he receives the call regarding the death of his partner; the camera remains focused on the phone's cradle on the bedside table next to him. This lack of information, plus Spade's curt ordering of his partner's name struck from his office and his former affair with his partner's wife, acts to initially present him as a suspect, thus increasing his distance from the law. Only later, with the introduction of more plausible suspects, do we gradually stop suspecting Spade. Marlowe, also, is not only antagonistic to the police but also allied with his client with a criminal past. In the opening shot of Marlowe's narration, he looks up from his desk to see in the window not his own reflection but that of the ex-con Moose Malloy, suggesting that one is the double of the other. Moose does things Marlowe would like to do but cannot. When Marlowe escapes from the doctor's asylum, he cannot get a cabbie to take him home until Moose appears and threatens the driver, and it is Moose who kills Marlowe's torturer, Dr. Amthor. Thus, both films feature a lawman more outside than inside the law.

25. Later, in the book Chandler had originally titled *Law Is Where You Buy It*, Marlowe is summoned to the office of the police chief. "Our city is small but very clean," the chief tells Marlowe. "I look out my western windows and I see the Pacific Ocean. Nothing cleaner than that, is there?" To which Marlowe, in his own reverie, adds, "He didn't mention the two gambling ships that were hull down on the brass waves just beyond the three-mile limit" (220), a perfect description of the chief's corruption, and one that was struck from the film.

26. Both films feature a hunt for a treasure that proves a chimera. But the Falcon goes no further than impugning the greed of the treasure hunters, while the hunt in *Murder My Sweet* for the (Holy) Grayle jewels calls attention to the corrupting power of the rich.

27. It is worth noting the pattern in Chandler. In the three novels that deal most explicitly with wealth, *Farewell My Lovely*, *The Big Sleep*, and *The High Window*, the villains are, respectively, the wife, daughter, and the mother of the patriarchs, in the end cumulatively rendering the patriarch invisible.

28. Spade and Marlowe also through their heightened masculinity affirm

the sexual norm against women's desire and the various other kinds of sexualities that float through the films, including Cairo's and Marriot's presentation as "perfumed dandies" and Gutman and the "gunsole" Wilma's perverse "father/son" relationship, which, given that "gunsole" is a 1940s term for male prostitute, also suggests pimp/hustler.

Chapter 2: Noir Part 1: Socialism in One Genre: Wildcat Strikers, Fugitive Outsiders, and a Savage Lament

1. Ironically, the Communist Party had initially opposed the strikes, supporting the continuation of the wartime no-strike pact. It was only after Truman's openly hostile moves against the Soviet Union that, late in the strike period, the party backed the strikes (Lichtenstein, 209).

2. That the "Communist" epithet when linked to the presence of the federal government worked to break strikes was established in an October 1945 strike of New York dockhands that closed New York harbor. The union leader, Joseph Ryan, invoked the "Communist" label to describe the rank and file who had been aided in the past by two left-leaning unions. This label fractured support and confused the workers so that they agreed to arbitration with the federal government, which took advantage of this newly generated antagonism against the strikers to rule against them on the issue over which they had started the strike. Here the "Communist" label turned a winning strike into a losing one and proved the efficacy of such a tactic (recounted in Lipsitz, *Rainbow* 103–8).

3. As an example of how these organizations worked in concert, the attack on one of the most radical unions, the United Electrical Workers, consisted of a joint effort by the FBI, the president, HUAC, and even the Atomic Energy Commission, which declared the union a security risk and asked General Electric not to renew its contract with the union for this reason (Rosswurm 15).

4. The International Longshoreman's and Warehousemen's Union, for example, was 50 percent non-white, and the Food Tobacco Agricultural and Allied Workers Union was both 50 percent women and 75 to 80 percent African American (Rosswurm 3).

5. A key unacknowledged reason for the blacklist was the decline in industry profits after 1946, which necessitated layoffs—layoffs that could be concealed by the blacklisting of "Communists." Crafts union employment shrank from 22,100 in 1946 to 13,500 in 1949 (Horne 8).

6. While younger writers, often employed for the harder work of pounding out a first draft, were paid little and were pitted against those who built

up résumés over several years, "high- (or moderately-) priced writers were brought in at the low end of the scripting process for a brief and not especially remunerative polish" (Buhle and Wagner 270).

7. Buhle and Wagner give the apt example of the Henry Fonda character in *The Long Night*, ex-GI, now a worker at a factory, whose uniform is punctured by cops' bullets in a shootout for his actions in killing the better-off rival of his love interest. The bullet-strewn uniform here accents that the state, supposedly an ally during the war, would no longer be an ally to the worker in the postwar (358).

8. In *Working Stiffs, Union Maids, Reds, and Riffraff: An Organized Guide to Films about Labor*, Tom Zaniello lists only four films that specifically dealt with labor in the period 1945–50. For the 1940s he lists only eight films, the fewest number of any decade in Hollywood history.

9. The Hollywood studio mode of production was of course also referred to as an assembly line, and Dassin in particular felt imprisoned in it, noting that before working for Hellinger he was under contract at MGM, where he described himself as going "stir crazy" and explained in language that paralleled the prison film that he started work on *Brute Force* "just a few days after I escaped from bondage" at MGM (Dassin interview).

10. This sympathetic treatment of prisoners contrasts sharply with the police procedural prison film *Canon City* (1948), written and directed by Crane Wilbur, the writer of *I Was a Communist for the FBI* (1951). Here, prisoners are jackals whose escape threatens the law-abiding community; the sadistic warden is replaced by a warm, fuzzy, paternal, southern "old boy" who orders his guards to shoot to kill; and the heroic prisoner is the one who does not want to escape, the equivalent of the stoolie in *Brute Force*.

11. See Sobchak for a description of the importance of the club or lounge and of "lounge time" to the chronotype of noir.

12. She may also be the fugitive herself, or she may be a class competitor, as in the femme fatale.

13. As the fugitive sees society turning against him or her, he or she can express what has often been (falsely) labeled existential anguish, that is, free-floating anxiety. Famous examples are the detective framed for murder, Bradford Gault's "I'm backed up into a dark corner and I don't know who's hitting me" in *The Dark Corner* (1946), and the following exchange between Joyce and Johnny:

> Joyce: It all blows up in your face, doesn't it?
> Johnny: What?
> Joyce: Whatever you're doing.

14. In describing the desperate political situation at the time of the production of *Force of Evil*, its director, Abraham Polonsky, rattles off the usual

litany of the Hollywood Ten on the defensive after the HUAC hearings, the disbanding of the anti-HUAC, liberal Committee for the First Amendment, and Churchill's Iron Curtain speech at Fulton, Missouri, which announced the cold war. After that speech, Polonsky says, "the fight was lost" (45). Polonsky also relates this defeat locally to the loss of the CSU strike in Hollywood and nationally to the defeat of the more radical unions of the CIO. This loss, he says, "made McCarthyism possible" because the unions were the main allies of the New Deal. At that time he believed there was little hope, because where previously the spirit of the New Deal "did exist in some of the big CIO unions," that spirit was "destroyed in the internal struggles within those unions" (44).

15. Thom Andersen concentrates on the critique rather than the lament for a lost opportunity in his characterization of this period as "film gris."

16. This is another reference, like the gangster/corporatists triumphing on July 4 by a scam involving the number 776, to the betrayal of the original ideals of the country in this new corporate era.

Chapter 3: Noir Part 2: Fugitive Kinds

1. In terms of truckers' reluctance to organize, it is salient that the overthrow of Allende in Chile in 1973 begins with a truckers strike against the Socialist government (Blum).

2. After receiving this treatment, it is no wonder that Steve and Ann flee a sheriff who lies unconscious after crashing his car. This sequence also features an early use of the all-points bulletin, the staple of the police procedural, but here, since focalized through the fugitive couple, occasioning fear of their being caught by a cold and unforgiving law.

3. With the rise of the McCarthyite police procedure, the positive spirit of the convict fugitive film survives only in the caper film, beginning with noir veteran John Huston's *Asphalt Jungle* (1950), in which crime is pointedly referred to as a "left-handed form of human endeavor." These films, in being focalized through the gang's robbery attempt, often concentrate on the element of work in pulling off the heist, culminating in the masterful, semi-silent, magnificently detailed cooperative working sequence of the heist in *Rififi* (1955), a French film from Hollywood director-in-exile Jules Dassin.

4. That Alton had a special feel for this trapped feeling is shown in his own description of prison from his book *Painting with Light*: "Life in captivity is dark. Although modern prisons are well lit in the daytime, the light source for daylight scenes remains the traditional prison cell window high up on the

wall. Through this window comes a shaft of sunlight to remind one of the precious freedom that exists outside, in contrast to the gloomy interior" (55).

5. This point is reiterated later when Ann calls Joe "something from under a rock," to which he replies: "I am something from underneath a rock, a whole pile of them: Corkscrew Alley; Dean's Orphanage; that famous rock that hits you in the back of the head after you've tried to help someone. Not to mention that heap I busted out of called the state pen. Yeah, a whole tiny little pile of rocks."

6. The stress on class conflict begins with the opening scene, where the character's poverty is accented: Eddie Stanford in *Fallen Angel* has to get off the bus in the northern California town where the action takes place because he doesn't have enough money to pay the fare to go any farther; Chuck Scott in *The Chase* doesn't have enough money for a hamburger when, as if from heaven, he finds the wallet of a powerful gangster and returns it, prompting his hiring by the gangster; and a wizened Johnny Farrell in *Gilda*, clothes in tatters and a few days' stubble on his face, finally wins a craps game but is about to be beaten up for the money when he is rescued by the cane-wielding Ballin, whose tuxedo Johnny admires and who then asks Johnny to make the class shift upward from shooting craps on the waterfront to being a croupier in Ballin's swank casino, with the transition emphasizing that the activity is the same, only the class status has shifted.

7. Toni Marichek's deliberately ethnic name is a marker, as is the marriage ceremony in *Desperate*, of the ethnic urban immigrant enclaves that, along with the already established working class, à la Sam's factory-worker father in the town, constituted the backbone of the CIO in the 1930s and 1940s.

8. The countering of this (upper-) class gaze is a main feature of the noir with its often unconscious depiction of working-class manners, though it is equally possible for the gaze to reassert itself as it does very stridently in the middle-class "looked-at-ness" at the "poor, downcast fighter" in *The Set-Up*, resulting in a maudlin mood that partially undercuts the effectiveness of the documentary-like reality of the boxing milieu in the film.

9. Which, as Marx maintains in *Capital*, is only an acceleration of the industrial process going on in the rest of Iverstown whereby workers like Sam's father are, over a lifetime, slowly consumed for the gain of the owner.

10. Martha's father's name, Pitt, summons the memory of the miners, one of the period's most radical groups of workers.

11. Jaibo, the character most interpolated into the criminal lumpenproletariat, who kills the boy who attempts to leave that life, Pedro, is still at his death given an extremely subjectivized moment where his mother's voice calls to him.

12. The most deviant film of the period, *So Dark the Night* (1945), "a film that should stand at the summit of those films that deal with the degraded detective" (Porforio qtd. in Silver and Ward 261), has the repressed older inspector himself as both detective and jealous murderer of a young woman engaged to him but who instead falls for a man her own age.

13. Mainwaring also wrote the screenplay for *The Lawless* (1950), in which the cop's corruption is a stand-in for that of society as a whole. He was fired from RKO by Howard Hughes for refusing to work on Hughes's anti-Communist vehicle *The Woman on Pier 13* (1949) and was later investigated by HUAC.

14. Spade's zealous "When his partner's killed a man's supposed to do something about it" is here answered by Markham's cynical "I buried him up there—I wasn't sorry for him or sore for her—I wasn't anything."

15. Mitchum's cynicism was the hard core he developed in dealing with the commercial film industry from a perspective of having himself been one of the "wild boys of the road" who rode the rails in the Depression. His line about his forty-plus-year Hollywood career was that he was just there "between trains" (Server).

16. There are a number of direct references to Janoth as Hitlerian. Pauline describes Janoth's office as "the Bertchsgarden of the publishing world," evoking Hitler's retreat where he took his mistress, and in the same conversation she declares that Janoth is "the only superman around here," the Nietzschean reference often taken as denoting Hitler's will to power. Janoth, whose mustache twitches a bit like Chaplin's caricature of Hitler in *The Great Dictator* (1940), also calls the artist Louise Patterson's abstract painting "a decadent-looking thing," recalling the Nazis' view of modernist art.

Chapter 4: The McCarthyite Crime Film: The Time of the (Quasi-Scientific) Toad (Criminal/Informer/Vigilante Cops versus Psychotic Fugitives)

1. By 1949 the unemployment rate climbed to 5.9 percent (Moody, *Injury* 42) and private investment fell 23 percent as the country began "skidding toward depression" (Boyer and Morais 349).

2. The argument that when foreign markets fail to absorb increased production, capital, which must constantly expand, works to preserve itself by creating a noncompetitive sector of the economy that produces goods (weapons) whose characteristic is that they constantly become obsolete and need to be renewed was expounded as early as 1912 by Rosa Luxembourg in *The Accumulation of Capital*.

3. For the role of the United States in the creation of the cold war as a solution to the postwar economic crisis see McCormick, who quotes Secretary of State Dean Acheson as claiming that in terms of rationalizing the cold war, "Korea came along and saved us" (98).

4. The direct enlistment of labor consisted at one point in AFL president George Meany and the CIO's James Carey being sent by the State Department on an elaborate ocean cruise and paid fifty dollars a day as consultants to introduce American speed-up techniques into British mills and plants (Radosh 415).

5. The most famous case of this disintegration was the role of U.S. labor and the CIA in splitting the French Communist union, the Confédération générale du travail or CGT, by the creation of the alternative Force Ouvriere (Renshaw 123).

6. For example, the International Longshoreman's and Warehousemen's Union was 50 percent nonwhite, the National Union of Marine Cooks and Stewards was at least 50 percent African American, and the Food Tobacco Agricultural and Allied Workers Union was both 50 percent female and 75–80 percent African American (Rosswurm 3).

7. In assessing the plan in 1951, the president of the expelled Amalgamated Clothing Workers said, "Our money has been used primarily to strengthen the governments in power and the industrialists," with U.S. industry the primary beneficiary of the "unbelievably high profits and low wages" (Boyer and Morais 353).

8. The 3,606 strikes in 1949 were the most since the peak strike year of 1946 (Lipsitz, *Rainbow* 243).

9. This shift was aided and abetted by a forced geographic shift of workers (promoted by massive government programs, the most prominent of which was a shift of funds away from mass transit toward highway construction) from the social, urban enclaves, the base of union organizing, to a more atomized existence in single-family homes in the suburbs (Lipsitz *Rainbow*).

10. After completing its work, HUAC boasted that "no major industry in the world today employs fewer members of the Communist Party than does the motion-picture industry" (Cogley 101).

11. Ironically, left directors sometimes contributed the prototypes of these changes, with Dassin's *Naked City* (1948) quickly stripped of its class content in Hughes's RKO films such as *Armored Car Robbery* (1950), setting the stage for the pursuit procedural, and John Berry's *He Ran All the Way* (1951) converting Garfield's HUAC-induced anxiety to a psychosis, resulting in the terrorizing of a middle-class family that proved a fine model for the psychotic fugitive. Popular Front themes, on the other hand, were often given expression only outside the United States, where the English television series

Robin Hood boasted scripts by Ring Lardner Jr., Gordon Kahn, and Waldo Salt, among the most prominent of the blacklistees (Neve 175).

12. In the early 1950s the Kefauver hearings applied the HUAC ethic of menace to crime, treating it as a hidden threat to be uncovered rather than as a social phenomenon to be analyzed (Straw 117).

13. Also carried over from HUAC was the validation of all forms of informing against "traitors" as opposed to the previous, opposite discourse (say, in *Brute Force*), which treated informers as snitches and traitors against a collective that viewed the law as encroaching.

14. Hathaway was throughout the period connected with the right-wing crime film (see *Niagara* later in this chapter), and de Rochemont, famous for the RKO *March of Time* (1951) documentary series, was employed by the CIA as the producer who "fronted" for the agency's involvement in its production of an animated version of *Animal Farm* (Saunders 294).

15. The script for *The Naked City* was originally written by Marvin Wald, who learned screenwriting during the war for the Air Force, where his scripts explained the use of and need for "sophisticated weaponry" to "combat the enemy." Wald was given access to New York Police Department files (Richardson 95), and it is no surprise that his script is about the use of surveillance weaponry to combat a domestic "enemy." The second version of the script, by Hollywood Ten writer Albert Maltz, accented the city as confluence of social classes.

16. The film was highly publicized as the first Hollywood film shot entirely on location, with the New York City locations seen as the mark of its "realism." However, director Jules Dassin claimed that what had happened was that on location in New York he had shot one film, with a more definite emphasis on social inequality, which then was completely altered in the editing in Los Angeles to emphasize the crime element to the point where Dassin claimed that upon seeing the movie he "walked out of the theater in tears" (Dassin interview).

17. Halloran's "Irishness," formerly a mark of an ethnic working class, is now disappearing as the classless society absorbs all distinctions. His bland ethnicity, marked by name only, is contrasted to the archaic lilt of his superior, Lieutenant Muldoon, whom, it is implied, Halloran will supplant.

18. Indeed, "Police detectives had told Wald that the Lower East Side looked unfavorably on cops" (Richardson 101).

19. For an alternative view of the film stressing the Popular Front aspects, see Kozloff.

20. Otto Preminger directed a crime film in each of the three periods with Dana Andrews: as a wise-cracking detective whose obsession for the victim of a murder overtakes his allegiance to the law in *Laura* (1944), and as a quint-

essential fugitive suspected of murder in a small town in California in *Angel Face* (1946), which begins with him having to get off the bus in the town because he doesn't have bus fare to continue.

21. For a slightly revisionist view see *L.A. Confidential* (1997), and for a description of the Los Angeles Police Department in the 1950s see J. Hoberman's review of the film (*Village Voice* 26 July 2004).

22. Kingsley spent two years researching the play in New York's Twenty-first Precinct (Leff and Simmons 185).

23. The script also bears this divided trace; it was written by John C. Higgins, who penned Mann's ultimate sympathetic fugitive film, *Raw Deal*, and Borden Chase, a noted HUAC supporter who in the crime film also scripted *Canon City*, the right-wing antidote to *Brute Force*, in which the escaped prisoners terrify the populace.

24. The remaining Spillane adaptation is Robert Aldrich's *Kiss Me Deadly* (1955). While this film, like Lang's *The Big Heat*, calls attention to the coldness of the character, it also, as Barton Palmer notes, partially recoups that character as a male model through the discourse of the playboy (*Dark Cinema* 96). In noting the film's balancing act, James Naremore quotes Aldrich's comment that ultimately "We kept faith with 50 million Mickey Spillane readers" (*More Than Night*, 152).

Chapter 5: The Neo-noirers: Fugitives, Surrealists, and the Return of the Degenerate Detective

1. His description of the system itself as bigger than and alien to the people in it echoes that of the patriarch in *The Strange Love of Martha Ivers*: in custody, the lead character realizes that the "wheels of justice weren't wheels at all. They were just people, living in a world in which it is far easier to be and do wrong than it is to be and do right" (Huggins 114).

2. The success of *77 Sunset Strip* prompted a host of other detective agency shows whose locations also connoted pleasure: *Bourbon Street* (New Orleans), *Hawaiian Eye* (Honolulu), and *Surfside Six* (Miami).

3. Huggins did not actually produce the series; he merely created it, sketching the film noir opening sequence. However, the producers faithfully followed his lead until the last year of the series. The examples here are mostly from "Fear in a Desert City," the series pilot, which closely hewed to Huggins's concept.

4. Of course, there were also ways of gilding the lily. In the pilot his alias is Jim *Lincoln*, and at the end, as he is racing out of town to avoid capture, he stops to pick up and comfort a stray kitten.

5. A useful precedent besides film noir was the early French poetic realist work (these films themselves seen as progenitors of film noir) by Jean Renoir *The Crime of Monsieur Lange* (1936). Here, more radically, a jury of Lange's peers allows him to cross the French border to freedom after his lover, Valentin, demonstrates in flashback that Lange's killing of a publishing company's tyrannical owner was necessary to save the cooperative the employees had created.

6. Noir novelist David Goodis so strongly felt the series' similarity to his own work during the classic film noir period on *Dark Passage* that he sued *The Fugitive* for plagiarism (Robertson 18).

7. See Hurd for a full treatment of this aspect of the ideology of the procedural.

8. This image of Kimble, which became the series' frozen-image trademark, can be seen as an exact rewriting of the "criminal" in profile as the last shot of *Dragnet*.

9. In contrast, in the 1993 film *The Fugitive*, starring quintessential Hollywood right-winger and Tom Clancy enthusiast Harrison Ford, Kimble's upper-middle-class doctor's rage at being hounded through urban settings reads more like white rage at the inner cities over loss of total enfranchisement than as righteous indignation at being hounded by the law.

10. In, respectively, "Landscape with Running Figures" (16 and 23 Nov. 1965) and "Ill Wind" (9 Mar. 1966).

11. The show, with its falsely convicted, death-row-bound murderer, also actively contested the death penalty at a time when it was being challenged in the United States as a whole. Kimble's home state was originally to be Wisconsin, but that had to be changed to Indiana because Wisconsin abolished capital punishment in 1963. By the end of the run, in 1967, Kimble's being brought back to Indiana to be executed was an anomaly, as that state too had abolished the death penalty (Robertson).

12. Reagan's supply-side economics, dubbed at the time "voodoo economics," fetishized a "trickle-down" approach to income distribution that never materialized. Its chief strategist, David Stockman, who later admitted the concept was fraudulent, was recently arraigned for attempting to embezzle a company for which he was hired as a consultant (*New York Times* 27 Mar. 2007).

13. Disney's *Newsies* (1992), appearing at the end of the Reagan-Bush era, was a nostalgic "celebration" by the notoriously anti-union company of turn-of-the-nineteenth-century unionizing which, in the light of the contemporary attack on labor, read as a kind of interment and mocking of the inability of unions to any longer pose a threat.

14. The other two films in the cycle, both 1990, were the studio-produced *The Grifters*, which simply dislocated a vague angst, and the far more interesting indie *The Kill-Off*, which caught the desperation of a New Jersey town given up for lost. Thompson was thus the equivalent in the neo-noir period of Hammett in World War II, Woolrich in the postwar, and Spillane in the cold war, stressing the importance in terms of noir of the film cycle having a precedent in the literary world.

15. Much as Paul Schrader had noted that mediocre directors such as Preminger had done their best work in noir, so too Clint Eastwood, subsequently celebrated like Preminger for a string of films that may hold up no better than Preminger's big-budget extravaganzas, made perhaps his best film at the beginning of the period in the underrated *Tightrope* (1984). From its startling cut from the sneakers of the serial killer who sadistically enjoys taunting his victims to the sneakers of Eastwood's detective who cannot hide his hard-edged affect from his kids, the film relentlessly equates the loneliness and alienation of cop and criminal, including the similarities in their inability to communicate with women and their consequentially violent sexual behavior. *Tightrope* rewrites the cartoonish *Dirty Harry* series, casting doubt on Eastwood's mythical creation in the same way his other masterful film, *Unforgiven* (1992), casts doubt on the mythical character Eastwood embodied in the spaghetti Westerns.

16. Morris, too, it might be added à la Schrader, makes his finest film by placing the ambiguous cinema verité techniques in the service of the noir conviction that the man on death row whom he is profiling is innocent.

17. This section is partly taken from a chapter in a proposed book on the history of film noir titled *Film Noir: The Dark Side of America*, coauthored by myself and Michael Bentley.

18. This dualistic nature is also present in the music and the dialogue. The 1950s Bobby Vinton song "Blue Velvet," as sung by Dorothy and played throughout the film on Jeffrey's ascending the stairs to the perversity he finds in Dorothy's apartment, calls attention to the fetishistic quality of the song that lurked even in its "innocent" 1950s initial appearance. The dialogue also is often an alternation of the most inane superego language, as when Sandy responds to Jeffrey's query about what she knows from her father about the ear he has found with "I don't know nothing but bits and pieces, I hear things" and with the absolute language of the id as Frank bleats at Dorothy during sex, "Baby wants Blue Velvet."

19. The ending also recalls the ending of one of Buñuel's Mexican films, *Susana*, in which an entire feudal hacienda has been overturned by a woman's (Susana's) desire. She is finally led off, and the next morning all is returned to

"normal," with the absurdity being that "normal" within the hacienda system of power is a situation in which all desire is repressed or narrowly channeled into patriarchal "marriage."

20. According to Stevenson, "What is distinctive about *Twin Peaks* is the way it connects all sexuality and violence to the abuse of a daughter by a father in a middle-class home. It's as if every person in town were but a part of a multiple personality generated by that abuse—as if not just an individual but a society has been formed in that incestuous cradle" (77).

21. The minor characters also play out this trauma. The drug dealer, Leo, remains in a coma, while the woman with the patch, Nadine, has regressed to high school, before she married her husband, Ed Hurley. He meanwhile continues his equally regressive adolescent romance with the waitress at the diner, who recalls her high school days with him when she was a cheerleader.

22. In the mid-1990s, likewise, New York's East Village, a former perennially resistant center of first labor consciousness and then the alternative movements of the 1960s, began to transform to a hip neighborhood ripe with property speculation which called itself "Boho" (conversation with Michael Pelias).

23. *The X-Files* spawned series even more openly critical of government, most notably *Nowhere Man* (1995–96), a combination of *The X-Files'* paranoid government plot with a drifter right out of *The Fugitive* who could not remember his own former life, which the secret government had stolen from him.

24. Statistics derived from the *New York Post* TV Week, 11–17 May 2003.

25. The first tentative step in this direction was ABC's 2007 summer series *Traveler*, in which two Yale graduate students are wrongly accused of a terrorist bombing and must find their Yalie roommate who may have set them up.

26. Both novelists are working in the wake of Walter Mosley, whose male detective Easy Rollins excavates the class and racial tensions of Los Angeles from the 1940s to the 1970s in novels such as *The Red Death*, which is about the uneasy relationship between black progressives and the Communist Party at the time of the blacklist.

27. The following interchange lays bare the sentiment underlying Bush II social engineering, the actuality of "No child left behind":

> Developer: Government should be run like a business, Dan. The university is in the black for the first time in years.
> Reles: Half the kids in Texas can't afford public college anymore.
> Developer: (Showing his dimples.) There are always jobs for caddies. (Simon 252)

Bibliography

Adorno, Theodor. *Critical Models*. New York: Columbia University Press, 2005.

Adorno, Theodor, and Max Horkheimer. "The Culture Industry: Enlightenment as Mass Deception." In *Dialectic of Enlightenment*, by Max Horkheimer and Theodor W. Adorno. Translated by John Cumming. 120–67. New York: Continuum, 1972.

Althusser, Louis. *Lenin and Philosophy and Other Essays*. New York: Monthly Review Press, 1971.

Alton, John. *Painting with Light*. Berkeley: University of California Press, 1995.

Andersen, Thom. "Red Hollywood." In *Literature and the Visual Arts in Contemporary Society*, edited by Suzanne Ferguson and Barbara Groseclose. 141–96. Columbus: Ohio State University Press, 1985.

Anderson, Terry H. *The Movement and the Sixties*. London: Oxford University Press, 1996.

Anobile, Richard J. *The Maltese Falcon*. New York: Avon, 1974.

Arthur, Paul. "The Gun in the Briefcase: Or, the Inscription of Class in Film Noir." In *The Hidden Foundation*, edited by David E. James and Rick Berg. 90–113. Minneapolis: University of Minnesota Press, 1996.

———. *Shadows on the Mirror: Film Noir and Cold War America, 1945–1957*. Ann Arbor: University Microfilms, 1985.

Barthes, Roland. *S/Z*. New York: Hill and Wang, 1974.

Bartlett, Donald L., and James B. Steele. *Empire: The Life, Legend, and Madness of Howard Hughes.* New York: Norton, 1979.

Bassinger, Jeanine. *Anthony Mann.* Boston: Twayne, 1979.

———. *The World War II Combat Film: Anatomy of a Genre.* Wesleyan University Press, 2003.

Belton, John. *Howard Hawks, Frank Borzage, Edgar G. Ulmer.* New York: A. S. Barnes, 1974.

Bernstein, Matthew. *Walther Wanger: Hollywood Independent.* Berkeley: University of California Press, 2000.

Biskind, Peter. "The Mind Managers." *Seeing Is Believing: How Hollywood Taught Us to Stop Worrying and Love the Fifties.* 137–44. New York: Pluto Press, 1983.

———. "They Live by Night by Daylight." *Sight and Sound* (Autumn 1976): v. 45, no. 4.

Blum, William. *Killing Hope: U.S. Military and C.I.A. Interventions since World War II.* Monroe, Maine: Common Courage Press, 2004.

Borde, Raymond, and Étienne Chaumeton. *Panorama du Film Noir Americain.* Paris: Les Editions De Minuit, 1955.

———. "Towards a Definition of *Film Noir*." In *Film Noir Reader*, edited by Alain Silver and James Ursini. 17–26.

Bordwell, David, Janet Staiger, and Kristin Thompson. "The Stability of Film Noir." *The Classical Hollywood Cinema.* 74–77. New York: Columbia University Press, 1985.

Bordwell, David, and Kristin Thompson. *Film History: An Introduction.* New York: McGraw-Hill, 1994.

Boyer, Richard O., and Herbert M. Morais. *Labor's Untold Story.* New York: Cameron Associates, 1955.

Bracher, Karl Dietrich. *The German Dictatorship.* New York: Praeger, 1970.

Brecher, Jeremy. *Strike.* Boston: South End Press, 1980.

Brecht, Bertoldt. *The Resistible Rise of Arturo Ui. Brecht Collected Plays*, edited by Robert Manheim and John Willett. vol. 6. New York: Vintage, 1957.

Britton, Andrew. "Blissing Out: The Politics of Reaganite Entertainment." *Movie* 31–32 (1986): 1–42.

Broe, Dennis. "Class, Crime, and Film Noir: Labor, the Fugitive Outsider, and the Anti-Authoritarian Tradition." *Social Justice* 30.1 (2003): 22–41.

———. "Class, Labor, and the Homefront Detective: Hammett, Chandler, Woolrich, and the Dissident Lawman (and Woman) in 1940s Hollywood and Beyond." *100* 32.2 (2005): 167–85.

———. "Fox and Its Friends: Global Commodification and the New Cold War." *Cinema Journal* 43.4 (2004): 96–102.

———. "Genre Regression and the New Cold War: The Return of the Police Procedural. *Framework: The Journal of Cinema and Media* 45.2 (2004): 81–101.

———. *Outside the Law: Labor and the Crime Film, 1941–55*. Ann Arbor: University Microfilms, 2001.

———. *Silent Film and the Shaping of Class in America*. Rev. ed. *Science and Society* 63.2 (1999): 271–74.

Brooks, Tim, and Earl Marsh. *The Complete Directory to Prime Time Network TV Shows, 1946–Present*. New York: Random House, 1980.

Browne, Nick. Preface, *Refiguring American Genres*, ed. Nick Browne. Berkeley: University of California Press, 1998: xi–xiv.

Buford, Kate. *Burt Lancaster: An American Life*. New York: Knopf, 2000.

Buhle, Paul, and Dave Wagner. *Radical Hollywood: The Untold Story behind America's Favorite Movies*. New York: The New Press, 2002.

Cawelti, John. *Adventure, Mystery, and Romance: Formula Stories as Art and Popular Culture*. Chicago: University of Chicago Press, 1976.

Ceplair, Larry, and Steven Englund. *The Inquisition in Hollywood: Politics in the Film Community, 1930–1960*. Berkeley: University of California Press, 1983.

Chandler, Raymond. *Farewell, My Lovely*. New York: Vintage Books, 1992.

———. *The High Window*. New York: Vintage Books, 1992.

———. "The Simple Art of Murder." *The Simple Art of Murder*. 1–18. New York: Vintage, 1950.

Ciment, Michel. *Conversations with Losey*. London: Methuen, 1985.

Clarens, Carlos. *Crime Movies: From Griffith to the Godfather and Beyond*. New York: Norton, 1980.

Coates, Paul. *The Gorgon's Gaze: German Cinema, Expressionism, and the Image of Horror*. Cambridge: Cambridge University Press, 1991.

Cogley, John. *Report on Blacklisting*. New York: Fund for the Republic, 1956.

Committee on Un-American Activities, U.S. House of Representatives. "Annual Report, 1952." *Film Culture* 50–51 (Fall and Winter 1970): 39–56.

Cook, Jim, and Alan Lovell 1982. "Coming to Terms with Hollywood: Aesthetics and Politics in 40s Cinema." Excerpts from F.B.I. Dossier No. 11.

D'Amico, James. "Film Noir: A Modest Proposal." In *Film Noir Reader*, edited by Alain Silver and James Ursini. 95–106.

Dassin, Jules. Interview with Cary Roan. *Brute Force* Laserdisc, Roan Group, 1995.

Davis, Mike. *City of Quartz: Excavating the Future in Los Angeles*. New York: Vintage Books, 1992.

Denning, Michael. *Cultural Front: The Laboring of American Culture in the Twentieth Century*. New York: Verso, 1996.

Dick, Bernard F. *Radical Innocence: A Critical Study of the Hollywood Ten*. Lexington: University Press of Kentucky, 1989.

Dooley, Dennis. *Dashiell Hammett*. New York: Frederick Ungar, 1984.

Durgnat, Raymond. "Paint It Black: The Family Tree of Film Noir." In *Film Noir Reader*, by Alain Silver and James Ursini. 37–52.

Dyer, Richard. *Stars*. London: British Film Institute, 1979.

Edwards, Grace F. *A Kiss before Dying*. New York: Bantam, 1998.

Elsaesser, Thomas. "Film History as Social History: The Dieterle/Warner Brothers Bio-pic." *Wide Angle* 8.2 (1986): 15–31.

———. "German Silent Cinema: Social Mobility and the Fantastic." *Wide Angle* 5.2 (1982): 15–25.

———. *Weimar Cinema and After: Germany's Historical Imaginary*. London: Routledge, 2000.

Englehardt, Tom. *The End of Victory Culture: Cold War America and the Disillusioning of a Generation*. Amherst: University of Massachusetts Press, 1995.

Erickson, Glenn. "Expressionist Doom in *Night and the City*." In *Film Noir Reader*, edited by Alain Silver and James Ursini. 202–7.

Everson, William. *The Detective in Film*. London: Citadel Press, 1974.

Fearing, Kenneth. *The Big Clock*. New York: Ballantine, 1946.

Field, Syd. *Screenplay: The Foundations of Screenwriting*. New York: Dell, 1994.

Flynn, Tom. "*The Big Heat* and *The Big Combo*: Rogue Cops and Mink Coated Girls." *Velvet Light Trap* 11 (Winter 1974): 23–28.

———. "Out of the Past." *Velvet Light Trap* 10 (Fall 1973): 38–43.

———. "Three Faces of Film Noir: *Stranger on the Third Floor, Phantom Lady* and *Crisscross*." In *Kings of the Bs: Working within the Hollywood System*, edited by Todd McCarthy and Charles Flynn. 155–66. New York: Dutton, 1975.

Foley, Barbara. *Radical Representations: Politics and Form in U.S. Proletarian Fiction, 1929–1941*. Durham: Duke University Press, 1993.

Fore, Steve. "Howard Hughes' 'Authoritarian Fictions': RKO, *One Minute to Zero*, and the Cold War." *Velvet Light Trap* 31 (Spring 1993): 15–26.

Foucault, Michel. "Panopticism." In *The Foucault Reader*, edited by Paul Rabinow. 206–13. New York: Pantheon, 1984.

Friedrich, Otto. *City of Nets: A Portrait of Hollywood in the 1940's*. New York: Harper and Row, 1987.

Gaer, Joseph. *The First Round: The Story of the CIO Political Action Committee*. New York: Duell, Sloane, and Pierce, 1944.

Genette, Gérard. *Narrative Discourse: An Essay in Method*. Ithaca: Cornell University Press, 1980.

Gifford, Barry. *The Devil Thumbs a Ride and Other Unforgettable Films*. New York: Grove Press, 1988.

Gomery, Douglas. *The Hollywood Studio System*. New York: St. Martin's Press, 1986.

Gordon, Bernard. *Hollywood Exile, or How I Learned to Love the Blacklist*. Austin: University of Texas Press, 1999.

Green, Marcus. "Gramsci Cannot Speak: Presentation and Interpretations of Gramsci's Concept of the Subaltern." *Rethinking Marxism* 14.3 (2002): 1–24.

Greene, Graham. *Stamboul Train*. Middlesex, UK: Penguin Books, 1932.

Grist, Leighton. "Out of the Past, a.k.a. Build My Gallows High." In *The "Movie" Book of Film Noir*, edited by Ian Cameron. 203–12. London: Studio Vista, 1992.

Gunning, Tom. *The Films of Fritz Lang: Allegories of Vision and Modernity*. London: British Film Institute, 2000.

Hall, Jasmine Yong. "Jameson, Genre and Gumshoes: *The Maltese Falcon* as Inverted Romance." In *The Critical Response to Dashiell Hammett*, edited by Christopher Mettress. 78–88. Westport, Conn.: Greenwood Press, 1994.

Harris, Howell John. *The Right to Manage: Industrial Relations Policies of American Business in the 1940s*. Madison: University of Wisconsin Press, 1982.

Harvey, Sylvia. "Woman's Place: The Absent Family of Film Noir." In *Women in Film Noir*, edited by E. Ann Kaplan. 22–34. London: British Film Institute, 1978.

Higham, Charles. *Trading with the Enemy: An Exposé of the Nazi-American Money Plot, 1933–49*. New York: Delecorte Press, 1983.

Himes, Chester. *If He Hollers Let Him Go*. London: Pluto Press, 1986.

Hirsch, Foster. *The Dark Side of the Screen*. New York: A. S. Barnes, 1981.

Hitchens, Gordon, ed. *Film Culture Special Double Issue on Hollywood Blacklisting* (Fall–Winter 1970): 50–51.

Hobsbawm, E. J. *Bandits*. New York: Delecorte Press, 1969.

———. *Primitive Rebels: Studies in Archaic Forms of Social Movement in the 19th and 20th Centuries*. New York: Praeger, 1959.

Horne, Gerald. *Class Struggle in Hollywood, 1930–1950: Moguls, Mobsters, Stars, Reds, and Trade Unionists*. Austin: University of Texas Press, 2001.

Horowitz, Daniel, ed. *American Social Classes in the 1950s: Selections from Vance Packard's* The Status Seekers. Boston: Bedford Books, 1995.

Horowitz, David, ed. *Corporations and the Cold War*. New York: Monthly Review Press, 1970.

Huggins, Roy. *Lovely Lady, Pity Me*. New York: Avon, 1949.

Hurd, Geoffrey. "The Television Presentation of the Police." In *Popular Television and Film, edited by Tony Bennett et al. 53–70. London: British Film Institute, 1981.

Inglis, Fred. *The Cruel Peace: Everyday Life in the Cold War*. New York: Basic Books, 1991.

Irwin, Lew. "The Breakdown of the Blacklist: A Broadcast on the Hollywood Blacklist by KPOL, Los Angeles." *Film Culture* 50–51 (Fall–Winter 1970): 74–77.

Izod, John. *Hollywood and the Box Office, 1895–1986*. New York: Columbia University Press, 1988.

Jameson, Fredrick. "On Raymond Chandler." In *The Poetics of Murder: Detective Fiction and Literary Theory*, edited by Glenn W. Most and William W. Stowe. 210–29. San Diego: Harcourt Brace Jovanovich, 1983.

Jarvie, Ian. "Hysteria and Authoritarianism in the Films of Robert Aldrich." *Film Culture* 22–23 (Summer 1961): 100–103.

Jensen, Paul. "Film Noir: The Writer Raymond Chandler, the World You Live In." *Film Comment* (Nov. 1974): 18–26.

———. "The Return of Dr. Caligari: Paranoia in Hollywood." *Film Comment* 7.4 (1971): 36–45.

Jewell, Richard B., with Vernon Harbin. *The RKO Story*. New York: Arlington House, 1982.

Johnston, Clare. "*Double Indemnity*." In *Women in Film Noir*, edited by E. Ann Kaplan. 100–111. London: British Film Institute, 1978.

Jones, Dorothy B. "Communism and the Movies; A Study of Film Content." In *Report on Blacklisting*, by John Cogley. 196–304. New York: Fund for the Republic, 1956.

Kaplan, E. Ann. "Fritz Lang and German Expressionism: A Reading of *Dr. Mabuse, der Spieler*." In *Passion and Rebellion: The Expressionist Heritage*, edited by Stephen Eric Bronner and Douglas Kellner. 398–408. South Hadley, Mass.: J. F. Bergin, 1983.

Kast, Pierre. "A Brief Essay on Optimism." In *Perspectives on Film Noir*, edited by Barton Palmer. 44–49. New York: Prentice Hall, 1996.

Kellner, Douglas. "Expressionism and Rebellion." In *Passion and Rebellion: The Expressionist Heritage*, edited by Stephen Eric Bronner and Douglas Kellner. 3–40. South Hadley, Mass.: J. F. Bergin Publishers, 1983.

Kelly, Keith, and Clay Steinman. "*Crossfire*: A Dialectical Attack." *Film Reader* 3 (1978): 106–27.

Kemp, Philip. "From the Nightmare Factory: HUAC and the Politics of Noir." *Sight and Sound* 55, no. 4 (Autumn 1986): 266–70.

Kerr, Paul. "Out of What Past? Notes on the B *Film Noir*." In *Film Noir Reader*, edited by Alain Silver and James Ursini, 107–27. 1996.

Kessler-Harris, Alice. "*The Life and Times of Rosie the Riveter* (U.S., 1980): The Experience and Legacy of Wartime Women Wage Earners." In *World War II Film and History*, edited by John Whiteclay Chambers II and David Culbert. 107–22. Oxford: Oxford University Press, 1996.

Kozloff, Sarah. "Humanizing 'The Voice of God': Narration in *The Naked City*." *Cinema Journal* 23.4 (1984): 41–53.

Kracauer, Sigfried. "Hollywood's Terror Films: Do They Reflect an American State of Mind?" *Commentary* (Aug. 1946): 132–36.

Krieger, Joel. *Reagan, Thatcher, and the Politics of Decline*. New York: Oxford University Press, 1986.

Krutnik, Frank. *In a Lonely Street: Film, Genre, Masculinity*. London: Routledge, 1991.

Langman, Larry, and Daniel Finn. *A Guide to American Crime Films of the Forties and Fifties*. Westport, Conn.: Greenwood Press, 1995.

Lasky, Betty. *RKO: The Biggest Little Major of Them All*. Santa Monica: Roundtable, 1989.

Lears, Jackson. "A Matter of Taste: Corporate Cultural Hegemony in a Mass-Consumption Society." In *Recasting America: Culture and Politics in the Age of Cold War*, edited by Lary May. 38–57. Chicago: University of Chicago Press, 1989.

Leff, Leonard, and Jerold L. Simmons. *The Dame in the Kimono: Hollywood, Censorship, and the Production Code from the 1920s to the 1960s*. New York: Grove Weidenfeld, 1990.

Levine, Rhoda F. *Class Struggle and the New Deal: Industrial Labor, Industrial Capital, and the State*. Lawrence: University Press of Kansas, 1988.

Lévi-Strauss, Claude. *Structural Anthropology*. Garden City, N.Y.: Doubleday, 1967.

Lichtenstein, Nelson. *Labor's War at Home: The CIO in World War II*. Cambridge: Cambridge University Press, 1982.

Lipsitz, George. "The New York Intellectuals: Samuel Fuller and Edger Ulmer." In *Time Passages*. 179–207. Minneapolis: University of Minnesota Press, 1990.

———. *Rainbow at Midnight: Labor and Culture in the 1940s*. Urbana: University of Chicago Press, 1994.

Luhr, William. *The Maltese Falcon*. New Brunswick, N.J.: Rutgers University Press, 1995.

———. *Raymond Chandler and Film*. New York: Frederick Ungar, 1982.

Luxembourg, Rosa. *The Accumulation of Capital*. New York: Routledge, 2004.

MacArthur, Colin. *Underworld USA*. New York: Viking, 1972.

MacDonald, Scott. "The City as the Country: The New York City Symphony from Rudy Burckhardt to Spike Lee." *Film Quarterly* 51(2): 2–20.

Mainwaring, Daniel. "Screenwriter Daniel Mainwaring Discusses *Out of the Past*." *Velvet Light Trap* 10 (Fall 1973): 44–45.

Maltby, Richard. "*Film Noir*: The Politics of the Maladjusted Text." *Journal of American Studies* 18 (1984): 49–71.

Maltz, Albert. "The Happiest Man on Earth." In *Years of Protest: A Collection of American Writings of the 1930s*, edited by Jack Salzman with Barry Wallenstein. 29–37. Indianapolis: Bobbs-Merrill, 1967.

Mandel, Ernest. *Delightful Murder: A Social History of the Crime Story*. Minneapolis: University of Minnesota Press, 1984.

Marc, David, and Robert J. Thompson. *Prime Time Prime Movers*. Syracuse: Syracuse University Press, 1995.

Marcus, Steven. Introduction and "Dashiell Hammett and the Continental Op." In *The Critical Response to Dashiell Hammett*, edited by Christopher Mettress. 194–202. Westport, Conn.: Greenwood Press, 1994.

Marling, William. *The American Roman Noir: Hammett, Cain, Chandler*. Athens: University of Georgia Press, 1995.

Marx, Karl. *Capital*. Vol. 1. London: Penguin Books, 1992.

———. *Early Writings*. London: Penguin Books, 1992.

Marx, Karl, and Friedrich Engels. *The German Ideology*. *The Marx-Engels Reader*, edited by Robert C. Tucker. 2nd ed. New York: Norton, 1978.

May, Lary. "Movie Star Politics: The Screen Actors' Guild, Cultural Conversion, and the Hollywood Red Scare." In *Recasting America: Culture and Politics in the Age of Cold War*, edited by Lary May. 125–53. Chicago: University of Chicago Press, 1989.

McCormick, Thomas J. *America's Half Century*. Baltimore: Johns Hopkins University Press, 1989.

McGrath, Patrick J. *John Garfield: The Illustrated Career in Films and On Stage*. Jefferson, N.C.: McFarland, 1993.

Melman, Seymour. *The Permanent War Economy*. New York: Touchstone, 1974.

Mettress, Christopher. "Dashiell Hammett and the Challenge of the New Individualism: Rereading *Red Harvest* and *The Maltese Falcon*." In *The Critical Response to Dashiell Hammett*, edited by Christopher Mettress. 89–108. Westport, Conn.: Greenwood Press, 1994.

Milkman, Paul Allen. *PM: A New Deal in Journalism, 1940–48*. New Brunswick, N.J.: Rutgers University Press, 1997.

Miller, Don. "Eagle-Lion: The Violent Years." *Focus on Film* (Nov. 1978): 27–38.

Mills, C. Wright. *The New Men of Power: America's Labor Leaders*. New York: Harcourt, Brace, 1948.

Milward, Alan S. *War, Economy, and Society, 1939–1945*. Berkeley: University of California Press, 1979.

Moody, Kim. *An Injury to All: The Decline of American Unionism*. New York: Verso, 1988.

———. "Is Bureaucracy Best For Unions?" *New Politics* 7.2 (1999): 126–32.

Mosley, Walter. *The Red Death*. New York: Pocket Books, 1991.

Mulvey, Laura. "Visual Pleasure and Narrative Cinema." *Screen* 16.3 (1975): 6–18.

Naremore, James. *The Magic World of Orson Welles*. Rev. ed. Dallas: Southern Methodist University Press, 1988.

———. *More Than Night: Film Noir in Its Contexts*. Berkeley: University of California Press, 1998.

Navasky, Victor S. *Naming Names*. New York: Viking, 1980.

Neale, Steve. *Genre*. London: British Film Institute, 1980.

Neve, Brian. *Film and Politics in America: A Social Tradition*. London: Routledge, 1992.

Nevins, Francis M. "Translate and Transform: from Cornell Woolrich to Film Noir." In *Film Noir Reader 2*, edited by Alain Silver and James Ursini. 137–57. New York: Limelight Editions, 1999.

Nielsen, Mike, and Gene Mailes. *Hollywood's Other Blacklist: Union Struggles in the Studio System*. London: British Film Institute, 1995.

Onosko, Tim. "RKO Radio: An Overview." *Velvet Light Trap* 10 (Fall 1973): 2–5.

Palmer, Barton. "*Film Noir* and the Genre Continuum: Process, Product, and *The Big Clock*. *Persistence of Vision* 3–4 (Summer 1986): 51–60.

———. *Hollywood's Dark Cinema: The American Film Noir*. New York: Twayne, 1994.

———. Introduction. *Perspectives on Film Noir*, edited by Barton Palmer. 3–17. New York: Prentice Hall, 1996.

Parenti, Christian. *Lockdown America: Police and Prisons in the Age of Crisis*. New York: Verso, 1999.

Peacock, Steven, ed. *Reading 24: TV against the Clock*. London: I. B. Tauris, 2007.

Pells, Richard H. *The Liberal Mind in a Conservative Age: American Intellectuals in the 1940s and 1950s*. Middletown, Conn.: Wesleyan University Press, 1989.

Pendo, Steven. *Raymond Chandler On Screen: His Novels into Film*. Metuchen, N.J.: Scarecrow Press, 1976.

Place, Janey. "Women in Film Noir." In *Women in Film Noir*, edited by E. Ann Kaplan. 35–67. London: British Film Institute, 1978.

Platt, Tony. "Street Crime: A View from the Left." *Crime and Social Justice* 9 (Spring/Summer 1978): 26–34.

Polon, Dana. *Power and Paranoia: History, Narrative, and the American Cinema, 1940–1950.* New York: Columbia University Press, 1986.

Polonsky, Abraham. "How the Blacklist Worked in Hollywood." *Film Culture* 50–51 (Fall–Winter 1970): 41–48.

Porforio, Robert G. "No Way Out: Existential Motifs in the Film Noir." In *Film Noir Reader*, edited by Alain Silver and James Ursini. 77–94.

Pratley, Gerald. *The Cinema of Otto Preminger.* New York: Castle Books, 1971.

Radosh, Ronald. *American Labor and United States Foreign Policy.* New York: Random House, 1969.

Reid, David, and Jayne L. Walker. "Strange Pursuit: Cornell Woolrich and the Abandoned City of the Forties." In *Shades of Noir*, edited by Joan Copjec. 57–94. New York: Verso, 1993.

Reiman, Jeffrey. "The Marxian Critique of Criminal Justice." In *Radical Philosophy of Law: Contemporary Challenges to Mainstream Legal Theory and Practice*, edited by David S. Caudill and Steven Jay Gold. 111–39. Atlantic Highlands, N.J.: Humanities Press, 1995.

Renshaw, Patrick. *American Labor and Consensus Capitalism, 1935–1990.* Jackson: University Press of Mississippi, 1991.

Rey, Henri-Francois. "Hollywood Makes Myths Like Ford Makes Cars (last installment): Demonstration by the Absurd: Films Noirs." In *Perspectives on Film Noir*, edited by Barton Palmer. 28–29. New York: Prentice Hall, 1996.

Richardson, Carl. *Autopsy: An Element of Realism in Film Noir.* Metuchen, N.J.: Scarecrow Press, 1992.

Richter, Irving. *Labor's Struggles, 1945–1950.* Cambridge: Cambridge University Press, 1994.

Rimoldi, Oscar. "Detective Films of the Thirties and Forties." *Films in Review*, Part 1, May–June 1993, 164–73; Part 2, July–Aug. 1993, 164–73; Part 3, Sept.–Oct. 1993, 164–73.

Robertson, Ed. *The Fugitive Recaptured.* Introduction by Stephen King. Universal City, Calif.: Pomegranate Press, 1993.

Roffman, Peter, and Jim Purdy. *The Hollywood Social Problem Film: Madness, Despair, and Politics from the Depression to the Fifties.* Bloomington: Indiana University Press, 1981.

Rogin, Michael. "Kiss Me Deadly: Communism, Motherhood, and Cold War Movies." *Ronald Reagan: The Movie and Other Episodes in Political Demonology.* 236–71. Berkeley: University of California Press, 1987.

Rosenfelt, Deborah. *Salt of the Earth.* New York: Feminist Press, 1978.

Ross, Andrew. "Containing Culture in the Cold War." *No Respect: Intellectuals and Popular Culture*. 42–64. New York: Routledge, 1989.

Ross, Steven. "Beyond the Screen: History, Class, and the Movies." In *The Hidden Foundation: Cinema and the Question of Class*, edited by David E. James and Rick Berg. 26–55. Minneapolis: University of Minnesota Press, 1996.

———. *Working-Class Hollywood: Silent Film and the Shaping of Class in America*. Princeton, N.J.: Princeton University Press, 1998.

Rosswurm, Steve. "An Overview and Preliminary Assessment of the CIO's Expelled Unions." *The CIO's Left-Led Unions*. 1–17. New Brunswick, N.J.: Rutgers University Press, 1992.

Sacks, Arthur. "An Analysis of the Gangster Movies of the Early Thirties." *Velvet Light Trap* 1 (June 1971): 5–11, 32.

Sarris, Andrew. "Big Funerals: The Hollywood Gangster, 1927–1933." *Film Comment* 13 (1977): 6–9.

Saunders, Frances Stonor. *The Cultural Cold War: The CIA and the World of Arts and Letters*. New York: New Press, 1999.

Sayre, Nora. *Running Time: Films of the Cold War*. New York: Dial, 1978.

Schatz, Thomas. *Boom and Bust: American Cinema in the 1940s*. Berkeley: University of California Press, 1997.

Schrader, Paul. "Notes on Film Noir." In *Film Noir Reader*, edited by Alain Silver and James Ursini. 53–64.

Schrecker, Ellen. "McCarthyism and the Labor Movement: The Role of the State." In *The CIO's Left-Led Unions*, edited by Steve Rosswurm. 139–57. New Brunswick, N.J.: Rutgers University Press, 1992.

Schroeder, William R. *Continental Philosophy*. Oxford: Blackwell, 2005.

Schwartz, Sheila. *The Hollywood Writers' Wars*. New York: Knopf, 1982.

Server, Lee. *Robert Mitchum: Baby I Don't Care*. New York: St. Martin's Griffin, 2001.

Shadoian, Jack. "Focus on Feeling: 'Seeing' through the Fifties." *Dreams and Dead Ends: The American Gangster/Crime Film*. 209–33. Cambridge: MIT Press, 1977.

Shindler, Colin. *Hollywood in Crisis: Cinema and American Society 1929–39*. New York: Routledge, 1996.

Silver, Alain. "*Kiss Me Deadly*: Evidence of a Style." In *Film Noir Reader*, edited by Alain Silver and James Ursini. 209–36.

Silver, Alain, and James Ursini, eds. *Film Noir Reader*. New York: Limelight Editions, 1996.

———. "John Farrow: Anonymous Noir." *Film Noir Reader* 145–60.

Silver, Alain, and Elizabeth Ward, eds. *Film Noir: An Encyclopedic Reference to the American Style*. 3rd ed. Woodstock, N.Y.: Overlook Press, 1992.

Simon, Michael. *Dirty Sally*. New York: Viking, 2004.

Simpson, David. "Feelings for Structures: Voicing History." In *Cultural Materialism: On Raymond Williams*, edited by Christopher Prendergast. 29–50. Minneapolis: University of Minnesota Press, 1995.

Sklar, Robert. *City Boys: Cagney, Bogart, Garfield*. Princeton, N.J.: Princeton University Press, 1992.

———. *Movie-Made America: A Cultural History of American Movies*. New York: Vintage Books, 1975.

Smith, Murray. "Altered States: Character and Emotional Response in the Cinema." *Cinema Journal* 33.4 (1994): 34–55.

———. *Engaging Characters: Fiction, Emotion, and the Cinema*. Oxford: Clarendon Press, 1995.

Smith, Robert E. "Mann in the Dark: The *Films Noir* of Anthony Mann." *Bright Lights* 2.1 (1977): 8–14.

Smith, Susan. *Hitchcock: Suspense, Humor, and Tone*. London: British Film Institute, 2000.

Sobchak, Vivienne. "Lounge Time: Postwar Crisis and the Chronotope of Film Noir." In *Refiguring American Genres*. 70–129, edited by Nick Browne. Berkeley: University of California Press, 1998.

Stam, Robert. *Unthinking Eurocentrism*. New York: Routledge, 1994.

Starobin, Joseph R. *American Communism in Crisis, 1943–1947*. Berkeley: University of California Press, 1972.

Stead, Peter. *Film and the Working Class*. London: Routledge, 1989.

Stevenson, Diane. "Family Romance, Family Violence, and the Fantastic in Twin Peaks." In *Full of Secrets: Critical Approaches to* Twin Peaks, edited by David Lavery. 70–81. Detroit: Wayne State University Press, 1995.

Stones, Christopher. "Vandalism: Property, Gentility, and the Rhetoric of Crime in New York City, 1890–1920." *Radical History Review* 26 (Oct. 1982): 13–36.

Straw, Will. "Urban Confidential: The Lurid City of the 1950s." In *The Cinematic City*, edited by David B. Clarke. 110–28. London, Routledge, 1997.

Sussman, Warren. "Did Success Spoil the United States? Dual Representations in Postwar America." In *Recasting America: Culture and Politics in the Age of Cold War*, edited by Lary May. 19–37. Chicago: University of Chicago Press, 1989.

Swidorski, Carl. "Constituting the Modern State: The Supreme Court, Labor Law, and the Contradictions of Legitimation." In *Radical Philosophy of Law: Contemporary Challenges to Mainstream Legal Theory and Practice*, edited by David S. Caudill and Steven Jay Gold. 162–78. Atlantic Highlands, N.J.: Humanities Press, 1995.

Tailleur, Roger. "*The Pink Horse* or the Pipe Dreams of the Human Condition."

In *Perspectives on Film Noir*, edited by Barton Palmer. 39–43. New York: Prentice Hall, 1996.

Talbot, David, and Barbara Zeutlin. *Creative Differences: Profiles of Hollywood Dissidents*. Boston: South End Press, 1978.

Thompson, E. P. *The Making of the English Working Class*. New York: Vintage Books, 1963.

Tomlins, Christopher. *The State and the Unions: Labor Relations, Law, and the Organized Labor Movement in America, 1880–1960*. Cambridge: Cambridge University Press, 1985.

Trumbo, Dalton. "The Time of the Toad." *Film Culture* 50–51 (Fall and Winter 1970): 31–41.

Ursini, James. "Angst at Sixty Fields per Second." In *Film Noir Reader*, edited by Alain Silver and James Ursini. 275–88.

Van Der Pijl, Kees. *The Making of an Atlantic Ruling Class*. London: Verso, 1984.

Vanneman, Reeve, and Lynn Weber Cannon. *The American Perception of Class*. Philadelphia: Temple University Press, 1987.

Vernet, Marc. "*Film Noir* on the Edge of Doom." In *Shades of Noir*, edited by Joan Copjec. 1–32. London: Verso, 1993.

Walsh, David. *Hollywood Honors Elia Kazan, Filmmaker and Informer*. Oak Park, Mich.: Mehring Books, 1999.

Ward, Elizabeth. "The Unintended *Femme Fatale*: *The File on Thelma Jordon* and *Pushover*." In *Film Noir Reader 2*, edited by Alain Silver and James Ursini. 129–36. New York: Limelight Editions, 1999.

Whitehall, Richard. "Some Thoughts on Fifties Gangster Films." *Velvet Light Trap* 11 (1974): 17–19.

Willet, John, and Ralph Mannheim. Introduction. *Life of Galileo*, by Bertolt Brecht. vii–xxii. New York: Arcade, 1994.

Williams, Raymond. *The Country and the City*. New York: Oxford University Press, 1973.

———. "Structures of Feeling." *Marxism and Literature*. 128–35. Oxford: Oxford University Press, 1977.

Winkler, Allan M. *The Politics of Propaganda: The Office of War Information, 1942–1945*. New Haven: Yale University Press, 1978.

Winslow, George. *Capital Crimes*. New York: Monthly Review Press, 1999.

Wood, Robin. "Norms and Variations: *The 39 Steps* and *Young and Innocent*." *Hitchcock's Films Revisited*. 275–287. New York: Columbia University Press, 1989.

Zaniello, Tom. *Working Stiffs, Union Maids, Reds, and Riffraff: An Organized Guide to Films about Labor*. Ithaca: Cornell University Press, 1996.

Index

Page numbers in italics indicate illustrations.

The Accused, 73
Across the Pacific, 144n21
Adam-12, 109
Adorno, Theodor, xxviii, 46, 76, 141
AFL. *See* American Federation of Labor
After Dark My Sweet, 115
Agee, James, 43–44, 66
The Agency, 123
Alias, 123
Alignment, xxxi
Allegiance, xxxi–xxxiv
Allied State Organization, 44
Alton, John, 56, 148n4
American Federation of Labor (AFL), 81–84
Amnesiac war veteran, 76–77; films of, 134–35
Among the Living, 14–15
Andrews, Dana, 94
Angels with Dirty Faces, 10
Appel, Benjamin, 17
Appointment with Danger, 108
Asphalt Jungle, 148n3
Atlas, Leopold, 60
Audience decline, 87

Bad Lieutenant, 116
Bandits (Hobsbawm), xxii–xxiii
The Best Years of Our Lives, 44
B-film, 106–7
The Big Clock, xix, xxiii; class fear in, 74–75; film v. book, ending of, 76; Laughton's impact in, 73
The Big Heat, 102–4
The Big Sleep (Chandler), 22–23
Bioff, Willy, 7
Black Angel (Woolrich), 28–29
Blacklisting, 39–40, 70; impact of, 86; unacknowledged reason for, 146n5
Blanke, Henry, 12
The Blue Dahlia, xxiii, 42; plot of, 49–50; protagonist in, 48–49
Blue Velvet, 106; neo-noir and, 118–19; opening sequence of, 117–18; *Twin Peaks*'s sexual abuse compared to, 120
"Blue Velvet" (song), 155n18
Body and Soul, 51, 56
Bogart, Humphrey, 12, 15, 22, 99; Mitchum compared to, 71–72; persona of, xxxiii, 19. *See also* "Sam Spade"

Borde, Raymond, xxvi
Boxing, 56, 92
Boy's Town, 44
Brecher, Jeremy, 32
Brewer, Roy, 39, 85–87
Brodie, Steve, 57
Brother Orchid, 10
Browne, George, 7
Brute Force, 47–48
Buffy the Vampire Slayer, 123
Buhle, Paul, 42
Build My Gallows High (Mainwaring), 70
Bullets and Ballots, 10
Burr, Raymond, 57, 60
Bush, George H. W., 114–16, 119

Cagney, James, 10, 99
Cain, James M., 43
Cassavetes, John, 108
Cat People, 143n13
Chance of a Lifetime, 16
Chandler, Raymond, 13, 24, 50; class and corruption in novels of, 22–23; women in novels of, 145n27
Charlie Chan, 16
The Chase, 149n6
Chaumeton, Étienne, xxvi
CIO. *See* Congress of Industrial Organizations
Citizen Kane, 65
City symphonies, 90–91
Class: *The Big Clock*, fear with, 74–75; Chandler's novels, corruption by, 22–23; crime film and, xxi–xxiv; defining, xix–xx; Depression-era drifter and conflicts in, 64; detective films highlighting contradictions in, 13, 16; film noir and, xvi–xvii, xx–xxi, xxv–xxvi; *The Maltese Falcon* and, 19–20, 22; middle-class fugitive's fears of, 72–73; *The Naked City*'s statements on, 92–93; opening sequences and conflict in, 149n6; "Philip Marlowe," *Murder My Sweet*, antagonism towards, 23–24; *The Strange Love of Martha Ivers*, conflict in, 65–67, 69; women in *The Maltese Falcon*, *Murder My Sweet* and, 28
Cole, Lester, 14, 39
Colman, Ronald, 11

Communism: INS fighting, 82; strikes being associated with, xvii, 34–35, 146n2; SWG linked to, 38; terrorism replacing, 106
Confederation of Studio Unions (CSU), 9, 84–85; strikes of, 35–37
Congress of Industrial Organizations (CIO), 33, 35, 83–84
Conrad, William, 112
Control, 89
Convict fugitive: features of, 59; films of, 132; in *Raw Deal*, 60–63
Corruption: Chandler's novels, class and, 22–23; in *Murder My Sweet*, 21–22; *The Strange Love of Martha Ivers*, laws and, 67–68
Cortez, Ricardo, 12
Cotton, Joseph, 99
Craft unions. *See* Unions
Creative guilds. *See* Guilds
Crime film: banishment of, 10; class and, xxi–xxiv; detective toughened in, 15; directors' attraction to, xxiii–xxiv; turned into documentary, 90; doom and, 77–78; evolution of, 43–45, 81; as genre, xxiii; Hollywood, 1930s and, 9–11; Italian neorealism's techniques in, 90; labor and, xxvii; laws portrayed in, 11, 16; paranoia/guilt in, 86; politics in, 21–22; revitalization of, 55; social content in, 46; socialism removed from, 88; social problem films, 131; viewer perspective as compared to Westerns, 87–88. *See also* Detective films; Film noir; Police procedural film
The Crime of Monsieur Lange, 154n5
Crime Wave, 96
Criminal cops, 93–95; films of, 136; vigilante cops compared to, 101. *See also Where the Sidewalk Ends*
Criminal detective. *See* Detectives
Crossfire, xxiv, 44–46
CSI, 123
CSU. *See* Confederation of Studio Unions
"Cultural front," xix–xx, xxviii

Dark City, 108
The Dark Corner, 70, 147n13
Dassin, Jules, 78, 148n3, 152n16

172 ··· Index

Davis, Bette, 12
Death to Smoochy, 139n3
Defense Mediation Board, 4
de Havilland, Olivia, 7
Demarest, William, 97
Denning, Michael, xxviii–xxix
Depression-era drifter: characteristics of, 63–64; class conflict and, 64; films of, 132. *See also The Strange Love of Martha Ivers*
Dern, Bruce, 115
Dern, Laura, 118
Desperate, xxiii, 50; darkness in, 58; working-class fugitive in, 56–58
Desperate Hours, 99
Destination Tokyo, 14
Detective films, 129–30; class contradictions in, 13, 16; gender equality in, 29; labor and, 19–20; laws harassing detectives in, 24–25; women as evil in, 27–28; WWII impacting, 11–12
Detective novel: circular nature in evolution of, 127–28; labor and, 18–19
Detectives, 1; characterization of, 11; crime film, toughening of, 15; detective film, laws harassing, 24–25; evolution of, xviii; postwar changes to, 70. *See also* "Philip Marlowe"; "Sam Spade"
Detective Story, 96–98
Detour, 78
Dirty Sally (Simon), 127
Disney, Walt, 35, 143n7
Dmytryk, Edward, 45, 45–46
Docks of New York, xxi
Documentary, 89. *See also* Pre-period documentary procedurals
Doom, 77–78
Double Indemnity, xix, xxxiii, 43
Douglas, Kirk, 65, 96, 98
Dragnet, 96, 106; *The Fugitive*'s narration compared to, 111–12; success of, 107
Drifter. *See* Depression-era drifter
Dunne, Philip, 43

Eagle-Lion, 59
Eastwood, Clint, 155n15
Edwards, Grace F., 126
Enterprise Studios, 51
ER, 123

Fallen Angel, 149n6
Farewell My Lovely (Chandler), 22
Farrell, James T., 87
Farrow, John, xx, xxv
Fascism, 143n7
Fearing, Kenneth, 73
Federal Bureau of Investigation (FBI), 89–90
Film and Politics in America (Neve), xxix
Film industry: amnesiac war veteran in, 76–77; WWII, profits of, 8–9
Film noir: boxing in, 56; class and, xvi–xvii, xx–xxi, xxv–xxvi; defining, xvi; despair in, 51–52; endings in, 50; end of, 88; genre changes in, xxix–xxx; labor and, 31; master plots of, 42–43; perspective of, 41; point of view in, xxvi; politics of, 30; prison and, 47–48; protagonist in, 41–42; score in, xxxiii; socialism and, xxiv–xxvi; women in, 43; WWII impacting, 14. *See also* Neo-noir
Finger Man, 96
Fleming, Rhonda, 71
Flynn, Errol, 14
Foley, James, 115
Fonda, Henry, 11, 147n7
Force of Evil, 51–53
Ford, Glenn, 103
France, xvi, 139n1
Freud, Sigmund, xvi, 139n2
The Fugitive, xxxii, 105–6; criticism of, 110; *Dragnet*'s narration compared to, 111–12; portrayal of laws in, 113–14; plots of, 110–11; success of, 107; sympathy and, 113
Fugitive couple, 101
Fugitives, 54–55. *See also* Amnesiac war veteran; Convict fugitive; Depression-era drifter; Middle-class fugitive; Psychotic fugitive; Working-class fugitive
Fury, 10–11

Galileo, 73
Gangster films: evolution of, 139n3; softening of, 15–16
Garfield, John, 51
Garner, James, 109
Gender, 28–29. *See also* Male gaze; Women
Gilda, 149n6
The Glass Key, 15–16
G-Men, 10

Government: Hollywood and propaganda for, 8; labor attacked by, 82–83; labor management and corporate policy backed by, 3–4; strikes arising from actions of, xviii–xix
Graham, Gloria, 103
Gramsci, Antonio, xxvii–xxviii
Grant, Cary, 14
The Grapes of Wrath, 58
Great Depression, 10
Greene, Graham, 15
Greer, Jane, 71
Grey's Anatomy, 126
Griffith, D. W., xxi
The Grifters, 155n14
Guilds, 7–8; attacks on, 80. *See also* Screen Actors Guild; Screen Directors Guild; Screen Writers Guild

Halloween, 142n18
Hammett, Dashiell, 17, 20, 24
Hathaway, Henry, 89, 99
Heflin, Van, 65
Hellinger, Mark, 42, 47
He Walked by Night, 56–57, 99, 108
Higgins, John C., 60
High Sierra, xxxiii, 15
The High Window (Chandler), 16, 22–23
Himes, Chester, 5
Hitchcock, Alfred, 124
Hitler, Adolf, 141n14
Hobsbawm, Eric, xxii–xxiii
Hollywood: audience decline and efforts of, 87; Brewer leaving, 86–87; crime film, 1930s, in, 9–11; government propaganda in, 8; HUAC investigating, 35, 38–41, 85–86; labor divisions, 1940s, in, 6–7; creative artist currents in 1940s and, xxviii–xxix; WWII, strikes in, 9
Hollywood Ten, 37, 39–41, 44, 98
Hollywood Writers Mobilization (HWM), 8
Hoover, J. Edgar, 81–82
Hopper, Dennis, 118
Houseman, John, 48–49
House on 92nd Street, 89
House Un-American Activities Committee (HUAC), xvii, xix, 51; Cole on hearings of, 39; Hollywood investigated by, 35, 38–41, 85–86; Polonsky on hearings of, 147n14; societal impact of, 84–85; SWG, impact of, 40; Trumbo on reasoning of, 37; unions investigated by, 34–35; unions terrorized by, 81
HUAC. *See* House Un-American Activities Committee
Huggins, Roy, 105, 107–10
Hughes, Howard, 86
Huston, John, 12–13, 148n3
HWM. *See* Hollywood Writers Mobilization

IATSE. *See* International Association of Theatrical and Stage Employees
If He Hollers Let Him Go (Himes), 5
Immigration and Naturalization Service (INS), 82
In a Lonely Place, 59
Income, 17–18
Independent production: beginning of, 47; downturn in, 51
Informer cops, 95–97
INS. *See* Immigration and Naturalization Service
International Association of Theatrical and Stage Employees (IATSE), 6–7, 9, 36, 84
Investigation, 89
The Irresistible Rise of Arturo Ui, 143n6
Italian neorealism, 90
I, the Jury, 102
I Was a Communist for the FBI, 96
I Was a Fugitive from a Chain Gang, 47, 58
I Wouldn't Be in Your Shoes, 29

Janssen, David, 108
Johnny Staccato, 108
Johnston, Eric, 40
Jones, Dorothy, 44

Keith, Brian, 114
Kemp, Phil, xxix–xxx
The Killers, 47
The Kill-Off, 155n14
King, Stephen, 112
Kingsley, Sidney, 96, 98
A Kiss Before Dying, 126
Kiss Me Deadly, 153n24
Kiss the Blood Off My Hands, xv–xvi

Labor: crime film and, xxvii; detective films and, 19–20; detective novel and, 18–19; film noir and, 31; government's role in corporate policy and, 3–4; government's attack on, 82–83; Hollywood, 1940s, division of, 6–7; strikes in WWII, 4–5; in WWII, 2; as impacted by WWII's end, 31–32
Labor's Untold Story, 2
Ladd, Alan, 14–16, 49
Lake, Veronica, 15, 50
Lancaster, Burt, xvi, 47, 49
Lang, Fritz, xxiv, 10–11, 72, 102
Lang, Hope, 118
Language, 20–21
Latimer, Jonathan, 73
Laughton, Charles, 73
The Lawless, 150n13
Laws: crime film's portrayal of, 11, 16; detective film, detectives harassed by, 24–25; *The Fugitive*'s portrayal of, 113–14; morality v., 1; *The Strange Love of Martha Ivers*, corruption in, 67–68; WWII, patriotism enforced in, 3–4. *See also* Police
Lawson, John Howard, 39, 87
Lens, Sidney, 83
Lewis, John L., 81
Lewton, Val, 143n13
Liotta, Ray, 116
Lipsitz, George, xxvi, 41–42, 105
Little Caesar, 10
The Long Night, 147n7
Lorre, Peter, 15
Lovely Lady, Pity Me (Huggins), 107
Loy, Myrna, 11
Lynch, David, 106, 114; style of, 117; concept of time in *Twin Peaks*, 122

Mainwaring, Daniel, 70
The Making of the English Working Class (Thompson), xxii
Male gaze, 67
Maltby, Richard, 41
The Maltese Falcon, xxxiii, 11, 12, 14, 22, 24, 70; class and, 19–20, 22; first versions of, 12; Huston adapting, 12–13; money concerns in, 17–18; narration and, 145n24; compared to *Out of the Past*, 71–72; police antagonism in, 25–27; women and class mobility in, 28. *See also* "Sam Spade"
Maltz, Albert, 14
Mann, Anthony, 56
Marshall Plan, 82
Marvin, Lee, 103
Maverick, 109
Mayer, Louis B., 39
McCarthyism, 80
Meany, George, 84
Metro-Goldwyn Mayer (MGM), 39, 51
MGM. *See* Metro-Goldwyn Mayer
Middle-class fugitive: class fears of, 72–73; films of, 132–33. *See also The Big Clock*
"Mike Hammer," 102
Milestone, Lewis, 64
Mitchum, Robert, 71–72
Monroe, Marilyn, 100
Morality, 1
More Than Night (Naremore), xx
Morgan, Harry, 108
Morris, Errol, 116
Mosley, Walter, 156n26
Motion Picture Alliance, 40
Motion Picture Association of America (MPAA), 40
Motion Picture Industry Council, 86
MPAA. *See* Motion Picture Association of America
Mr. Moto, 16
Mulholland Drive, 139n3
Murder My Sweet, 14; class antagonism in, 23–24; corruption in, 21–22; first-person perspective of, 25; money concerns in, 18; police antagonism in, 25–27; women and class mobility in, 28
Murray, Philip, 33, 84
Muscuraca, Nicholas, 70
The Musketeers of Pig Alley, xxi, xxiv

The Naked City, xxi, 91, 93, 152n15; city symphony styling of, 90–91; class statements of, 92–93; narration in, 91–92
Naremore, James, xx
Narration: *Dragnet* compared to *The Fugitive*, 111–12; *The Maltese Falcon* and, 145n24; in *The Naked City*, 91–92; psychotic fugitive and, 98–99; sympathy and, xxx

Neff, Walter, 107
Nelson, Donald, 4
Neo-noir: *Blue Velvet* and, 118–19; defining, 106; Reagan/Bush politics and, 114–16
Neorealism. *See* Italian neorealism
Neve, Brian, xxix
New Deal, 3, 51, 143n2
Newsies, 154n13
Niagara, xxxiv, 99–101
Night and the City, 78–79
Noir. *See* Film noir
Nolan, Lloyd, 89
Notorious, 124
Nowhere Man, 156n23

Objective Burma, 14
O'Keefe, Dennis, 60
One Lonely Night (Spillane), 102
Order, 89
Out of the Past, 70–72

Painting with Light (Alton), 148n4
Panic in the Streets, 96
Panorama du Film Noir Americain (Borde and Chaumeton), xxvi
Parks, Larry, 85
Passos, John Dos, 3
Patriotism: profit and, 9; WWII, laws enforcing, 3–4
Phantom Lady (Woolrich), 29
"Philip Marlowe," 16, 25–27; class antagonism of, 23–24; income and, 17–18; language of, 21
Pitt, Brad, 122
Platoon film, 14
Police: *The Maltese Falcon, Murder My Sweet*, antagonism of/toward, 25–27; *Raw Deal*, absence of, 63; "Sam Spade" antagonized by, 25. *See also* Criminal cops; Informer cops; Vigilante cops
Police procedural film, 41; allegiance in, xxxiv; changes in, 81, 88; FBI influencing, 89–90; mainline, 136–37; pre-period documentary procedurals, 136. *See also* *The Naked City*
Politics: in crime film, 21–22; of *Crossfire*, 45–46; of film noir, 30; in Hammett's work, 17; Huggins and, 107–8; of Reagan/Bush and neo-noir, 114–16
Polonsky, Abraham, 36, 51–52; on HUAC hearings, 147n14; on McCarthyism, 80
The Postman Always Rings Twice, 43
Powell, William, 11
Preminger, Otto, xxv, 152n20, 155n15
Pre-period documentary procedurals, 136
Prison, 47–48
Proletarian novels, 17
Propaganda, 8
The Prowler, 116
Psychotic fugitive, 92, 93; films of, 137–38; genre of, 99; narration and, 98–99. *See also Niagara*
Public Enemy, 10
Pushover, 107

Quinn, Anthony, 78

Raft, George, 19
Rainbow at Midnight (Lipsitz), 42
Rand, Ayn, 40
Raw Deal, xxi, xxxii, 56, 61; convict fugitive in, 60–63; police absence in, 63; style of, 60; sympathy in, 62–63
Ray, Nicholas, 59
Reagan, Ronald, 86, 114–16, 118–19
"Reaganite Entertainment," 115
The Red Death (Mosley), 156n26
Red Harvest (Hammett), 17
Renoir, Jean, 154n5
Retreat into genre. *See* Fugitives
Reuther, Walter, 33
Richard Diamond, Private Eye, 108
Ride the Pink Horse, 41
Rififi, 148n3
RKO, 44, 56, 70, 86
Roaring Twenties, xxxiii, 19
Robinson, Edward G., 10
Rockford Files, 109
Roosevelt, Franklin D., 2–3
Rossellini, Isabella, 118
Rossen, Robert, 13, 51, 64
Russell, Kurt, 116
Ryan, Joseph, 146n2
Ryan, Robert, 46

SAG. *See* Screen Actors Guild
"Sam Spade," 12, 19, 22, 26–28, 70; income and, 17–18; language of, 20–21; police antagonizing, 25
Satan Met a Lady, 12
Schary, Dore, 44–46, 56–57
Schrader, Paul, xx, xxv
Scott, Adrian, 39, 98
Scott, Lizbeth, 65
Screen Actors Guild (SAG), 7, 36, 84
Screen Directors Guild, 7
Screen Writers Guild (SWG), 7, 37; communism linked to, 38; HUAC hearing's effects on, 40; Taft-Hartley Act, opposition of, 38
Selznick, David O., 44
The Set-Up, 56
77 Sunset Strip, 108–9
Side Street, 57
Simon, Michael, 127
Smith, Murray, xxx
Socialism, xxiv–xxvi, 88
Social problem films, 131
So Dark the Night, 150n12
Somewhere in the Night, 77
The Sopranos, 139n3
Sorrell, Herb, 6, 9, 35–37
So Well Remembered, 46
Spillane, Mickey, 102
Stanwyck, Barbara, 65
Stowe, Madeleine, 116
The Strange Love of Martha Ivers, 68; class conflict in, 65–67, 69; creative team behind, 64; laws/corruption in, 67–68; male gaze and, 67
Stranger on the Third Floor, 14–15
Strasberg, Lee, 77
Street with No Name, 89–90
Strike (Brecher), 32
Strikes: communism associated with, xvii, 34–35, 146n2; of CSU, 35–37; government actions prompting, xviii–xix; in Hollywood during WWII, 9; postwar, 31–34; of UAW, 33; WWII, labor and, 4–5
Stroud, George, xix
"Structure of feeling," xix, xxvii
"Structure of sympathy," xxx–xxxi

Surveillance, 89
SWG. *See* Screen Writers Guild
Sympathy: allegiance and, xxxi–xxxiii; *The Fugitive* and, 113; narration and, xxx; in *Raw Deal*, 62–63. *See also* "Structure of sympathy"

Taft, Robert, 34
Taft-Hartley Act, xvii, xix, xxiv, 31, 51; purpose of, 33–34; Section 9h loyalty test in, 81; SWG's opposition of, 38
Tailleur, Roger, 41
Television: B-film compared to, 106–7; Huggins's Western work in, 109; 9/11's impact on, 123–27; terrorism and, 124–27
Terrorism: communism replaced by, 106; television and, 124–27
They Drive By Night, xxxiii, 19
Thieves Highway, 56
The Thin Blue Line, 114, 116
Thin Man, 11, 16
This Gun for Hire, 14–15
Thompson, E. P., xxii
"Thuggish," 145n23
Tightrope, 155n15
Time to Kill, 16
T-Men, 60
Too Late for Tears (Huggins), 107
Tourneur, Jacques, 70
Tracy, Spencer, 10–11
Trevor, Claire, 60
Truman, Harry, 33
Trumbo, Dalton: on freedom of artist, 38; on HUAC's reasoning, 37
Try and Get Me, 56
24, 123–25
Twin Peaks, 106, 117, 121, 156n20; *Blue Velvet*'s sexual abuse compared to, 120; criticism of, 119; Lynch's concept of time in, 122

UAW. *See* United Auto Workers
UE. *See* United Electrical Workers
Ugly Betty, 126
Ulmer, Edgar, 78
Unforgiven, 155n15

Unions, 6–8; HUAC investigating, 34–35; HUAC terrorizing, 81. *See also* Confederation of Studio Unions; International Association of Theatrical and Stage Employees
United Auto Workers (UAW), 32–33
United Electrical Workers (UE), 35
Unlawful Entry, 116

Veteran. *See* War veteran
Vigilante cops: criminal cops compared to, 101; films of, 138; violence and, 102. *See also The Big Heat*
Vinton, Bobby, 155n18
Violence, 102; in *The Big Heat*, 103–4
"Voodoo economics," 154n12

Wagner, Dave, 42
Wald, Marvin, 152n15
Waldorf Statement, 39–40, 70
Wallis, Hal, 12, 64
Walsh, Richard, 9
War Board, 3, 5, 27
War film, 14
Warner Brothers, 36, 38
Warner, Jack, 7, 35–36, 39, 48
War Production Board, 4
War veteran, 134–35. *See also* Amnesiac war veteran
Webb, Jack, 105–6, 107; early career of, 108; Huggins competing with, 109
Westerns: Huggins's work in television and, 109; viewer perspective as compared to crime film, 87–88

Where Danger Lives, xxx
Where the Sidewalk Ends, 94–95
White Heat, xxv
Widmark, Richard, 78
Wild Boys of the Road, 98
Williams, Raymond, xxvii
Wilson, Charles, 4
Wilson, Michael, 90
The Window, 55–56
Women: in Chandler's novels, 145n27; detective film, evil of, 27–28; in film noir, 43; *The Maltese Falcon*, *Murder My Sweet*, class mobility and, 28
Woolrich, Cornell, 28–29, 133–34
Working-class cop. *See* Informer cops
Working-class fugitive: in *Desperate*, 56–58; films of, 131–32; professions of, 56; scarcity of, 55
World War II (WWII): corporations profiting during, 2–3; detective films impacted by, 11–12; film industry profiting from, 8–9; film noir impacted by, 14; Hollywood strikes during, 9; labor impacted by end of, 31–32; labor in, 2; labor strikes during, 4–5; patriotism in laws during, 3–4
WWII. *See* World War II
Wyler, William, 44, 96

The X-Files, 122–23

You Only Live Once, xxiv, 11, 72

Zanuck, Darryl, 7–8, 77

www.ingramcontent.com/pod-product-compliance
Lightning Source LLC
Chambersburg PA
CBHW032024230426
43671CB00005B/195